Ronald Reagan and the Public Lands

Number 10
THE ENVIRONMENTAL HISTORY SERIES
Martin V. Melosi, General Editor

COLLEGE STATION

Ronald Reagan and the Public Lands

AMERICA'S CONSERVATION DEBATE, 1979–1984

C. Brant Short

TEXAS A&M UNIVERSITY PRESS

The paper used in this book meets the minimum requirements of the American National Standard for Permanence of Paper for Printed Library Materials, Z39.48-1984. Binding materials have been chosen for durability.

Library of Congress Cataloging-in-Publication Data

Short, C. Brant (Calvin Brant), 1955–
    Ronald Reagan and the public lands : America's conservation
debate, 1979–1984 / C. Brant Short. – 1st ed.
        p. cm. – (The Environmental history series ; no. 10)
    Bibliography: p.
    Includes index.
    ISBN 0-89096-411-4 (alk. paper)
    1. United States–Public lands. 2. Conservation of natural
resources–Government policy–United States. 3. Environmental
policy–United States. 4. United States. Dept. of the Interior.
5. Watt, James G. 1938–   . 6. Reagan, Ronald. I. Title.
II. Series.
HD216.S58   1989
333.1'0973–dc19   88-32639
                                                           CIP

For my wife, Dayle

Contents

Preface

America's frontier experience may be the nation's most enduring collective myth. Raised in a popular culture filled with cowboys, cattle drives, and wagon trains, Americans recall with pride the nation's westward expansion. Few would question Frederick Jackson Turner's hypothesis that free land beckoning in the West fostered the development of American democracy. "This proposition does not sound novel now," observes Henry Nash Smith, "because it has been worked into the very fabric of our history."[1] In the final decades of the twentieth century, a vast western wilderness continues to stir passions. With millions of acres of public domain under federal management, Americans face a great dilemma. Should the public lands continue to serve as an economic Eden, in the tradition of a "Manifest Destiny," with its oil, timber, and mineral treasures captured for human consumption? Or should Americans, acknowledging an age of limits, preserve the shrinking wilderness for its inherent values? This dilemma, which estranged John Muir and Theodore Roosevelt during the first stages of the conservation movement, continues to call for resolution.

Articulate advocates on both sides of the issue debate the merits of preservation versus development. Wendell Berry, for example, believes that some tracts of wilderness must be preserved because the land provides a necessary cultural model, a standard of civilization for future generations. "Only if we know how the land *was*," writes Berry, "can we tell how it *is*. Records, figures, statistics will not suffice; to know, in the true sense, is to see." However, he concedes that for practical and humane reasons most of the land in the United States will be developed and used for human purposes. Both a farmer and a philosopher, Berry lucidly identifies the central dilemma of the public lands: Americans need to develop their natural resources for economic well-being; Americans need to retain their wilderness intact for spiritual and cultural well-being.[2] Each generation therefore confronts the political question: how *will* the public lands be used, with the answer becoming increasingly difficult as the human community grows ever larger, the undeveloped lands ever more scarce.

Americans have debated how to manage the public lands since the dawn of the republic, and although the frontier has been officially closed for nearly a century, the stakes in public land decisions remain high. Over 700 million acres of land, one-third of the total landmass of the United States, are owned and managed by the federal government. The public lands hold valuable treasures: one-quarter of the nation's coal reserves; half of the uranium, oil, and gas reserves. These lands represent the nation's "best prospect for future supplies of strategic minerals including cobalt, titanium, and molybdenum."[3]

Greater development of public lands became a primary theme in Ronald Reagan's 1980 bid for the presidency, illustrating the importance of the wilderness. After Reagan's electoral victory, new Secretary of the Interior James Watt systematically redirected federal land policy toward increased use of the nation's natural resources. Watt "interpreted the landslide Reagan victory in November 1980 as a mandate for resource development," observes Roderick Nash. "Any wilderness not legally protected . . . appeared to be fair game for both resource and recreational exploitation." By speaking out with such fervor, Watt and Reagan "drew attention as never before to the constant conflict in federal resource policy between development and preservation." Because of this unprecedented attention, America's public lands policy offered front-page headlines throughout Reagan's first term.[4]

The contemporary conservation debate has featured organized and widespread attempts by various factions to influence public attitudes and behavior. Multitudes of speeches, essays, editorials, and books reveal how advocates attempted to shape federal land policy. Leaders from both factions, demanding increased preservation or increased development, eagerly sought national as well as local and regional forums to help persuade audiences that government policy must be changed. This volume describes, interprets, and evaluates the rhetoric in the public lands debate from 1979 to 1984. This time frame provides an excellent period for a case study, as the public discourse progresses from the initial stages of campaign sloganeering to the later stages of policy implementation. A rhetorical analysis of the public lands debate offers several insights. By viewing the debate as process, readers will be able to perceive the dynamics of argument and counterargument within the confines of the historical situation. Furthermore, analyzing the issues from the perspective of the participants offers a means of understanding how the advocates saw themselves and how they defined their particular cause. This study will also help evaluate Joseph Petulla's claim that both environmentalists and their critics tend to "cluster in closed societies and build walls around themselves through the language of their arguments and the tactics of their struggles."[5] A historical overview of the conservation movement will provide perspective on the current debate.

I would like to thank those persons and organizations who have helped make this project possible. The following individuals and institutions provided research material: Cecil Andrus, Bruce Babbitt, Steve Hanke, Richard Lamm, Paul Laxalt, Wallace Stegner, the Institute of the American West, the Western Committee on Public Lands, the Political Economy Research Center, Sagebrush Rebellion, Inc., the Audubon Society, and the Wilderness Society. Staff members from the following libraries provided useful assistance: Montana State University, University of Montana, Montana College of Mineral Science and Technology, Montana State Library, Carroll College, University of Utah, and Idaho State University.

I would like to thank Robert G. Gunderson, the director of my doctoral dissertation, for his comments and suggestions on this manuscript, as well as his demand for "news." Additionally, I would like to thank the other members of my dissertation committee for their help: Ronald E. Lee, James R. Andrews, and Walter T. K. Nugent. My appreciation also goes to J. Jeffery and Eleanor Auer for their encouragement, hospitality, and friendship over the years.

Finally, I would like to thank my family and friends, especially my wife, Dayle, who has given her time, counsel, and love.

Ronald Reagan and the Public Lands

1. America's Conservation Consensus

ORIGINS OF THE PUBLIC LANDS DEBATE

In examining the origins of conservation, Grant McConnell identified the movement's two separate sources: the mystics, such as John Muir, who considered wilderness preservation to be an "act and obligation of worship," and the more pragmatic utilitarians, such as Theodore Roosevelt and Gifford Pinchot. In contrast with the preservationist notion that nature should remain undeveloped for the good of the human soul, the utilitarians emphasized that "natural resources must be developed and preserved for the benefit of the many, and not merely the profit of the few."[1] During the earlier stages of the conservation movement, Pinchot modified utilitarianism by adopting a chronological qualifier: "the greatest good of the greatest number for the longest time." To seek this ideal of utility in public policy, conservationists promulgated the standard of multiple use, suggesting that diverse use of the public lands inherently benefited a greater number. Conversely, single use of the lands, whether for mining, recreation, grazing, or logging, somehow compromised societal interests. The adoption of the multiple-use standard, concludes McConnell, had an important consequence: it created a "bias toward *measurable* benefits," with the dollar offering a "practical unit of measurement."[2] Such a bias minimized preservationist efforts to justify wilderness protection on the basis of spiritual benefits.

Viewing conservation as a moral rather than an economic problem, preservationists rejected resource development no matter how scientific and rational it appeared. Roosevelt and Pinchot, on the other hand, differed greatly from the wilderness worshipers of the early twentieth century. Even though serious differences separated conservationists, many observers did not at first recognize the degree of this schism. However the perception of unity among conservationists was short lived. "As concrete issues became clarified," wrote Samuel Hays, "diverse interests revealed this superficial unity and shattered the unified crusade into particularistic groups."[3] A decade-long struggle to make the Hetch Hetchy Valley a part of Yosemite National Park rigidified the split within the conservation movement. Arguing that the aesthetic side of conservation should not supersede the "economic and moral aspects of the case," Pinchot wanted to dam the valley. The failure of preservationists to save Hetch Hetchy became an important symbol for both factions during later public land debates.[4] The origins of the conservation movement help demonstrate a fundamental dichotomy: one faction committed to orderly public land development and the other devoted to preserving the wilderness intact. Under the rubric of "conservation," each group sought to control public perceptions of what the movement really meant.

Discussing the broader implications of conservation, Hays suggested that a "gospel of efficiency–efficiency which could be realized only through planning, foresight, and purpose," characterized the utilitarian conservation of the Progressive Era. As a result, the conservation movement helped transform a decentralized, nontechnical society into a "highly organized, technical, and centrally planned and directed social organization."[5] Significantly for future generations of Americans, utilitarians believed that conservation would lead to economic prosperity and material growth; conservation symbolized abundance, not scarcity.

In the 1950s and 1960s, "decisions for permanence" in public lands policy suggested a reinvigorated preservationist faction. Roderick Nash listed several factors which helped the preservationists successfully shape public policy. First, they carefully reformulated their rationale for preserving the wilderness, generating more easily grasped arguments and appeals for the general public. Second, they developed a better understanding of how to influence the political process. More politically astute than wilderness advocates at the turn of the century, contemporary conservationists learned that influence was gained in a variety of ways. Positive public reception of wilderness preservation confirmed that a change in American values was indeed taking place.[6]

In a move illustrative of their growing political acumen, the preservationists achieved a significant victory in the Echo Park controversy.[7] Their prevention of the construction of a series of dams in Utah helped launch a national move toward wilderness preservation. Conservationists employed several rhetorical strategies to save Echo Park. According to Nash, they argued that traditional aesthetic and spiritual values inherent in the wilderness must be preserved in a nation of growing materialism. Furthermore, the preservationists challenged "reclamationists and engineers with their own tools: statistical data concerning the efficiency of a dam at Echo Park."[8] Clearly a coupling of the scientific and the spiritual worldviews appeared to be taking place.

The merger of the preservationists and utilitarians into a newly formed environmental movement during the 1960s changed the character of the conservation movement. An altered definition of the human place in the universe provided the fulcrum for this reconciliation. Both the preservationists and utilitarians traditionally held a human-centered worldview; for them, as Nash put it, "either man's stomach or man's spirit is the paramount concern." In contrast, the emerging new ecological view radically transformed this perspective by defining humans as part of the biotic community. According to Leopold, an ecological perspective changed the role of "*Homo sapiens* from conqueror of the land-community to plain member and citizen of it." Working from this vision, conservationists concerned themselves with the survival of the ecosystem rather than the spiritual or economic benefits of the wilderness. In the 1960s, concluded Nash, there "occurred a convergence of the utilitarian and aesthetic streams toward the ecological. The intellectual collision toward the end of the decade helps to explain the gospel of ecology."[9]

At the center of the contemporary environmental movement stood Leopold's "land ethic" and his calls for an "ecological conscience." A world of pollution, overpopulation, and nuclear weapons motivated many Americans to reconsider their relationship with the environment. Calling for a new commitment to the environment in the 1960s, Interior Secretary Stewart Udall concluded, "It is our relationship with the American earth that is being altered by the quiet crisis, our birthright of fresh landscapes and far horizons."[10]

Leopold's essays helped environmentalists reorient traditional American worldviews. For example, he claimed that people need to maintain a balance between wilderness and civilization to achieve a worthwhile existence. A life-style tilted too far toward either extreme missed what he believed to be the ideal state. Observation taught Leopold that an interdependence among all living beings characterized our environment. This knowledge implied a new approach to wilderness management, an approach that reflected a "conviction of individual responsibility for the health of the land. Health is the capacity of the land for self-renewal."[11]

In describing the land ethic, Leopold noted that ethics always rested upon a simple premise: "that the individual is a member of a community of interdependent parts." But in his view, the land ethic "enlarges the boundaries of the community to include soils, waters, plants, and animals, or collectively: the land." As a result, humans were asked to consider more than economic benefits in their use of the wilderness. Using the land ethic to judge human actions, Leopold found that a "thing is right when it tends to preserve the integrity, stability, and beauty of the biotic community. It is wrong when it tends otherwise."[12]

By helping to restructure the worldview of the conservation movement, Leopold's philosophy created a new conservation rhetoric. Instead of justifying wilderness in terms of human benefits (whether spiritual or economic), ecologists demanded that the well-being of the biotic community itself should be considered when making public land policies. Although Leopold died in 1948, his ideas had a dramatic impact upon public land policy-makers in the 1960s. Asking for public support in 1962 for new conservation laws, Interior Secretary Udall reiterated many of the same appeals advanced by Leopold a decade earlier. Udall warned that wilderness "is not a renewable resource. Man can only shrink or destroy the primeval – he cannot recreate it once it is gone." Moreover, Udall pointed to the new science of ecology, which taught that humans "are not outside nature, but in it; that it is not a commodity which we can exploit without restraint, but a community to which we belong." Later, in his bestselling book, *The Quiet Crisis,* Udall called for a land ethic that stressed the "oneness of our resources and the live-and-help-live logic of the great chain of life." Calling Leopold an "American Isaiah," Wallace Stegner pointed to that writer's importance among environmentalists: "He was one who made us begin to understand that wilderness is indispensable for science and survival."[13]

Policy changes in the 1960s and 1970s affirming an ecological perspective broadened the public land managers' understanding of their guiding light – the notion of multiple use to provide the "greatest good of the greatest number." As federal land managers embraced the land ethic in developing policy regulations, they sought an optimum mixture of uses that would add to the criterion of multiple uses the requirement that they not damage the land's biological capacity.[14]

A large amount of public land, about 60 percent of the total, is now reserved for multiple use, including recreation, grazing, logging, mining, watershed control, and fish and wildlife sport.[15] A string of legislative victories, beginning with the Wilderness and Multiple Use acts in 1964, displaced the utilitarian brand of multiple use in federal land management. Calling the Wilderness Act an "environmental Marshall Plan," Nash claims that it institutionalized the philosophical concept that wilderness should be an "ongoing part of American civilization."

The federal government explicitly defined a policy of permanent land ownership with the Multiple Use Act, officially changing the traditional goal of land disposal. The 1973 federal Endangered Species Act, reports Tom Arrandale, "forced forest rangers and BLM managers to survey public lands for threatened wildlife and plants and to rule out use that could disrupt their habitat."[16] Another significant piece of legislation, the National Environmental Policy Act of 1969, greatly strengthened the evolving conservation consensus. Applicable to all federal agencies, the law ordered that environmental impact statements (EIS) be utilized to assess "potential damage to the environment from any government action." In a single decade, Leopold's land ethic had become an enforceable guide to public-land policy making. Environmental impact statements "forced public land managers to broaden the interests and values they weighed in balancing multiple use," observes Arrandale. "It required rangers and district managers to justify resource development in written documents, open to public scrutiny." Through the EIS process, environmentalists broke new ground in their efforts to redefine traditional uses of wilderness. According to Arrandale, "They seized the opportunity, at both local and national levels. Well-organized groups used public comment requirements to prod local rangers and district officials to take account of the environmental risks. Agency officials, anticipating environmentalist opposition, increasingly modified proposals to provide protection for wildlife and other values."[17]

Conservation's culminating victory came in 1976 with the passage of the Federal Land Policy and Management Act and the National Forest Management Act. These laws mandated "scientific land-use planning" as well as full consultation with "environmentalists, industry, state and local governments, and all parties with interests in federally owned lands."[18] Because these laws endorsed permanent federal ownership of the public lands, both Forest Service and BLM officials could confidently develop long-range plans using an ecological, rather than an economic, definition of multiple use.

A national commitment to public land preservation emerged in the
United States beginning with the Echo Park victory in 1954 and ending with the Alaska Land Bill of 1980. The rise of an ecological worldview, coupled with numerous laws implementing the land ethic as a
guide to wilderness policy making, resulted in a new conservation consensus. Both Republicans and Democrats endorsed the consensus, institutionalizing a national program of land management. In addition,
numerous environmental organizations sought to influence policy
through litigation, lobbying, and public communication. With a growing membership during most of the 1970s, major environmental groups
became a strong political force in America. By the end of the 1970s,
notes Stephen Fox, the environmental movement was "still making
gains in membership, income, and influence. With the combined
power of some three thousand groups, conservation seemed a permanent force in American political and social life."[19]

Why did the conservation consensus, after twenty years of victory,
come unraveled so quickly? Two important developments help explain
why the environmental community was on the defensive at the end
of the 1970s. Traditional resource users such as ranchers and loggers
were never happy with the so-called "lockup" of the public lands. As
the government continued to inventory specific tracts of land and restrict use, western groups attempted to stem the move toward stringent land-use guidelines. Moreover, the apparent indifference of the
Carter administration toward western concerns further exacerbated the
problem. Carter's cancellation of numerous western water projects provoked a massive outcry from both liberals and conservatives in the
region. Regarding public land issues in general, Richard Lamm and
Michael McCarthy conclude that the Carter administration "was a
western nightmare. . . . At no time did he have a western strategy.
Out of uninterest or contempt, or both, Carter went to the Rocky
Mountain West only four times in his term."[20] Some angry westerners
formed the Sagebrush Rebellion in order to call attention to "unreasonable" restrictions on livestock grazing, logging, and mining. Although membership in the group remained small, the rebels were endowed with wealth, status, and power. As a result, they commanded
national attention for their plan to transfer ownership of federally
owned public lands to the various state governments. Another problem that hurt the conservation consensus was the declining economic
condition of the United States in the late 1970s. A tight energy market

stimulated demands that the public lands be used to achieve energy independence from foreign oil sources.

Candidate Ronald Reagan and the rising New Right in American politics supported western calls for greater public land development in direct opposition to two decades of restricted use. Promising to get the federal government "off the backs of the people," candidate Reagan predicted a new era with oil and other minerals flowing freely from the vast public lands. After his election in 1980, Reagan repeated his support for the Sagebrush Rebellion in a telegram to rebellion leader Dean Rhodes, announcing, "I renew my pledge to work toward a 'sagebrush solution.' My administration will work to insure that the states have an equitable share of public lands and their natural resources."[21] With the Reagan administration promising radical changes in public land management, the national debate regarding the future of the public lands and resource development was in full swing.

Analyzing the rhetoric of the public lands debate should help illuminate the enduring historical and political importance of conservation and environmental concerns in contemporary America. From Henry David Thoreau and John Muir to Edward Abbey and David Brower, wilderness advocates have advanced public arguments to modify and change attitudes toward the public lands. Historically, public address has reflected the division among preservationists and utilitarians by helping each faction define publicly the goals and values of its particular brand of conservation. Rhetorical prowess helped advocates such as Aldo Leopold, Bob Marshall, Bernard DeVoto, and Wallace Stegner reconcile the competing forces in the conservation movement and forge the ensuing conservation consensus. With the intense reexamination of resource policy in the late 1970s, rhetoric once again assumed a preeminent role in national decision making. Because of this significance, this study presents a rhetorical history of the contemporary public lands debate, beginning in 1979 with the rise of the Sagebrush Rebellion and ending in 1984 with the completion of Ronald Reagan's first term in office and the resignation of his public lands alter ego, Interior Secretary James Watt.

2. "Western Men at Lexington Bridge"

THE RISE OF THE SAGEBRUSH REBELLION

Like a brilliant comet in the night sky, the Sagebrush Rebellion burst forth, seemingly unstoppable. Yet in two short years, the rebellion burned out, becoming a memory in Rocky Mountain history. Why did this phenomenon, endorsed by some of the nation's most powerful politicians and apparently popular with the general public, fade from view so quickly? Although several writers have started to dissect the movement's failure, no study has focused upon the rebellion's lifeblood, its rhetoric.[1]

Given the value attached to public advocacy by the rebels and their opponents in the environmental community, a rhetorical analysis seems an appropriate means of understanding the movement. Using the rhetorical and political strategies of the New Right as their model, the rebel leaders organized and presented a conservative alternative to the prevailing "ecological" view of public land management. In this manner, the rebellion offered a philosophical and intellectual rationale to complement their pragmatic demands for a land transfer to the individual states. An examination of the rebellion therefore may explain the nation's turn toward conservatism in the late 1970s as well as illuminate the rise of the Sagebrush Rebellion. This chapter will describe the rebellion's historical background, analyze key features of rebel discourse, and evaluate the rebellion's significance within the larger national public lands debate.

Demands that federally managed lands be taken over by the various states did not begin with the Sagebrush Rebellion of the 1970s. At least two other organized rebellions occurred in the twentieth century, each failing to generate significant changes in land policy. A brief examination of the two earlier rebellions reveals that the causes of the rebellions, and their rhetorical justifications, were remarkably similar to the more recent movement. Between 1907 and 1915, six public land conferences were held in the western states, each providing a forum for ranchers who demanded changes in the federal management of western rangelands. The conferences appeared to be a response to the rise of conservation, with cattlemen shocked that grazing fees might be charged in national forests. Invoking claims of states' rights, many ranchers hoped to get regional support for their cause. In an analysis of these conferences, Lawrence Rakestraw concludes that spontaneous and unanimous support for the ranchers never appeared, helping doom the first organized attempt to end federal control of the public lands.[2]

In the 1940s a second sagebrush rebellion emerged, this time representing a greater threat to continued federal control of the public lands. Senator Patrick McCarran of Nevada held numerous committee hearings in the western states, beginning in 1940 and going until 1943. The hearings, according to William Rowley, cast suspicion upon the "good will of the federal grazing administration and gained some publicity and support for a move to offer the grazing lands to state ownership."[3] Stockmen were angered by possible reductions of grazing, mandated in an effort to employ a scientific method of range management. Moreover, they were concerned that too much regard for wildlife might threaten grazing rights established for cattle and sheep earlier in the century. As a result, the ranchers proposed buying the public lands at rates from nine cents to $2.80 per acre. A typical justification for the land sale appeared in an editorial written by Elmer Brock in 1947. He argued that the livestock industry had to be freed of the "federal overlordship" that had "harassed the stockmen of the West for years and left them at the mercy of the whims and edicts of bungling officials." With bureaucrats in control of the public lands, Brock argued, ranchers were "denied the American form of government." In an impassioned plea, Brock declared that if the livestock industry, "the backbone of western economic life" was to survive, the public lands would have to be "returned" to state control.[4]

Although ranchers did not succeed in getting land "returned" to the western states, the lines of argument in the 1940s found new audiences in the 1970s when the Sagebrush Rebellion emerged. In another striking parallel with the most recent rebellion, the opponents of the ranchers in the 1940s came from throughout the United States. Led by *Harper's* editor Bernard DeVoto, influential Americans joined with the conservation community to oppose the land transfer. DeVoto's essay, "The West Against Itself," attacked the "land grab" and detailed for the general public the goals of the ranchers. By the early

1950s, opposition in Congress, in the western press, and among sportsmen doomed any bills intended to transfer public lands to state ownership.[5] DeVoto's friend and biographer, Wallace Stegner, continued the battle against the contemporary sagebrush rebellion, often repeating arguments advanced thirty years earlier.

Most observers agree that the conservation movement's crowning success, the Federal Land Policy and Management Act of 1976, represented the last straw for many western ranchers, miners, and loggers. By institutionalizing Aldo Leopold's land ethic as the guiding standard for public land policy, the act threatened traditional land uses. From 1977 until 1979, the Bureau of Land Management and the Forest Service inventoried public lands to determine how many acres should remain in multiple use and how many should receive wilderness designation, which would place significant restrictions on commercial activity. These land studies, collectively called RARE II (Roadless Area Review Evaluation) outraged many westerners. Because any commercial development was prohibited on the study tracts during the inventory, the lands became de facto wilderness areas, restricting any mining or logging until the final classification.[6] In 1979, the BLM and the Forest Service presented their final recommendations to the Congress: 15 million acres designated as wilderness areas, 36 million classified as multiple-use land, and almost 11 million subject to further study. This final recommendation set off angry protests throughout the West because the millions of acres awaiting further evaluation became de facto wilderness, not to be disturbed by human development.[7] Less than a month after the recommendations were announced, while Jimmy Carter prepared his "national malaise" speech at Camp David, the Nevada legislature declared a "sagebrush rebellion."

The Sagebrush Rebellion was a regional phenomenon centered in the Rocky Mountain West. Dissatisfaction with federal land policy emerged in the West, westerners organized the rebellion, and advocates shaped their rhetoric for a western audience. Although environmentalists portrayed public land management as a national question, the political battlefield was concentrated in the western states. Hoping to create a unified front for their cause, the rebels decided to lobby each state legislature in the region for an official endorsement of the rebellion's goals. Before analyzing rebel rhetoric, we should consider the particular worldview of the contemporary westerner. Several characteristics make the western audience ideal for an antigovernment crusade such as the Sagebrush Rebellion.

Most observers would agree that the Rocky Mountain West is a conservative region both politically and culturally. Raised on the myth of rugged individualism, many westerners pride themselves on their ability to thrive in a hostile environment, as is demonstrated by the recall of the pioneer heritage when federal regulation seems encroaching. Wallace Stegner claims that the Intermountain West is the "most politically reactionary part of the world because it's closest to the frontier." The Sagebrush Rebellion, he argues, caught "the people's imagination and [stirred] them to fight somebody, or throw somebody out," and assured westerners that the "old freedom still lasts, that it's still there."[8] Many in the West appear to accept a version of history distorted by a myth of "regional independence." This view, observe Lamm and McCarthy, ignores the fact that the western pioneers "received substantial help from the federal government in their frontiering years." The rise of western radicalism in recent years, they conclude, has deepened the West's "sense of paranoia and isolation."[9] Because westerners often define freedom in terms of space, land becomes a measure of individual liberty, and the restriction of the public lands exacerbates the region's antigovernment hostility.

In July, 1979, the Nevada legislature passed a resolution demanding the transfer of 49 million acres of federal land to state control. Within two months, the *Wall Street Journal*, the *Los Angeles Times*, and the *New York Times* highlighted the so-called "sagebrush rebellion," bringing national attention to the new movement.[10] In September *Newsweek* added more national attention in a cover story titled "The Angry West," and environmentalists were alerted to the rebellion in a *High Country News* feature.[11] During that same month, Senator Orrin Hatch of Utah introduced a national sagebrush rebellion bill into the U.S. Senate, cosponsored by conservative stalwarts Jake Garn, James McClure, Paul Laxalt, and Alan Simpson. Besides authoring this federal legislation, Hatch spoke to a public lands rally in Reno, Nevada, and presented the rebellion's philosophy in a speech appropriately titled, "A Second American Revolution." In less than three months, Americans witnessed the beginning of a new, possibly unique political crusade, in the words of one observer, a "right-wing land reform movement."[12]

Who were the sagebrush rebels? Was the movement a grass-roots response to federal indifference toward the West? Originally, the rebels appear to have been western ranchers, with energy officials and timber executives joining as the movement gained momentum.[13] More than five hundred rebels attended a conference in Utah, including state land commissioners, state legislators, and Senators Hatch, McClure, Ted Stevens, and Malcom Wallop. Sponsored by the League of States Equal Rights (LASER), the conference also included representatives from Conoco, Citizens for Mining, the National Inholders Association, U.S. Borax, the International Snowmobilers, and Louisiana Pacific Timber.[14] Financial reports from the various Sagebrush Rebellion organizations show the movement to be well endowed. LASER's 1981 budget of $1.5 million listed $550,000 for a "public information and media program," $50,000 for a conference in Washington, D.C., $175,000 for research, and $60,000 for congressional lobbyists. In Nevada, the state legislature appropriated $250,000 to establish the Committee on Public Lands to help pursue a successful rebellion. Idaho's Sagebrush Rebellion, Inc. (SRI), sponsored fund raisers and sold various materials, including a recorded speech by radio commentator Paul Harvey, in order to raise funds.[15]

Rhetorically, one of the most potent weapons of the rebellion lay in its colorful and memorable name. Rich in connotations, the phrase "sagebrush rebellion" conjures up powerful images, in the words of Lamm and McCarthy: "Sagebrush plains, wild and untamed as the men who ride them. . . . Strong, bronze-faced, steely eyed men. Zane Grey men. Pioneer men, American men. Western men at Lexington Bridge."[16] Although the movement's name came to be "one of the most important symbolic aspects" of the rebellion, Malcom Cawley observed that originally the term was "coined by the media as a somewhat derogatory characterization of the movement."[17] Rebels, sensing the powerful symbolism inherent in the term, adopted it as their own. The prorebellion National Association of Counties argued that, although the term was invented to ridicule Nevada's efforts to claim the public land, it came to symbolize a "greater voice in the management of all federal land, water and energy programs."[18] Early accounts of the rebellion in fact place the term in lower case and with quotation marks. Within several months, the title became a proper noun as the rebels claimed it for themselves.

The rebellion's name symbolized the New Right's activist approach to the issues. Instead of going to Washington, D.C., to criticize public land policy, rebels were in the field working to dismantle the conservation consensus and return land policy to the individual states. Rebellions demand action, not further study, and from that perspective the Sagebrush Rebellion presented an attractive solution to the com-

plexities of public land policy making. Various rebels noted the rich
symbolism in the movement's name. Vernon Ravenscroft, president
of SRI, characterized the rebellion as embodying the "spirit of resistance" caused by the "frustration and broken dreams" of many western Americans.[19] The word "sagebrush" reflected another important
aspect of the movement's philosophy. Seeking ownership of the arid,
desert lands of the West, rebels used the term to remove images of
pristine wilderness, beautiful mountain ranges, and acres of wildlife
habitat, being sold out from western citizenry.

Examining rebel discourse, one finds three consistent logical appeals used to justify land transfer to the states: first, the individual
states will be better land managers; second, economic growth in the
West is stifled by restrictive federal land management; and third, the
states have the right to control the land that falls within their borders.[20] Ironically, the advocacy of these specific arguments reveals an
inherent contradiction in rebel rhetoric. On the one hand, some rebels defined the issue as a states' rights question, making land ownership the point of contention, not the specific land use. On the other
hand, many rebels implicitly changed the terms of the debate by emphasizing the economic advantages to be afforded by state management of the public lands. These rebels envisioned more mining, more
logging, more energy exploration, and more grazing after a successful
land transfer. Some rebels even maintained that the state ownership
was only temporary and that sales to private individuals would soon
follow. Ravenscroft for example proclaimed that some land "without
apology, should be privately owned and used to build our state. The
important point is that we in Idaho ought to have the right to make
that basic determination."[21]

In contrast, environmentalists ignored the states' rights issue and
concentrated on potential land sales ("land grab") and development
("rapebellion") of the public lands. As a result, rebels were forced to
adopt a defensive rhetorical strategy, attempting to dispel opposition
charges and clear up misconceptions regarding the true intent of the
movement. The impact of the movement's contradiction will become
evident in a closer examination of rebel discourse.

Rebels selected a three-pronged attack to get the land transferred
to state ownership. Initially, they wanted state legislatures to pass resolutions demanding that BLM and Forest Service lands be transferred
to the individual states. In addition, the rebels began to build a financial war chest to launch a legal challenge in the federal courts.

Lastly, they initiated a broad "public education" campaign to persuade western voters to support the movement. Although the rebellion never had a large membership, many rebels held powerful positions in the states and brought attention and status to the movement.
Rebellion leaders were committed to an organized and widespread
program of public communication. The Nevada Committee on Public Lands provided followers with a sample speech that "may be used
in whole or in part, depending on the group to be addressed and the
amount of time available." The committee instructed followers how
to use local media and service organizations to get the rebel message
out to the public. The organizing material discussed letter-writing
campaigns, how to set up a telephone network, and how to target
local and national politicians. The committee's workbook also suggested that rebels needed to develop small working groups. Once a
work group was formed, it should "identify speakers within [the] group
to address community organizations. . . . Speakers should include informed members from local business, social and academic circles, and
other recognized leaders of the community."[22]

Other rebel groups also followed a systematic approach to public
communication. During 1980, John Harmer, president of LASER, addressed nine western state legislatures and numerous civic and business groups to explain the values and goals of the rebellion.[23] Idaho's
SRI told its followers that the "media loves the conflict! Service clubs
are curious as to just what is involved in this 'Rebellion' issue." Ravenscroft listed his rhetorical success during 1980: five guest editorials in
Idaho newspapers, two service club speeches, and speeches to numerous interest groups including the Oregon Cattlemen, the Idaho
Water Users, and the Idaho Cattlefeeders. In addition, the SRI newsletter observed that the group had available speakers for anyone in-
terested in the rebellion. "If you can arrange for your group to invite
one of our speakers," the newsletter promised, "we will supply a quality program."[24]

Rebel leaders continued to attract public attention in 1981. Idaho's
SRI passed out literature at thirty-six county fairs and two major state
fairs in Boise and Twin Falls. More important, rebellion speakers were
granted national audiences in addresses before the National Association of Counties in Louisville and the National Association of Realtors in Las Vegas. The 1981 SRI Speakers Bureau Report concluded
by listing the various events that speakers had attended, including the
Idaho Boys' State meeting, local chamber of commerce meetings, and

even "entrance into the 'lion's den' at the annual meeting of the Idaho Wildlife Federation."[25]

An examination of rebel rhetoric reveals consistent arguments and appeals employed by the various sagebrush organizations. The Revolutionary War became the movement's fundamental image for argumentation, finding expression in nearly every rebel speech, interview, essay, and pamphlet. A highly charged symbol, the American Revolution has been used rhetorically in numerous political causes. "Polemicists support their arguments by quoting from, and alluding to Revolutionary heroes," observed Ronald Reid. "By shaping the Revolutionary past in appropriate ways, polemicists can draw analogies between their ideas, goals, and actions and those of our Noble Forefathers."[26] Turning to the Sagebrush Rebellion, one finds the American Revolution once again exploited to persuade contemporary audiences that revolutionary values were alive and well in the Rocky Mountain West.

In one pamphlet describing the goals of the SRI, Thomas Jefferson is quoted prominently: "What country can preserve its liberties, if its rulers are not warned, from time to time, that its people preserve the spirit of resistance." Other examples of SRI literature also linked the current rebellion with the American Revolution. In a 1980 newsletter, Sandy Pinkard declared that "there's a story in the rebellion . . . we're talking about issues that haven't come up since the Boston Tea Party." A country-and-western singer, Pinkard penned the Sagebrush Rebellion's anthem, "A Down to Earth Proposition," with lyrics about "constitutional rights we don't have as 11 western states. Look at the bungler . . . the bureaucrats . . . managers who haven't been responsible to the people and haven't run things right."[27] In a 1981 newsletter the SRI presented a photograph of a Minuteman, on horseback, with Utah's Wasatch Mountain Range in the background. A caption describes the picture as a "rebel's dream come true." A colonist with his gun strikes a pose of classic "preparedness, vigilance, and determination." Some rebels even cited direct precedent for their cause in the actions of the founding fathers. Ravenscroft insisted that Thomas Jefferson "gave the nation one tax free year by selling the public lands in the Ohio River Valley. As such, he went beyond the clearly stated goals of the Sagebrush Rebellion."[28] From Ravenscroft's description, America's third president was also its first sagebrush rebel.

Western politicians, too, were eager to exploit the rhetorical link between the Revolution and the rebellion. Governor John List of

Nevada declared that antifederal hostility in his state was the "greatest in the U.S. since the time of the revolution against the King of England," while Senator Paul Laxalt claimed that the cause of the rebellion "is a simple one of being denied access to our lands, of being ruled like some faraway colony by uncaring and unknowledgeable bureaucrats more than 3000 miles distant." Another rebel proponent, Sen. James McClure, charged that the "original colonies got complete dominion over their own lands by revolution. We have not got complete dominion over our own future in Idaho." Calvin Black, a county commissioner from southern Utah, also employed the Revolutionary War analogy. Adding two more states to those typically considered to be "western" (apparently North Dakota and South Dakota), he asserted that environmental legislation "effectively disenfranchises the people who live in the thirteen western colonies from equal economic, political, and human rights as compared to Americans who live in the thirty-seven sovereign states."[29]

In a revolutionary gesture on July 4, 1980, outside the small Utah community of Moab, three hundred people saw the American Legion present the flag and heard the national anthem played. County Commissioner Harvey Merrill "warned the crowd of the 'cancerous' growth of the federal bureaucracy—a bureaucracy which continually failed to listen to the people." In a striking peroration, he announced, "We will take control of our destiny in Southeastern Utah and won't delegate it to a bureaucracy." At that point, a D-6 Caterpillar (which had served as the speaker's platform) was started and plowed an illegal road into a BLM wilderness area. Although the action had no direct impact on federal policy, Marilyn Cooper, a local political leader, suggested the importance of the event: "Let's keep the Sagebrush Rebellion alive, and every three or four months, when everybody has nothing to do, we'll stir up something."[30]

Hatch's 1979 speech in Reno is the likely origin of the rebellion's obsession with the symbolism of the Revolutionary War. The Carter administration's disdain for "private property rights and just plain decency," argued Hatch, "has not been equalled since the first American Revolution threw out the archetype of such oppression, pompous George the Third." The same forces that produced America's first revolution, he advised, "are felt again, not from an outside oppressor, but from an internal enemy." He detailed the parallel between the rebels and the revolutionaries, claiming that the issues "are the same: Equality of rights, dignity for the individual and protection of the citizen's private property." Concluding that the Sagebrush Rebellion "is perfectly consistent with the principles which our Founding Fathers established through their sacrifice," the senator offered an appealing symbol that pervaded rebel argumentation among the diverse and independent organizations.[31]

What made the Revolution so attractive to the rebels? Was it a convenient symbol for any grass-roots group in the United States seeking public support? Examining the broad goals of the Sagebrush Rebellion, one finds that the Revolutionary War analogy served an important function in the movement's evolving ideology. More than just an advertising slogan, the Revolutionary War became the foundation for rebel rhetoric. Several factors explain this development. Appeals to America's shared acceptance of the Revolution helped to legitimize the rebellion's primary goal, a transfer of power from one government to another. Although the rebellion could never be termed a real revolution, the agenda employed by rebels strongly deviated from typical conservative politics. Rebels therefore had to justify to fellow conservatives this new approach to political change.

In previous decades, while single-issue activism thrived on the political left, conservatives paid little attention to this style of politics. Richard A. Viguerie, a leader of the New Right, concluded that all his movement had done was "copy the success of the old Left." The success of the environmental movement, consumerism, and antinuclear groups, he believed, confirmed that single-issue groups exercised "power and influence" in the United States.[32] The Revolutionary War analogy helped justify the rebellion's status as a single-issue crusade. Traditional conservatives, the Old Right, unfamiliar with the activist approach taken by the New Right, could identify with Jefferson and the founding fathers and endorse this new style of shaping public policy.

The Revolutionary War theme helped distinguish the Sagebrush Rebellion from other cases of federal-state conflict. Although the term "states' rights" occasionally appeared in their rhetoric, most rebels avoided this emotionally loaded phrase. As recently as 1980, Jimmy Carter had characterized the term "states' rights" as a code word for racism. Although the western states had no connection with segregation, rebels eschewed possible comparisons with an earlier American rebellion, the Civil War. Some advocates openly rejected comparison between the antebellum South and the contemporary West. John L. Dobra and George A. Uhimchuk, business professors at the Univer-

sity of Nevada–Reno, asserted that the legal theories of the Sagebrush Rebellion "are substantially different from political theories of
John C. Calhoun." The rebellion, they claimed, was "states' rights vis-
à-vis other states, and not states' rights vis-à-vis the central government."[33] Environmentalists, however, ignored such a distinction in
making their case against the Sagebrush Rebellion.

Surprisingly, the rebels avoided use of the western myth in their
public discourse. A proven rhetorical device in many types of contemporary communication, the myth would seem to be an appealing
symbol for rebel advocates.[34] Almost no rebel, however, mentioned
the frontier thesis, the pioneer spirit, or the cowboy as a symbol of
western independence, an omission that seems unusual given the per-
vasiveness of the western myth in advertising, entertainment, literature, and political rhetoric. Several factors help explain this phenomenon. The rebellion called for cooperative, organized measures to halt
government regulation, while the western myth tends to sanctify in-
dividuality. A lonely cowboy drifting from place to place fails to adequately symbolize the unity of the rebellion. The western myth glori-
fies wilderness as the maker of "rugged individuals," affirming Turner's
thesis that the frontier transformed the American character into something noble and unique. In contrast, the Revolutionary War analogy
better represented the Sagebrush Rebellion's notion that Americans
should be guaranteed economic freedom from government repression.
Just as America's founders sought less governmental control over their
economic life, the sagebrush rebels sought similar freedom to use "their"
land as they wished.[35]

Sagebrush rebels employed the Revolutionary War analogy in their
rhetoric to arouse and unify public opinion toward less preservation
and greater access to the public lands. By placing their philosophy in
the larger framework of the American ideology, the rebels could "present culturally defined truths . . . that simplify, highlight, or drama-
tize basic cultural premises and prescriptions."[36] In this manner, use
of the Revolutionary War continued an American tradition of exploiting history to justify controversial causes. "We have seen the
Revolution," concluded Ronald Reid, "shaped to justify slavery and
abolitionism, secession and a war against secession, socializing the
American economy and keeping things as they are."[37] The Revolution therefore builds a group ideology which may justify extreme action by persuading followers that the movement upholds traditional
American values. Additionally, the analogy provides a rich resource

for arguments and appeals, allowing the use of highly emotive cultural symbols to engage public interest. As a result, advocates pointed to Jefferson, Madison, and Washington as the true ancestors of the Sagebrush Rebellion.

Although the western myth is missing in sagebrush discourse, rebel rhetoric conveys a strong anti-eastern impulse. The rebels maintained that mismanagement of the public lands resulted from bureaucratic ignorance and arrogance, two problems inherent among the eastern establishment. Such an anti-eastern sentiment, claimed Alan Crawford, "finds increased expression in New Right politics," which hopes to "revenge the resentments of the South and West" against the East.[38] This viewpoint is endorsed by many rebels, including Senator McClure, who criticized eastern environmentalists because they did not understand the need to hunt wild horses in order to reduce overpopulation. Demands to stop the hunting of horses on public lands, which came from places like New York City and Philadelphia, demonstrated typical eastern ignorance to McClure. Moreover, the senator attacked federal land managers, calling them well-intentioned do-gooders "who would protect us to death" and "smother us with their care and attention to the point we were no longer permitted to lead our own lives in the West." This bureaucratic attitude, McClure insisted, was the "genesis of the Sagebrush Rebellion."[39]

Senator Hatch used a similar tale in his "Second American Revolution" speech in Reno. To describe bureaucratic ignorance at its worst, he told a story of a Nevada rancher who "experienced the ultimate in federal bureaucratic idiocy." For over twenty years the rancher used Forest Service lands for his spring lambing. Told that no livestock would be allowed on federal lands until May 20, he protested that his lambs would start dropping about May 1. The rancher received this reply from the secretary of agriculture: "We suggest you postpone lambing until after May 20." Hatch offered no evidence of the authenticity of this story noting that it "may or may not be true." However, when he later endorsed the Sagebrush Rebellion in a letter to the *Washington Post,* he repeated the story as fact, omitting his qualifier. Fact or fiction, this anecdote needed little corroboration among the Nevada ranchers who were fed up with federal land management.[40]

Some rebels argued that liberalism, not ignorance, was the real root of the problem. Ravenscroft charged that federal officials, committed to a liberal political agenda, naturally opposed the best interests of the miner, logger, and rancher: "Expanding regulations, endless studies, red tape, and abrupt arbitrary decisions on the part of federal agencies have caused these frustrations. Contesting with a bureaucracy is akin to wrestling with a tub of taffy." Indeed, the "no growth" politics of America's "planned" economy, argued Ravenscroft, had stagnated the western states.[41] Rebel disaffection with the East was aptly summarized in a *Wall Street Journal* report. Believing that "urban preservationists" had little understanding of public land issues, the report concluded, westerners "resent Eastern implications that they . . . are not to be trusted to manage their ranches and businesses" without harming the public lands.[42]

Many rebels claimed that eastern bureaucrats ignored the best interests of the West in making resource-use decisions. State Senator Richard E. Blakemore of Nevada observed that even "well-intentioned" federal land managers lack the "omniscience to develop adequate national standards to meet the diversity of terrain and resource characteristics that make up the expansive West."[43] Calling federal officials "arrogant" in dealing with state leaders, Jac Shaw of the Nevada Governor's Office charged that such an attitude makes "it very difficult for rational people to sit across the table and discuss issues." In fact, the western states, Shaw concluded, are subjected to greater federal indifference than other regions of the country because the West has so much land: "The more land in any State that Federal bureaucrats control, the less interest they have in the concerns of the inhabitants of that state."[44]

Graphically supporting this view, Senator McClure concluded that western resources are "under-utilized and over-managed by hordes of bureaucrats sitting on their fat backsides." Calling the federal bureaucracy "extreme and inflexible," Senator Hatch charged that federal land management "benefits and fertilizes the inflationary growth of the Federal bureaucracy; the only true function of which is to preserve and proliferate itself at the public's expense."[45] McClure's and Hatch's polemics against government bureaucracy typify the philosophical common ground shared by the New Right and the Sagebrush Rebellion. The two groups became nearly interchangeable in 1980 when Ronald Reagan, the symbolic leader for many in the New Right, declared that he too was a sagebrush rebel.

Growing out of the rebellion rhetoric are several "persuasive slogans," words and phrases that are the building blocks of the movement's ideology.[46] A frequently used phrase in rebel discourse insisted that federal ownership had "locked up" public lands. Who is more

selfish, asked Hatch, than the "dandelion worshippers who unnec-
essarily lock up millions of acres of scenic beauty . . . not because
the lock up will enhance the beauty, but simply to lock it up, to
meet some mysterious quota of land deposited in a no interest, costly
bank?"[47] Marlene Simmons, a Wyoming legislator, told a congressional
hearing that she supported the rebellion because of the "lock-up
of our natural resources by over-protective, selfish, and sometimes
narrow-minded special interest groups."[48] The "lock-up" label lumped
all public lands together as though they were designated wilderness
areas, ignoring that two-thirds of the federal land was classified for
"multiple use."[49] By applying the "lock-up" label to all federally managed lands, rebels could avoid overwhelming audiences with the com-
plexity of environmental laws and simplify the issue into a development-
versus-preservation controversy. As a result, the public perceived two
powerful, albeit distorted, alternatives in the debate: the public lands
locked up by uncaring bureaucrats from the East *or* the public lands
opened for the free and equal use of all Americans.

Another important persuasive slogan for the rebels claimed that
the western states deserved "equal footing" with the other states in
determining how their land ought to be managed. Although some
applied the equal-footing argument in a constitutional context, many
rebels advanced the slogan with no reference to the legal theory itself.
As a result, rebel rhetoric abounds with calls for equal footing as a
matter of basic fairness and civil liberty. Hatch argued that his Sagebrush Rebellion bill would place "all States on an equal footing as the
Founding Fathers intended."[50] A sample letter distributed by the Nevada Committee on Public Lands asserted: "In order that (name the
state) and other western states be placed on 'equal footing' with eastern, southern, and midwestern states, the Sagebrush Rebellion advocates state control of the unappropriated public lands."[51] In addition,
pamphlets from the various rebel groups highlighted the equal-footing
argument. A pamphlet distributed by Idaho's SRJ demanded a Supreme
Court ruling to answer the question, "Were all states admitted to the
Union on a true 'Equal Footing'?" Utah's LASER organization asserted
that federal land regulations "wrongfully deprive the western states of
equal footing guaranteed to all states under the Constitution."[52]

Rhetorically, the equal-footing slogan served several functions. It
reinforced the notion that the Sagebrush Rebellion was a continuing
American Revolution. By tracing the equal-footing doctrine to the
writing of the Constitution, rebels identified another link to Amer-

ica's founders. The appeal also supported the perceived colonial status of the western states. Forced to give up their territorial lands upon admission to the United States, rebels argued, western states were never equal with the rest of the country. This interpretation helped bolster the constitutional aspect of the equal-footing appeal and added legal stature to the rebellion's claims. With this argument, moreover, rebels invoked a powerful cultural symbol in their calls for equality among the states. The American public, observed Charles Elder and Roger Cobb, endorses and upholds certain values, including liberty, freedom, and equality.[53] In this manner, the equal-footing appeal reaffirmed a fundamental American value, the practice of equal treatment under law.

Rebels claimed that transfer of the public lands to the states would stimulate needed economic activity. In line with conservative calls to decrease government regulation as a means of achieving economic growth, the rebellion presented the ideology of the New Right in practice. Arguing that natural resource development could bring an "economic boom" to the western states, Senator Hatch declared, "Our standard of living will grow. Those who tell us we can never again grow are wrong." Lynn Shepard, chairman of Arizona's Association of County Supervisors, endorsed the rebellion because federal bureaucrats "dictate our policies and it stops us from any growth and makes it hard for us to manage our own affairs and create any kind of economic footing."[54]

Appeals to the panacea of economic growth fit comfortably into the optimistic rhetoric of the New Right. Viewing the limited-growth philosophy of the environmental movement with suspicion, the rebels rejected the ecological notion that all entities in the ecosystem be afforded certain inherent rights. Seeking greater balance in public land use, rebels wanted to make human needs the paramount consideration in allocating resources. Claiming that "we have gone overboard to protect endangered species to the detriment of human beings," Hatch demanded, "we've got to develop oil shale and tar sands. Those are God-given resources that can alleviate some of the suffering that this country faces."[55] With such appeals, the sagebrush rebels were able to present a human-centered view of the public lands. Among rebel supporters, the economic constraints imposed by an ecological view of the world appeared unreasonable in light of human needs.

The Sagebrush Rebellion presented the first organized and politically viable challenge to the conservation consensus since the early

1950s. Although concentrated in the West, the rebellion shared resources, leadership, and ideology with the New Right. It is no coincidence that senators such as McClure, Hatch, Garn, and Laxalt were considered leaders in both the New Right and the Sagebrush Rebellion. As a result, the rebellion's impact on policy making should be measured in light of the apparent resurgence of American conservatism in the late 1970s and early 1980s. Before examining the connection between the rebellion and the public land policy of the Reagan administration, another special interest group deserves attention. Environmentalists responded to the rebellion's challenge, and by the summer of 1980 a full-scale counterrebellion was forming in the Rocky Mountain states. Examining the clash between the rebels and the conservationists will help illuminate the Sagebrush Rebellion's role in the larger public lands debate and reveal the movement's impact upon policy making.

3. "Save Our Public Lands"

THE ENVIRONMENTAL RESPONSE

TO THE SAGEBRUSH REBELLION

An organized counterrebellion emerged in 1980, forcing advocates of the Sagebrush Rebellion to adopt a defensive rhetorical style and rely increasingly upon refutation as their principal mode of argument. Many opponents of the sagebrush movement lived and worked outside the West. Although the rebellion received financial aid from nonwestern sources, rebel writers and speakers were in almost all cases residents of the Rocky Mountain region. Examining the counterrebellion, one finds a dual rhetorical strategy designed first to refute rebel claims and second to rebuild public support for the threatened conservation consensus. While rebels attempted to distinguish the question of land ownership from that of land use in their appeals, environmentalists ignored this distinction and characterized the rebellion as an "antiwestern" measure from either perspective.

Opposition to the Sagebrush Rebellion formed among three different groups: government officials at the federal, state, and local levels, including Interior Secretary Cecil Andrus and Governor Bruce Babbitt of Arizona, organized environmental groups such as the Sierra Club and the Audubon Society, and, surprisingly, leaders in the hunting and fishing recreation lobby. Although some observers might expect sports enthusiasts and environmentalists to share the same agenda, significant differences exist between them. Sporting groups have become increasingly conservative in recent decades, especially since gun control issues alienated many hunters from traditionally liberal organizations and politicians. Many sagebrush rebels were therefore surprised to see their hunting and fishing friends leading the counterrebellion in the West. Richard Starnes and Ted Trueblood, national opinion leaders among America's sportsmen, helped organize active opposition to the Sagebrush Rebellion.[1]

Environmentalist discourse, supported with diverse logical proofs, often clashed directly with the appeals the rebels advanced. In this manner, environmentalists often employed research data in making their claims, an argumentation style that contrasts with the highly symbolic rhetoric of the sagebrush rebels. Environmentalists eschewed their own brand of symbolism (invoking the founding fathers, for example) in favor of evidence. Specific reactions by the environmentalists will illustrate this rhetorical stance.

Environmentalist opposition to the Sagebrush Rebellion was swift and direct. Staff members of leading organizations met in Denver, October 27–28, 1979, less than two months after Orrin Hatch's sagebrush bill was introduced into the Senate. Ultimately, seventeen environmental groups publicly opposed the legislation before Congress that would have approved a public land transfer to the individual states. Groups agreeing to fight the rebellion included the Friends of the Earth, the Izaak Walton League, the National Wildlife Federation, the Rocky Mountain Office of the Audubon Society, the Sierra Club, and the Wilderness Society.[2]

Dismissing the rebellion's central premise, that the movement simply "returned" public lands to state ownership, environmentalists argued that the western states had never held title to the disputed lands. Cliff Young, president of the National Widlife Federation, argued, "On admission to the Union, the states agreed in their constitutions what was to remain under federal jurisdiction." Cecil Andrus agreed, pointing out that upon entering the United States, the western territories "signed irrevocable agreements disclaiming all rights and title to federal public lands within their borders." Why did the federal government demand title to the lands in the first place? Because, Andrus explained, the western territories were "acquired by the national government through purchase and warfare, at the expense of all Americans living at that time." In a letter distributed to western newspapers, Donald Nelson of the Audubon Society refuted the notion that public lands were somehow preempted by statehood. For over one hundred years, he wrote, the federal government "attempted to dispose of this land, with the present public lands being areas no one wanted."[3] Western pioneers had decades to obtain the public lands, but with growing pressures to exploit the natural resources, environmentalists concluded, permanent federal ownership now seemed appropriate.

Refuting the states' rights appeal, James H. Pissot of the Audubon Society insisted that equal footing had never been recognized by the

Supreme Court as an economic or property question. "The fifty states differ widely in size, resources, and land types," claimed Pissot. "If lack of acreage is such an issue, are Utah and Nevada also less equal because of their lack of water?" Extending his argument, he asked, if the public lands are turned over to the western states, "will not the Eastern states cry out that, lacking equal *state-owned* acreage, now *they* are not on equal footing?"[4] Although the rebels presented the equal-footing appeal as an issue of fair play, they also emphasized its merits as a constitutional issue. Their initial challenge on constitutional grounds was rejected by a federal district court in Nevada.[5] If the rebels could not obtain a court hearing at the district level, a Supreme Court challenge appeared unlikely. Moreover, legal studies by the Department of Interior, the Arizona attorney general, and the *Utah Law Review*, reported Wallace Stegner, all "concur that the constitutional, equal-footing case is very weak." If the equal-footing doctrine were ever upheld by the Supreme Court, Stegner predicted, there would be national chaos: national parks, national forests, wilderness sanctuaries, "every part of the once-public domain would come under a cloud."[6]

Environmentalists maintained that the western states could not properly manage the vast tracts of public land and disputed rebel claims that state ownership would be more efficient than that of the Forest Service and the Bureau of Land Management. Advocates offered several lines of refutation to demonstrate the harmful consequences of a land transfer. In a message to the Arizona legislature, Governor Babbitt concluded: "Historically, the record of abuses in the State Land Department is not reassuring. State lands were sold off for a pittance . . . the State Land Department still does not have adequate statutes or personnel to do a truly effective job of land management." Andrus observed that western states have two institutional features that would lead to great problems. Many states constitutionally mandate that state lands be used to balance the state budget or finance the school system. For example, if Idaho followed its constitution, Andrus pointed out, "it would mean a lot of those lands would be sold, or leased for single-purpose harvest—either timber or mineral." In addition, political pressures from special interest lobbyists represented another threat to state ownership. Reflecting upon his experience as a two-term governor of Idaho, Andrus argued, "Economic pressure groups would put overwhelming, sometimes irresistible pressure on elected officials to sell off the lands for single-purpose use." Outdoor writer Ted Trueblood supported this conclusion. Quoting the Idaho Environmental Council, he noted that "almost all constitutions of the western states require that state lands 'shall be managed for their maximum economic value.' This requirement prohibits multiple-use management. . . . Wilderness, watershed, wildlife, recreation, and hunting are, at best, nearly illegal uses of state lands."[7]

With over 59 million Americans hunting and/or fishing in 1980, Trueblood's gloomy prediction suggested harmful consequences for this national pastime if the state gained title to the public lands.[8] To further document the inability of the states to properly manage forests and grazing lands, the Public Lands Institute reported that lands already "owned by Colorado and 10 other Western states are managed by agencies that are seriously understaffed." More important, the report charged that state land managers ignore conservation and wildlife concerns "because the land is managed solely for moneymaking."[9]

Environmentalists turned the rebels' claims back on them, arguing that the real "lock up" of the public lands would occur *after* a successful land transfer to state control. Invoking the legislated goal of multiple use, environmentalists argued that federal land statutes guaranteed public access to the lands. Mixing his metaphors, Andrus claimed that most westerners understood that the federal lands, "far from 'fencing them in,' are a major reservoir of freedom where they can hike, hunt, fish, prospect for minerals, graze livestock and share in numerous other recreational and economic activities."[10] Governor Babbitt also countered the rebels' position by noting that multiple use mandates that "no single interest is allowed to dominate the land." State ownership appeared to be a poor alternative because lands currently managed by the federal government would "soon be replaced by locked gates, barricaded roads, and 'No Trespassing' signs."[11] Such a frightening vision prompted many westerners, including some ranchers, to reassess their support for the rebellion.

Rejecting the notion that arrogant eastern bureaucrats forced numerous environmental laws upon an unsuspecting West, environmentalists argued that western senators and representatives were the principal architects of the conservation consensus. Andrus insisted that the Federal Land Policy and Management Act (FLPMA) of 1976 was the "result of a steady evolution of attitudes and values about the resources of the public lands and [was] shaped—and largely drafted—by Westerners in Congress." Johanna H. Wald and Elizabeth H. Temkin insisted that the FLPMA, often "alleged to have 'caused' the Sagebrush Rebellion, illustrates the dominant influence of the West on public land laws." Westerners conceived the legislation, westerners shaped the law in Congress, and the "majority of westerners in Congress voted in favor of its passage."[12] In fact, environmentalists claimed that westerners had written most of the conservation legislation passed in recent decades. During the twentieth century, wrote Cliff Young, most public lands legislation was "sponsored by western congressmen. If the laws were not wisely enacted, we can hardly blame westerners for supporting what we in the West have advocated."[13]

Environmentalists maintained that federal laws encouraged state and local participation in the development of public land policy. Contrary to observers who traced the rebellion's birth to the FLPMA of 1976, Babbitt suggested that the "Act took significant strides toward increasing the influence of state and local government on federal land use planning activities." How did this law provoke the rebellion if it indeed encouraged greater local and state participation in making policy? Frank Gregg, an official with the Bureau of Land Management, called the rebellion an "understandable reaction" by ranchers to the BLM's "steady progress in implementing the balanced multiple-use management program called for by the FLPMA of 1976." Even though ranchers had the opportunity to speak out, they were angered by efforts to create more varied use of the federal rangelands. Grazing restrictions seemed inevitable in light of land conditions. According to Gregg, 84 percent of the public rangelands "are in no better than fair condition; . . . almost half of its lands are in an unacceptable state of erosion; and . . . its wildlife habitats are deteriorating."[14]

Some rebels hoped to portray the public lands debate as a battle of good versus evil, western sportsmen against environmental extremists. Marlene Simmons, for example, argued that the American Dream of "the family that plays together stays together" was no longer possible because "excessive land withdrawals" greatly limited the amount of public land available for snowmobiling, skiing, and four-wheel driving. Instead of family use, she charged, "these wilderness areas can only be used by a fortunate few who are financially and physically able to enjoy them." She ended her polemic by concluding that Americans are "bombarded from every angle by the preservationist movement to lock up our public lands."[15]

In March, 1980, outdoor writers Trueblood and Starnes advised their respective audiences that the Sagebrush Rebellion was a land grab, plain and simple. The land in question, observed Trueblood, is "public land. We can wander on it at will to hunt, fish, camp, or enjoy its freedom in countless other ways." Calling the rebellion an attempt to "steal the public lands," he declared that the rebels "want it for nothing." Hunters, wrote Starnes, ought to have special interest in the controversy because much of the western wilderness would be "sold off to private interests, doubtless to be despoiled, raped, gutted and ruined in the search for a quick buck." Listing the vast numbers of wildlife, including moose, elk, deer, fish, ducks, and pheasants that inhabit the public lands, Starnes concluded that the biggest losers "will be the outdoorsmen of the West." Rebels understandably sought to quell such fears. Vernon Ravenscroft of Sagebrush Rebellion, Inc., told Idaho hunters that wildlife is "produced by favorable habitat—not by the name on the deed." In states with little public land such as Alabama, Mississippi, and Louisiana, he observed, hunters have "unbelievable deer hunting" thanks to a cooperative "hunter management program worked out by the owners of private timber lands." Hunters and fishermen, however, seemed unconvinced. In a strident editorial, *Outdoor Life* told its readers that "large corporations want absolute control so that they are free to use or abuse the land as they please without the federal government's control. In your wildest imagination can you honestly believe that these giant corporations won't strip you of your freedom to hunt and fish?"[16]

Adopting another rhetorical strategy employed by the sagebrush rebels, environmentalists also exploited the West's anti-eastern impulse. In so doing, they sought to separate the rebels from mainstream western Americans. Labeling the rebels as right-wing extremists, environmentalists portrayed the movement as the servant of various special interests. For example, a Montana Democratic Party briefing document observed that admission to the Sagebrush Rebellion conference held in Utah cost $145 per person, well beyond the financial reach of typical western sportsmen. In addition, the brief claimed that the Mountain States Legal Foundation, an early proponent of the rebellion, received funding from conservative private concerns such as Coors Beer, Amax Coal, Boise Cascade, Consolidated Coal, Stauffer Chemical, and "other big corporate pawns."[17] Some environmentalists announced that the high cost of the conference kept them from attending. Using the fee to attack the "elistist bent" of the rebellion, James Pissot of the Audubon Society observed, "If it costs $145 to get into a conference like this, we wonder what it will cost to get into these [public] lands (when the states take over)."[18] Portrayal as the pawn of big business seemed to contradict the rebellion's grass-roots image and shifted regional resentment to focus on eastern special interests attempting to shape public lands policy in the West.

Linking the rebellion to the desires of corporate America, Trueblood charged that its real motive was "to exploit the energy potential of the public domain." Recalling the 1980 Idaho Senate campaign between Steve Symms and Frank Church, he pointed out that sagebrush rebel Symms had received funding from numerous corporate sponsors, including Chevron, Atlantic Richfield, Conoco, Forest Oil, the American Gas Association, Independent Energy, Marathon Oil, Phillips Oil, Shell Oil, and Texaco. "You don't have to be a genius," concluded Trueblood, "to see who's really behind the Sagebrush ripoff."[19]

To substantiate the rebellion's dire consequences for the West, environmentalists accused rebels of secretly wanting to sell the public lands to private interests. The rebels "have made no secret of the fact that their goal is to see the public land converted to private ownership," claimed Idaho State Senator Ken Robison. To prove this charge, many advocates quoted Sen. Orrin Hatch's publicized comment that the public lands would eventually be sold. "My bill," said Hatch, "is designed to return control of our destiny to the people of Utah by transferring title to the unappropriated public lands to state control, and from there to the county authorities, and ultimately to private citizens."[20] The public lands would therefore eventually end up on the auction block, going to the highest bidder, regardless of the state of residence. Western ranchers faced the prospect of being outbid by oil and gas companies, real estate speculators, or corporate ranchers. Andrus charged that developers would like to "carve up choice western desert and mountain sites into subdivisions, private hunting preserves and exclusive recreational areas."[21]

For environmentalists, state ownership of the public lands presented a myriad of problems that overshadowed states' rights considerations. Ignoring appeals to fairness and federalism, advocates emphasized the potential threat posed by a successful rebellion, pointing to restrictions on hunting, fishing, hiking, and grazing. This rhetorical strategy forced rebels to defend the land-use consequences of a land transfer and allowed environmentalists to avoid becoming bogged down in an ideological debate. In this manner, environmentalists seemed to gain the advantage in the public lands debate as 1980 came to a close.

Frustrated by the rebellion's ability to capture media attention consistently, Trueblood and a "little group of old fishing friends in Boise" formed Save Our Public Lands, Inc., an Idaho-based group to combat the rebels. Trueblood received permission from *Field and Stream* to reprint his antirebellion essay in tabloid form.[22] Initially printing 30,000 copies at their own expense, members of the group were later able to publish 150,000 copies as private contributions grew. Save Our Public Lands distributed the tabloids door to door in many cities, called press conferences to denounce the rebellion, and sponsored rallies to unify antirebellion sentiments among Idahoans.

In addition, the group used bumper stickers, bulletins, and petitions to spread their message. Noting that some observers questioned the political impact of petitions, Trueblood declared, "We don't agree. We've used them several times and, believe me, when you stagger into a congressional debate or state legislative hearing carrying a big box of petitions and say, 'Here are the names and addresses of 50,000 Idaho people who support our cause,' you make a ripple on the pond." Members of Save Our Public Lands claimed to have stemmed the rebellion's momentum in Idaho. Using their petitions in legislative hearings and holding a rally at the Idaho State Capitol, the group helped kill a sagebrush bill in a senate committee. In 1981, Save Our Public Lands published a short book, *The Sagebrush Rebellion: A Bid for Control*, by Ken Robison. Reviewing typical environmental objections to the rebellion, Robison concluded that the public lands "represented freedom to the American people. It was freedom to explore new land, to tap its resources, to settle on it, that brought most of the settlers West. The large public land area of the West still represents freedom."[23] This conclusion illustrates the fundamental theme of the counterrebellion: continued federal ownership of the public lands protects individual freedom to use the nation's public lands in a variety of ways. The antirebellion sentiments expressed by sportsmen confirm the rhetorical strength of this argument. Other factors, however, help explain the rebellion's ultimate demise.

Did the Sagebrush Rebellion have any discernible effect on public policy or opinion? Public opinion polls showed contradictory results, suggesting either public indifference on the issue or a lack of consensus by westerners. One survey, conducted in eight Rocky Mountain states, found that 36 percent of the public favored the rebellion and that 60 percent opposed it. Critics attacked the survey as biased, noting that the rebellion was called a "seizure of the federal lands" in the questionnaire. On the other hand, a California survey found that 57 percent of residents wanted "greater control" over the public lands.[24] Even with the media's continuous coverage of the rebellion throughout 1980, enhanced by a political campaign that addressed the issue in many states, many westerners remained ignorant of the movement. A poll commissioned by the *Denver Post* found that 72 percent of those interviewed had never heard of the Sagebrush Rebellion.[25] Observing that the few opinion polls examining the rebellion "have proved inconclusive," the *Christian Science Monitor* concluded that the only tangible evidence of public opinion came in Washington, where voters rejected a Sagebrush Rebellion bill, 60 percent to 40 percent.[26]

The sagebrush rebels did, nevertheless, receive strong support for their cause in various western state legislatures, where favorable legislation was passed in Alaska, Arizona, California, Colorado, Hawaii, Idaho, Nevada, New Mexico, Utah, and Wyoming. Additionally, six of these states passed Nevada-style legislation demanding a transfer of the public lands to state control.[27]

Some writers explained that the sagebrush legislation passed easily because it was merely symbolic. Because the individual states were not prepared actually to seize the land, noted John G. Francis, state legislators could endorse the rebellion "without believing that the lands would be transferred forthwith and without viewing votes for the Rebellion as very meaningful."[28] Some rebels even admitted publicly that the movement's purpose was more symbolic than real. Sen. Paul Laxalt, a staunch rebel, stated that "it was never his intention to take over the federal lands—that the movement was more 'symbolic' and a 'cry for the West to have more say.'" Another rebel proponent, David Leroy, Idaho's attorney general, told a group that he saw the rebellion as "a plea for a more meaningful partnership between states and the federal government in making land management decisions." Moreover, several years after the rebellion had ended, Senator McClure recalled that transferring the federal lands to the states was not the "essence" of the rebellion. "I think a great majority of Idahoans have not wanted all the lands sold," noted the senator.[29]

As political conditions changed in 1980, the sagebrush advocates assumed a defensive posture. In a July, 1980, press release to Idaho newspapers, Vernon Ravenscroft structured his message to refute those critics who "repeatedly dredge up one of three inaccurate, misinformed, hypothetical arguments." He insisted that the western states could responsibly manage the public land after a transfer of ownership; that the rebellion was not a special interest land grab; and that hunters and fishermen should not be concerned by scare tactics of the environmentalists. His defense of the rebellion concluded that "strident emotional misrepresentation, and tar baby arguments" had no place in the public lands debate. Also in 1980, the Nevada Committee on Public Lands issued a question-and-answer fact sheet seeking to dispel arguments against the rebellion, rather than reiterating the economic and social arguments in its favor.[30]

Not all sagebrush rebels believed that public land would ever be transferred to the states. Evaluating the success of the movement therefore requires looking at its initial goals as well as its end results. In 1979, the National Association of Counties listed five different goals that could be used to evaluate the success of the Sagebrush Rebellion. Significantly, of the five criteria, only one dealt with a land transfer, while other goals included: focusing attention on "western water, land, energy," and other public land concerns; changing attitudes and gaining political concessions from the administration in office; changing attitudes in federal agencies, especially the BLM; and gaining congressional support for land sales and other public land issues.[31] Informed observers suggested that some of these goals were ultimately reached. One source noted that in conversations BLM personnel confirm that the "Rebellion is already putting federal land managers on the defensive. It is . . . undermining their ability to make and enforce professional management decisions."[32]

Political concessions favorable to the sagebrush rebels were also obtainable goals. "To a great extent, the Sagebrush Rebellion has been successful," reported Andrew Grose, chief of staff to the governor of Nevada. "[T]here is far greater public awareness of the public lands situation which is also to the benefit of the Western states."[33] James Haggard, representing the prorebel Phelps Dodge mining corporation, claimed that the movement had accomplished important goals for the West: "It has created an organization. It has inspired individuals to speak out. It has attracted the attention of the national news media, and it has had significant impact on past elections." With a new president, a restructured Senate, and a sympathetic interior secretary, Haggard concluded that there was "reason to hope that many of the wrongs suffered by the western land users will be remedied."[34] The manager of the Utah Mining Association agreed, pointing out that the federal agencies "are more responsive to western users because of the furore [*sic*] stirred up by the sagebrush rebellion." The Utah Foundation reported in January, 1980, well before Ronald Reagan's success in the Republican primaries, that the Sagebrush Rebellion "has generated pressures which have markedly improved relations between federal land administrators and local land users. Major problems and differences remain, but a new and improved climate for two-way discussion of these differences has emerged."[35]

Ironically, after Reagan's presidential victory in 1980, the rebellion went into a steady decline. Many rebels were euphoric after the election. Three weeks after the general election, a national headline reflected their satisfaction: "Sagebrush Rebels See Open Range in Reagan's Victory." Reagan's endorsement of the rebellion, wrote David Salisbury, had been "little noted by the national press," but his victory "may have set the stage for a revolution in national land policy." Two weeks after this report, *U.S. News and World Report* announced continued rebel hopes for a land transfer. With Reagan in the White House, westerners "believe that they will have a much better chance of winning the battle." The article also reported candidate Reagan's pledge that if elected, his administration would "reflect the values and goals of the Sagebrush Rebellion. Indeed, we can turn the Sagebrush Rebellion into the Sagebrush Solution."[36] In retrospect, it appears that his endorsement was less than absolute. Once the nation's highest placed sagebrush rebel assumed the presidency, a change of conviction started to take place.

The administration's efforts to distance itself from the movement began even before the president's inauguration. During his Senate confirmation hearings, interior secretary-designate James Watt suggested that many public land disputes could be resolved by a "good neighbor" approach, with continued federal management of the lands but eased land-use restrictions. Watt told one source that changing Washington's "arrogant" attitude toward the West would remove the need for a Sagebrush Rebellion.[37] Six months into office, Watt's good neighbor policy had indeed apparently defused the rebellion. His support for "more mining, more drilling, more grazing, more timber cutting, and more local control," wrote Brad Knickerbocker, meant that rebels "may not need outright confrontation to win much of what they are fighting for." Senator McClure echoed the same sentiments when he told an Idaho newspaper that with a friend in the White House, "the push for the Sagebrush Rebellion may dissipate."[38]

With little support from the administration and growing efforts by environmentalists to counter the movement, the Sagebrush Rebellion was in trouble. Sara Terry reported in August 1981 that environmentalists, "caught off guard by the initial momentum" of the rebellion, launched a powerful counterattack throughout the West. Rebel defeats in the Idaho and Montana legislatures, claimed Terry, were due to "lobbying efforts by a coalition of environmentalists, sportsmen's clubs, organized labor, senior citizens, and women voters."[39] By stressing the possible harms of a successful rebellion, environmentalists gained the upper hand in the sagebrush debate. In addition, Reagan's good neighbor policy allowed many rebel proponents to withdraw their support from a continued rebellion.

With Watt leading the administration's public lands policy, the rebellion lost its luster for many western politicians. In September, 1981, Watt told the Western Governors' Conference that although he and Reagan continued to be sagebrush rebels, "I hope to be a rebel without a cause." One national periodical interpreted this remark to be a "declaration that the Sagebrush Rebellion had all but collapsed" and that Watt "deserved much of the credit for defusing the rebellion."[40] More important, the federal district court in Nevada dismissed the state's claim against the public lands within the state. Noting that there was "little support in Congress for Sagebrush Rebellion legislation," William Endicott concluded that the movement "is on the verge of collapse."[41] Many western ranchers seemed pleased by Watt's efforts to minimize enforcement of grazing regulations imposed by the Carter administration. Ron Madsen, a member of Senator Hatch's staff, observed that Watt's policies are "sympathetic to the West, so the impetus has died down. Everywhere I go people are now saying that the federal government is a good landlord."[42]

By 1984 only a few diehards believed the rebellion could be saved. Idaho's Sagebrush Rebellion, Inc., continued to issue newsletters and hold public meetings, but with Reagan's sweeping reelection in 1984, it seemed unlikely that the rebellion could sustain the fervor of the late 1970s. The loss of political support from many conservatives and the eased public land restrictions removed the primary concern among many western land users. Ironically, "good neighbor" Reagan helped kill the Sagebrush Rebellion with kindness.

Different observers have proposed various reasons for the decline of the rebellion. Frank Popper claimed that the rebellion did not fail, but "ended because it achieved many of its goals." According to Popper, the Reagan administration provided an optimum solution for rebels, continued federal management but with eased use standards. "For many Westerners sympathetic to the Rebellion," concluded Popper, "restraining federal regulation became an acceptable substitute for selling federal land."[43] Robert H. Nelson, an economist with the Department of Interior, identified a different reason for the demise of the rebellion. Ranchers and mining interests backed away from the rebellion when they realized the impact of a successful land transfer: traditional public land users could lose their use rights or pay excessive fees if each state controlled the public lands. Indeed, Nelson concluded, many westerners recognized "the rewards of federal ownership to be worth the annoyances."[44]

While the Sagebrush Rebellion appeared finished as a significant factor in western politics by 1982, it provides an important link in the larger public lands debate. The rebellion presented the New Right in action, attempting to develop a new conservative ideology that could compete with the successful agenda of the conservation consensus. Significantly, rebel leaders were also those individuals who were so often identified with the rise of the New Right: Jake Garn, Orrin Hatch, Paul Laxalt, James McClure; even Sen. Jesse Helms of North Carolina expressed his support for the Sagebrush Rebellion. The activism inherent in the New Right philosophy typifies the genesis of the Sagebrush Rebellion. America's old conservatives, charged Senator Garn, "just made a record for the folks back home. . . . They were content to just sit back and oppose. . . . We feel we have to propose something."[45] Using Nevada's call to arms, the New Right found a pragmatic, albeit regional, goal: to challenge the liberal's public land policy.

The Sagebrush Rebellion reinstituted the political struggle over conservation that has raged periodically throughout the twentieth century. Samuel P. Hays observed that conservation brings into focus the "two competing political systems" of this century: those who endorsed "science and technology" and sought a centralized technocracy to make societal decisions; and those who sought more open decision making with a "wider range of alternatives open for choice."[46] As a result, the Sagebrush Rebellion debate presented a clash of competing systems of government, with the conservation consensus, stemming from a New Deal perspective, versus the rebellion, representing the New Right goal of limited government and an economy driven by private forces.

Because the Sagebrush Rebellion appeared and left the political landscape so abruptly, many observers might minimize its larger place in the American public lands debate. Looking closely at the rebellion, however, reveals that it changed the direction and momentum of the conservation consensus. First and most important overall, the Sagebrush Rebellion presented a viable political challenge to the conservation consensus that became a legislative reality in the 1970s. Federal public land policy became an issue once again in the Congress. The goals of an ecological conscience and a land ethic were no longer accepted as givens in making policy. Second, the sagebrush rebels demonstrated the effectiveness of economic arguments in countering the humane and ecological appeals of many environmentalists. The rebels had little reluctance in demanding that economic well-being be given higher priority than ecological well-being in some circumstances. Third, the rebellion reflected the New Right's successful adoption of liberal rhetorical and political strategies: single-issue, grass-roots organizations with speakers bureaus, media contacts, telephone networks, and letter banks. The rebels showed that political conservativism could be an activist philosophy. In this manner, the rebellion proved that the New Deal approach to government could be challenged by an alternative philosophy. The New Right's call for limited government, greater development of the public lands, and greater freedom for the individual states found clear expression in the Sagebrush Rebellion, an important lesson for those conservatives still a part of the Old Right. Lastly, the rebellion mobilized a complacent environmental community. Conservation leaders were slow to realize in 1980 that for the first time in twenty years an opponent to many of their goals could end up in the Oval Office. Recognizing the implications of a Reagan victory, twenty-two major environmental groups abandoned their nonpartisan stance and endorsed Jimmy Carter.

Although the direct effects of the Sagebrush Rebellion on land ownership appear minimal, the movement did alter the direction of the American conservation debate. It set the stage for a four-year struggle between the Reagan administration and the environmental movement to redefine public land policy. Although the rebellion dimmed after Reagan's reelection, a new breed of federal land manager emerged and a new challenge, the privatization of the public lands, entered the conservation debate. Among the many legacies of the Sagebrush Rebellion, the most important may be that the movement inspired Ronald Reagan and his new administration to dismantle the conservation consensus and provide a new program for managing America's public lands.

4. The Presidency and the Public Lands

CONSERVATION AND THE 1980 PRESIDENTIAL CAMPAIGN

Speaking to a group of Ohio Teamsters in 1980, Ronald Reagan captured the frustration and anger of the American working class in a single word. America, he charged, was in a "depression" and when challenged on the technical accuracy of that term, he capitalized on the distinction. Recalling an old joke, Reagan told the union members that it is a recession when your neighbor loses his job and a depression when you lose your job. Jimmy Carter's academically accurate "recession" appeared to be nitpicking compared with Reagan's common-sense approach.[1]

During the 1980 presidential campaign, the future of the public lands became a primary issue among Republicans and Democrats. Had no other issues been at stake the election could, in fact, have been viewed as a national referendum on whether the vast western wilderness ought to be preserved or developed, since the candidates discussed the issues in such extreme, polarized terms. In retrospect, the public lands controversy typified the choice voters were presented in 1980. In the tradition of the New Deal, Carter endorsed federal efforts to regulate and restrict public land use. Reagan proposed a different agenda: give private interests greater freedom to develop the lands in a quest for a strengthened economy. Again, voters faced a difficult question: at what cost does a society preserve its forests, rangelands, and mountains? Analyzing how the public lands became a salient issue in 1980 will help describe the political climate that accompanied the 1981–84 conservation debate. To further illuminate Reagan's intended land policy revolution, the implications of James Watt's selection as interior secretary will be examined.

The year 1980 was an unhappy time to be an incumbent president seeking reelection. American economic woes were indeed disturbing. Spendable weekly earnings had dropped steadily during Jimmy Carter's tenure, while the national unemployment rate had fluctuated between 12 and 14 percent. Moreover, the consumer price index rate of increase doubled under his leadership.[2] Inflation and federal budget deficits, twin demons for New Right ideologues, were both at record highs. Unemployment reached 15 to 20 percent in many industrial cities as steel mills and automobile plants closed their gates, while the national poverty rate started to grow after many years of steady decline. As the 1980 general election neared, noted Laurence Barrett, candidate Reagan's "apocalyptic predictions about the failures of big government were coming true."[3]

With the economy in dire straits, the 1980 campaign increasingly centered upon economic issues. Concurrently, foreign affairs were on hold: the SALT II talks with the Soviet Union were suspended; the Iranian hostage crisis remained at a stalemate; and the Camp David peace process was bogged down in delays. With energy, inflation, and unemployment dominating the campaign, the question of developing the public lands achieved increased prominence. The Carter administration, although taking some steps toward resource development, generally supported the conservation consensus of the previous two decades. The RARE II land inventory and the Alaska Land Bill of 1980 endorsed by Carter reaffirmed administration support for the values of wilderness preservation. More than any other presidential race in recent decades, the 1980 campaign placed the question of public lands preservation or development squarely before the American voters.

Surprisingly, before the 1980 primary season, many political experts considered Reagan to be a weak candidate. According to Elizabeth Drew, some observers believed Reagan "too old, too blunder-prone" to be a successful candidate. If he could indeed gain the Republican nomination, many pundits assumed, the "election of a Democrat is certain."[4] Ironically, aides to Carter hoped that Reagan would gain the nomination, believing the former movie actor to be the most vulnerable Republican in 1980. Considered the head of the Republican right wing after Barry Goldwater's defeat in 1964, Reagan had articulated a simple and consistent ideology over the years. His personal brand of conservatism, while embracing some aspects of the Old Right, the New Right, and even the Neoconservatives, was both "broader and simpler" than the ideologies of these groups. Voters found Reaganism to be politically engaging, claimed Barrett, because they seemed to know what it "favors or opposes at least on principle." The fundamentals of Reaganism, he concluded, were best summarized as radical, simple, and optimistic.[5] Looking at a nation beset by serious economic ills, Reagan argued that America must use the public lands to help rebuild the nation. Reagan's rhetorical style of speaking common sense to the American public, provided a glowing optimism in stark contrast with Carter's finger-pointing national malaise speech of the previous summer.[6]

A review of Reagan's campaign oratory shows that the candidate was remarkably in tune with the goals of the Sagebrush Rebellion. Speaking in modern America's village green, the urban shopping mall, Reagan blasted federal bureaucrats who have "no more faith and trust in the American people" and who think they must tell "us how to run our lives." In a peroration that became a staple of the campaign, he announced that America needed a president "who will take government off the people's backs and turn the great genius of the American people loose once again."[7] Reagan's political metaphors meshed comfortably with the Sagebrush Rebellion's notion that government had locked up the public lands, stifling economic growth and fueling inflation. America "doesn't have to be in the shape that it is in," Reagan declared in his televised debate with Carter. "We do not have to go on sharing in scarcity with the country getting worse off, unemployment growing. . . . All of this can be cured and all of it can be solved."[8]

Regarding the public lands, Reagan's campaign rhetoric suggested several conclusions for voters. He presented a simple plan to save the economy by opening the lands to greater exploration and development. In making such appeals, Reagan infused a strong sense of morality into his policy pronouncements. Ronald Dallek concluded that Reaganism combined "old-fashioned Republicanism" with a well-defined ideology "expressing strong feelings" about how Americans should think and act. Suggesting that Reaganites were caught up in symbolic politics, Dallek claimed that Reaganism was less a response to specific problems and more a "means of restoring traditional values to the center of American life."[9] In this manner, Reagan's public lands agenda fit into the New Right's larger mission of restoring work, family, and neighborhood as important values. And this sense of crusade had no better embodiment than the new president's public lands policy maker James Watt.

The issue of public lands often emerged in the campaign under the rubric of energy. In the Carter-Reagan race, one writer observed, "energy" represented the nation's "growing realization that inflation, unemployment, and foreign policy were strongly influenced by growing oil shortages."[10] Because of this recognition, public lands became linked to a wide array of national concerns.

Rhetoric from varied opinion leaders helped set the climate for the ensuing public lands debate. Commemorating the tenth anniversary of Earth Day, environmentalist Gladwin Hill attempted to answer the question, "What has happened to the environmental fervor of the early 1970s?" Public activism appeared less zealous, maintained Hill, because America's environmental concern "has become institutionalized; it is now an integral part of the national fabric." On the other hand, several negative stereotypes clouded the success of the conservation movement. Rejecting the belief that environmentalism represented the "elitist enthusiasm" of upper-class professionals, Hill argued that only a large, grass-roots constituency could have lobbied successfully for the many laws passed in the 1960s and 1970s protecting the environment and preserving the public lands. He also refuted the notion that environmentalism was a monolithic movement, placing wilderness preservation in an "Armageddon-like" conflict with other societal interests. Instead of demanding absolute wins and losses, environmentalists had learned to accept political "advances and setbacks" everyday. It would be simplistic to believe, Hill concluded, that all environmentalists endorsed the same policies.[11]

Several months later another national journal published a New Right criticism of the environmental movement that soundly rejected Hill's conclusions. In a detailed polemic, William Tucker attacked environmentalism for becoming America's own "aristocratic conservativism." In the 1960s, the nation's lower middle class and the upper middle class joined together to fight for numerous social reforms, such as civil rights and consumerism. However, in the 1970s, Tucker maintained, the upper middle class shifted priorities, seeking to preserve the status quo and deny any further redistribution of societal wealth. By supporting strict environmental standards and preservation of large tracts of wilderness, Tucker reasoned, environmentalists prevented America's lower middle class from making continued economic gains. Because of this economic paralysis, a new political alliance, the lower middle class and the business elite, emerged in 1980 to challenge the conservation consensus which appeared to threaten the well-being of both groups. This alliance, concluded Tucker, would force the victor in 1980, whether Carter or Reagan, to bring a "new pragmatic, optimistic approach to environmental problems." Frustrated by the environmental movement's long string of legislative victories, conservatives found in Tucker's essay an appealing intellectual justification for their prodevelopment crusade.[12]

Leaders in the organized conservation movement found Reagan's proposals to develop the public lands and relax environmental standards more frightening as the fall campaign progressed. In previous elections, environmentalists had remained nonpartisan in an effort to court both Republicans and Democrats. Indeed, the Theodore Roosevelt–Gifford Pinchot tradition still appealed to many Republicans, as demonstrated by the support of the Nixon and Ford administrations for key bills that furthered the conservation consensus.

In 1980, however, many environmental groups abandoned their nonpartisan tradition and endorsed Jimmy Carter. Representing more than 10 million members, the twenty-two different groups included the Sierra Club, the Audubon Society, the Wilderness Society, and the Friends of the Earth. Conservation leaders emphatically rejected Reagan's public lands agenda. Calling the Republican candidate hostile to environmental protection, Marion Edy of the League of Conservation Voters charged that "his ignorance of environmental issues is real, not a figment of the media's imagination." A former Republican governor of Delaware, Russell Peterson, representing Audubon, charged that both Reagan and the Republican Party platform showed a "basic misunderstanding of the important issues such as energy." Reaganites, claimed Peterson, sought to "free up industry so it can make a bundle today. They don't understand that a healthy economy depends on a healthy environment and a wise use of resources." Announcing his support for Carter, Brock Evans of the Sierra Club suggested that it was time that environmentalists "started acting like the other guys around town and started getting active on the political front." Indeed, the *New York Times* concluded that the endorsement of Carter "marks another step in the politicization of the environmental movement in recent years."[13]

During the campaign, Reagan stressed a variety of arguments concerning the future of the public lands under his administration. These appeals reaffirmed Reagan's link to the New Right and demonstrated the rhetorical strength of simple and optimistic solutions to complex problems. Significantly for the public lands debate, each theme advanced by the Republican candidate directly countered Carter's policy, offering voters two conflicting images: common-sense Reaganism or complicated Carter analysis. Speaking in Kokomo, Indiana, a Democratic stronghold with a 19 percent unemployment rate in 1980, Reagan argued that for the first time in American history, the nation faced "three grave crises at the same time." Each crisis by itself could destroy the United States, he asserted. "Our economy is deteriorating. Our energy needs are not being met. And our military preparedness has been weakened to the point of immediate danger. The Carter record is a litany of despair, of broken promises, of sacred trusts abandoned and forgotten."[14] Offering a distinct alternative to Carter's record, Reagan promised to solve each of the "grave crises" with little or no sacrifice for the voting public.

The United States, proclaimed Reagan, had multiple, untapped energy sources, in direct contrast with Carter's predictions of an extensive energy shortage. In his acceptance speech at the Republican National Convention, Reagan claimed that large amounts of oil had been trapped underground because the Carter administration "seems to believe the American people would rather see more regulation, taxes and control than more energy." Reagan also linked exploration of the public lands with his larger goal of saving the economy. Arguing that America must get to work producing energy, he concluded that his "program for solving economic problems is based on growth and productivity." In this manner, he linked his claim that America had an abundance of energy with the New Right economic savior: "growth and productivity." Debating Carter only days before the election, Reagan repeated his claim that the United States had explored only 2 percent of the outer continental shelf, "where it is believed by everyone familiar with that fuel and that source of energy, that there are vast supplies to be found." During the previous year, he continued, millions of acres of public lands "were taken out of multiple use" and locked up under the Carter administration. "It is believed," concluded Reagan, "that probably 70 percent of the potential oil in the United States is probably hidden in those lands. And no one is allowed to even go and explore to find out if it is there." Concluding his plans to find new energy, Reagan told the 100 million viewers that America does have the "sources here. We are energy rich."[15]

Claiming that a minuscule number of Americans, the "environmental extremists," were responsible for locking up the public lands, Reagan complained that the search for energy must not be "thwarted by a tiny minority opposed to economic growth which often finds friendly ears in regulatory agencies for its obstructionist campaigns."[16] A link between environmentalists and advocates of limited growth represented a common theme among New Right advocates. Believing that economic growth offered the best means of helping the nation's poor and unemployed, conservatives rejected calls for a limited life-style, reduced energy use, and redistribution of societal wealth. The "small is beautiful" philosophy that many social theorists embraced in the 1960s and 1970s was anathema to the New Right.[17]

When environmentalists attacked Reagan's conservation record, a campaign spokesperson replied that the Republican nominee had two goals for the public lands. First, seeking a balance in resource policy, Reagan planned to examine "every regulatory requirement with a commitment to simplify and streamline the process." Second, he wanted the federal government to "return to the states the primary responsibility for environmental regulation."[18] Such a response late in the campaign demonstrated Reagan's disinterest in courting the conservation vote and confirmed his plans to decentralize the bureaucracy at the level of resource management and environmental protection.

Proposing that the federal government should not be involved in the energy business, Reagan maintained that the energy crisis "could be solved if only the government would get out of the way and let the oil companies explore and drill and produce the oil we have."[19] Reflecting the political philosophy of the New Right, Reagan char-acterized the federal government as the real culprit behind the energy shortages of the 1970s. In the presidential debate he attacked Carter's energy program, observing that "free enterprise can do a better job of producing the things the people need than government can." To prove his assertion, Reagan charged that the Department of Energy's $10 billion budget "hasn't produced a quart of oil or a lump of coal or anything else in the line of energy."[20]

He also offered voters anecdotal evidence that the federal govern-ment should be barred from the energy marketplace. Noting that there had never been an energy crisis from the time of the "horseless car-riage until 1971," Reagan charged that since that year, consumers had faced "increasing scarcity and skyrocketing prices." What had happened? "Well, the simple difference is in 1971 the government injected itself into the energy industry," concluded Reagan. "Is it too difficult to suggest that we go back to what we were doing for seventy-one years and set the oil industry loose?"[21] Indeed, by getting government out of the market by decontrolling oil prices, Reagan promised, "we can be producing enough oil to be self-sufficient in five years."[22] Reagan's common-sense style of attributing fault and offering simple solutions apparently found a receptive audience among voters in 1980.

Human needs, stressed Reagan, must be given priority in public land decision making. He rejected the environmental notion that economic benefits should not outweigh the intangible qualities of wilderness or the rights of other forms of life. Although America's "environmental heritage" must not be jeopardized, Reagan acknowledged in his acceptance speech, "we are going to reaffirm that the economic prosperity of our people is a fundamental part of our environment."[23] In a single sentence, the Republican candidate suggested that economic development would become a primary consideration in his public lands policy. Once again a human-centered view of conservation was slipping back into vogue. Aldo Leopold's land ethic, in which humans were a small part of the more complex ecological system, was challenged by the New Right vision that placed humans at the top of the priority list.

In line with the New Right's faith in economic growth as the key to societal well-being, Reagan called the conservation of energy resources a weak and defeatist policy. Announcing his candidacy in 1979, he said that it was not in his program to say "use less energy." "At best it means we will run out of energy a little more slowly," he concluded. "As President I will not endorse any course which has this [conservation] as its principal objective." Eight months later, Reagan chastised those "who preside over the worst energy shortage in our history" and tell Americans to use less, "so that we will run out of oil, gasoline, and natural gas a little more slowly."[24] He dismissed Carter's conservation plan to help the United States achieve energy independence from foreign sources. As long as America had millions of acres of public land locked up, Reagan saw no reason to make the nation's consumers suffer.

Not known for his environmental record, Jimmy Carter supported the fundamental goals of the conservation consensus. Interior Secretary Cecil Andrus supervised the implementation of several major conservation laws, including the Federal Land Policy and Management Act of 1976, the RARE II inventory of the public lands, and major changes in federal grazing standards. Although Carter's synthetic fuel program and the MX missile system angered some conservationists, on the whole Carter received a positive performance rating. Kathy Fletcher echoed two familiar themes among environmentalists: even with some flaws, Carter was superior to Reagan on environmental issues; and Carter would be even more environmentally sensitive as a second-term president. Acknowledging that environmentalists could legitimately criticize Carter's resource record, Fletcher concluded, "Carter deserves and conservationists need a second term for him to complete his ambitious environmental agenda." Hesitation in supporting Carter, observed Fletcher, "could prove disastrous for environmental progress in the 1980s."[25] Significantly, the Alaska Land Bill, signed by Carter in 1980, may have sealed his place in environmental history. According to Roderick Nash, this bill represented the "greatest single act of wilderness preservation in world history."[26]

Carter's record represented nearly the opposite of Reagan's public lands agenda. In direct conflict with the New Right, Carter believed that the United States had a limited amount of energy available. "We have to accommodate inevitable energy shortages and inevitable energy price increases," announced Carter. "This country's just got to change its style of living, and it's a very difficult transformation for Americans even to acknowledge limits, much less live within them."[27] Reflecting Carter's belief that America had entered an era of limits, the 1980 Democratic platform called for a massive residential energy conservation grant program. In addition, the platform favored new efforts by the federal government to develop synthetic and renewable sources of energy. The platform concluded: "We must make conservation and renewable energy our nation's energy priorities for the future."[28] Perceiving a growing shortage of resources on the public lands, the Democrats looked to conservation of the finite fuels as a legitimate policy option.

Environmentalists were recognized by the Carter administration as an important voice in making wilderness policy decisions. Carter rejected Reagan's characterization of conservationists as an extremist element. One member of the Carter administration, in fact, was designated to work directly with environmental groups. The Democratic platform declared that the United States must move "decisively to protect our countryside and our coastline from overdevelopment and mismanagement."[29] Unlike his Republican counterpart, Carter openly courted and received the support of the nation's environmental community.

In direct conflict with Reagan, Carter promoted continued governmental efforts to develop new energy sources. He pointedly rejected Reagan's free market approach of allowing private enterprise to lead the search for energy. Instead of letting market forces dictate the amount of exploration and development, Carter sought a windfall profits tax on oil to fund government programs in solar and synthetic energy. In addition, Carter asked for the establishment of an Energy Mobilization Board to reduce bureaucratic delays in energy research. Exercising his habit of hyperbole, Carter characterized his energy program as "more ambitious than the space program, the Marshall Plan, and the interstate highway system combined."[30] Although such a combination of programs may be difficult to visualize, the image demonstrates the importance Carter attached to his energy program. He believed that this program continued an established tradition of allowing the federal government to lead the way in energy policy. In contrast, Reagan's free market approach to solving the fuel shortage appeared unreasonable to Democrats. At the Democratic convention, Carter claimed that the Republicans wanted to destroy the windfall profits tax and unleash the "oil companies and let them solve the energy problem for us." Calling this an outrageous program, he pledged that Democrats would "fight it every step of the way."[31]

Affirming his party's support for the land ethic, Carter did not believe that economic needs ought to take priority over the less tangible wilderness values. Defending restrictions on coal mining, for example, Carter observed that such regulations "affect the life and the health and the safety of miners, and also . . . protect the purity of our air and the quality of our water and our land. We cannot cast aside those regulations."[32] In addition, the Democratic platform reaffirmed the party's commitment to the environmental movement of the 1960s and the 1970s. Noting that the party had been "charged with the stewardship of an irreplaceable environment," the platform concluded, "the Democratic Party must continue to be as environmentally progressive in the future as it has been in the past."[33]

Believing energy sources to be in short supply, Carter made conservation a keystone in his energy program. In the presidential debate, he argued that energy independence could be achieved in only two ways: first, by conserving energy and two by producing more American energy.[34] Americans needed to learn to sacrifice by turning down their thermostats, by wearing sweaters around the house, and by using less energy in the pursuit of pleasure. If all Americans shared in the sacrifice, the public lands could remain unspoiled by oil rigs and strip mines. In contrast to Carter's call for reduced consumption, Reagan declared, "I do not believe that conservation alone is the answer to the present energy problem. . . . There are hundreds of mil-

lions of acres of land that have been taken out of circulation . . .
[that] contain probably more oil and natural gas than we have used
so far since we drilled that first well 121 years ago."[35]

The major campaign promises Reagan and Carter articulated in 1980
demonstrate the importance of the public lands question in that election year. In selecting a president, American voters ultimately had to
answer five questions concerning energy and the environment. Does
the United States have an abundance of energy sources locked up on
the public lands? Should the federal government be involved in energy production? Do environmentalists represent the views of most
Americans? Should human needs be given priority in determining
natural resource use? Is resource conservation a worthy plan for achieving energy independence? During the fall campaign, the candidates
took opposite positions on each of these questions. Regarding the
future of the public lands, informed voters had a true choice in candidates in 1980. By embracing Reaganism, the public seemingly rejected the conservation consensus and made public lands policy a de-
batable issue once again.

Understanding the public lands debate after Reagan's victory begins with James Watt. He represented the ideal true believer of the
New Right. Committed to promoting America's moral rebirth, Watt
relied upon narrow Protestant fundamentalism for a guide to political decision making. After confirmation, he announced, "We are on
a crusade, I kind of feel that mission."[36] Watt's pious language demonstrated the New Right effort to merge political conservatism with
moral rebirth. Some observers found Watt to be the perfect embodiment of Reaganism. If Watt did not exist, wrote Ron Wolf, the president would have had to invent him: "Watt is everything Reagan
wanted at Interior, a conservative hardliner, a business sympathizer
who would reduce government regulation and appease members of
the Sagebrush Rebellion, a tough administrator determined to stimulate more energy and mineral production from public lands."[37] Because substantive changes in policy had to go through Watt, the new
secretary became an integral force in the public lands debate. Reviewing the secretary's background will explain why the Interior Department became a key arena in the New Right attempt to dismantle the
conservation consensus.

Upon Senate confirmation, James Watt became one of the most
powerful individuals in the United States.[38] In less than a year, he also
became one of the most disliked. "I cannot recall a Cabinet member

since the days of FDR," wrote James J. Kilpatrick, "who has stirred up the antagonism that Watt has manifestly aroused."[39] Public opinion polls sponsored by Democrats and Republicans alike demonstrated the secretary's dramatically low approval ratings.[40] Although Watt developed a strong following among conservative Republicans, his polemical leadership style threatened many of Reagan's public land initiatives. By 1982, changes in Interior Department policy supported by Watt were in trouble. Numerous members of congress, as well as the nation's leading environmental groups, were prepared to fight any proposal Watt advanced.

A noted proponent of New Right conservatism before he joined the Reagan administration, Watt promised radical changes in Interior Department policy. Members of the national news media seized upon this theme early in his tenure. The *Los Angeles Times* reported that after less than three months on the job, Watt had "jerked the Interior Department into a sudden reversal toward environmental protection that has been building for two decades."[41] Watt even conceded that he had to "shock" department employees to "bring about the changes we wanted."[42] At a fund raiser in South Dakota, Watt explained his political philosophy: "You have to strike fast in this business. Influence is a very perishable commodity. You can lose it practically overnight. You have to use what you've got when you've got it. For me that's right now."[43]

The secretary's personal history suggests a man of intelligence, conviction, and ambition. Born and raised in Wyoming, he left behind an impressive record: Boys' State governor, high school valedictorian, honors graduate in business, and law review editor at the University of Wyoming. He joined Milward Simpson's 1962 campaign for the U.S. Senate and upon Simpson's victory, Watt was appointed as a legislative aide. In his four years serving Simpson, Watt became the Wyoming senator's principal speech writer as well. In 1964 he became a born-again Christian, joining the Assembly of God Church. In 1966, after Simpson's retirement from the Senate, Watt became a lobbyist for the U.S. Chamber of Commerce. He joined Richard Nixon's presidential transition team in 1968 and played a major role in preparing Interior Secretary nominee Walter Hickel for confirmation hearings.[44] For ten days Watt wrote out detailed answers to potential questions for Hickel, a land developer from Alaska who was under fire for his lack of environmental concern. For guiding the "gruff, coarse Alaskan developer through five grueling days of televised hearings,"[45] Watt was rewarded with a position as a deputy secretary of interior, responsible for water and power.

After serving in a number of federal positions from 1969 to 1977, Watt returned to the West to become director of the Mountain States Legal Foundation (MSLF). Representing the broad goals of the New Right's political philosophy, the MSLF was founded, observed Watt, to fight "those bureaucrats and no-growth advocates who challenge individual liberties and economic freedoms."[46] He established a notable record of conservatism at the MSLF by opposing the Sierra Club and the Interior Department in court, as well as taking issue with the Equal Rights Amendment, affirmative action guidelines, OSHA regulations, and other social policies.[47] Moreover, Watt made the foundation a respected and successful New Right power broker. During the years he directed the foundation, Watt increased the annual budget from $194,000 to $1.2 million and hired more lawyers to support conservative causes in the courts.[48]

The success of the MSLF concerned some members of the environmental community. Noting that the foundation used the tactics and vocabulary of many environmental groups in their legal challenges, the *High Country News* observed that if the MSLF had a motto, it would be: "private rights, private freedoms, and private enterprise." Moreover, some observers attacked the "public interest" label of the foundation. "My idea of a public interest lawyer is someone who isn't funded by special interests and who is guided by his conscience," argued Ralph Nader. "Not these guys. They're in it for the money."[49]

At the MSLF, Watt's rhetoric was noted for a strident view of both liberals and environmentalists. A 1978 speech in Dallas is typical of his confrontational style. Calling the environmentalist a "zealot for his cause," Watt suggested that an underlying goal of some environmental groups was to "weaken" the United States: "Today, there is a new political force in the land—a small group of extremists who don't concern themselves with a balanced perspective or a concern about improving the quality of life for mankind—they are called environmentalists. . . . What is the real motive of these extreme environmentalists? Is it to simply protect the environment? Is it to delay and deny energy development? Is it to weaken America?"[50] The Dallas speech provides a glimpse into the rhetorical genesis of the counter-environmental movement. Numerous arguments Watt articulated found receptive audiences in 1980 when advanced by candidate Reagan. Watt argued, for example, that conservationists and environmentalists were really two different creatures. Conservationists were the people of the West who developed the frontier with an "orderly and balanced perspective." On the other hand, environmentalists, charged Watt, were single-minded and willing to pursue their objectives "at whatever cost to society." The desire among environmentalists to prevent public land development is "so strong that any means is justified," including "frivolous court actions" and the formation of activist groups with millions of dollars to spend. The end result of environmentalism, Watt declared, would be severe energy shortages and the loss of hundreds of thousands, even millions of jobs. Watt concluded the Dallas speech by appealing for "orderly development" of the vast western public lands and by calling the environmental movement "the greatest threat to the ecology of the West."[51]

During confirmation hearings, Watt claimed that he could take political positions that were more moderate than the MSLF had advocated. When senators pointed out that some of the foundation's legal positions were even more conservative than Reagan's agenda, Watt replied, "My loyalties shifted because of my commitment to Reagan." When asked directly about his endorsement of the Sagebrush Rebellion, Watt announced that he planned to defuse western anger through a good neighbor policy. Indeed, he claimed that pending sagebrush legislation in Congress "would be premature and a divisive force in Congress and there's not much chance of its passing."[52] Less than two months after the Sagebrush Rebellion helped elect a supporter to the presidency, the Reagan administration was redefining its call for a rebellion.

Watt told reporters during confirmation hearings that he and the president-elect had four major goals regarding the public lands: "to make more public lands available for multiple uses rather than limiting them to wilderness or recreation; to develop a policy for production of strategic minerals; to maintain public access to and upgrade the management of parks and recreational lands; and to work toward national self-sufficiency in energy."[53] Significantly, the goals suggested that the secretary intended to implement Reagan's campaign pledges as policy. Emphasizing the need to change existing department policies, Watt claimed that the real extremists in the debate were those "who would deny economic development and the balanced management of our resources for the benefit of consumers and all of America." The United States, reasoned Watt, could not afford to lock up the natural resources for the use of any single-interest group. In this manner, the Sagebrush Rebellion's primary metaphor, that of a public land lock up, survived the 1980 campaign even if the movement itself appeared to be finished.

Ronald Reagan's ability to transform the public lands question into a major issue in 1980 revealed some growing cracks in the conservation consensus. Reagan's plan to decentralize the scope of federal government appeared to have a ripe candidate in the great bureaucracy charged with public land management. Relying upon the advice of western senators in the selection of an interior secretary, the president-elect pleased conservatives by choosing James Watt, whose nomination confirmed that public land development would become a central goal in Reagan's first term. Declaring that Watt "is not 'middle-of-the-road,'" an environmental lawyer told the *High Country News* after Watt's nomination, "he is a constant advocate of corporate access to public lands – very pro-development."[54]

Conversely, leading environmental groups decided to enter the presidential campaign in 1980 by supporting Jimmy Carter's candidacy. Moreover, they were prepared to fight Reaganism after the election – in court, in Congress, and in public forums. By the time of Reagan's first inauguration, the lines were being drawn for the most important public land debate since conservationists prevented the Eisenhower administration from developing Echo Park in Utah. Only this time the prodevelopment faction had a shrewd leader at the Interior Department and an incoming president committed to reversing fifty years of New Deal land management. The conservation debate was ready to begin anew.

5. "Paralysis by Analysis"

THE CONSERVATION RHETORIC OF JAMES WATT

James Watt believed that Ronald Reagan's election in 1980 represented a clear mandate for greater development of the public lands. "Paralysis by analysis," Watt's poetic characterization of the conservation consensus, would end, he believed, in the Reagan Revolution. Outlining his public lands agenda for the president-elect, Watt bluntly told Reagan that such a plan of action would cause tremendous controversy if implemented. "You'll have to back me and back me until you have to fire me," he prophetically advised Reagan.[1]

With all the enthusiasm of a faith healer, Watt accepted the cabinet appointment. "God calls each of us to our different missions," he told reporters after the nomination. "I'm prepared emotionally, spiritually and intellectually to withstand the onslaught."[2] Reagan's victory, he believed, presented an "opportunity to make the massive change"[3] essential to the survival of the United States. Revealing his New Right credentials, Watt charged that meaningful reforms in government could not be made in a "traditional Jerry Ford manner. The old establishment working it out."[4] Instead, America needed leaders with a sense of mission and moral courage, individuals such as James Gaius Watt of Lusk, Wyoming.

After Senate confirmation in January, 1981, Watt moved quickly to organize his department. A seasoned federal bureaucrat, he pleased the president by being the first cabinet member to make major staff appointments. In the first months of 1981, Watt had virtually a free hand in shaping federal public lands policy. Reagan's wound from an assassin's bullet in March and subsequent absence from daily policy meetings gave Watt even greater independence. As a result, Reagan's public lands policy, in most cases, represented the vision of one man.[5]

Compared with other members of the cabinet, Watt appeared to be an unusual selection. At forty-three, he was much younger than other Reagan appointees. Moreover, as a vocal born-again Christian, Watt was the only member of the religious right appointed to a high-level position in the Reagan administration. During his first year in office, Watt granted several press interviews in order to explain administration policy as well as reveal his personal philosophy. The biography that emerged from such interviews illuminates the fervor that guided his tenure. Watt grew up distrusting liberals and Democrats; indeed, he saw little distinction between the two. His father, an attorney and the county Republican Party chairman, told one reporter: "You could see the New Deal, the left-wing taking over. . . . We were Republican, rabid Republican."[6] Echoing his father, Watt recalled that in the 1930s and 1940s, conservatives sought to hold onto the "dignity of the individual." But the liberals won those battles, and in the 1980s, they "want to hold onto their Great Society programs, and FDR's programs, the Fair Deal or whatever he called it."[7] Whether Watt's historical error was intentional, it demonstrates an abiding antagonism toward New Deal liberalism. With no romantic notions of Franklin Roosevelt (such as Reagan sometimes alluded to), Watt symbolized the maturation of the Goldwater wing of the Republican Party, those disgruntled conservatives who wanted to purify party dogma.

Watt overtly embraced the New Right's dedication to a religious revival, a third Great Awakening in modern America. Openly witnessing his faith, Watt preached a brand of Christianity laced with large doses of patriotism. "I'm a fundamentalist in my commitment to the Judeo-Christian principles of America," he proclaimed.[8] Responding to critics of his religious views, Watt charged that he and his family were "persecuted evangelical Christians" who experienced hatred and a "Holocaust-like mentality here in America." Persecution at the hands of the news media and special-interest groups, he observed, "makes us all the more aware of fighting continually for political liberty and [spiritual] freedom."[9]

Promising to remain faithful to his conservative heritage, Watt ridiculed the compromise and bargaining that often accompanied governmental policy making. He entered office prepared for public confrontation, asserting that partisanship had destroyed the administrations of two earlier interior secretaries, Walter Hickel and Stanley Hathaway.[10] With a clear mission in mind and a free hand from the president, Watt set out to restore America to its previous "greatness." In so doing, he made development of the nation's public lands a front-page story for nearly three years.

One of the busiest public speakers in the administration, Watt possessed unusual rhetorical prowess. On the one hand, his vocal outbursts caused numerous political problems for the administration. On the other, he became the leading fundraiser (except for Reagan) among Republicans and helped placate New Right leaders unhappy with the administration's moderate pace on many social issues. In numerous speeches, the secretary linked the broad goals of the New Right agenda with the specific changes he hoped to make in public land policy. Besides concentrating on natural resource issues, Watt also used public forums to attack administration opponents. Unlike other cabinet officers, Watt could afford to be controversial. Because most policy changes at Interior were administrative in nature, Watt needed only congressional inactivity in order to implement substantial changes. Not needing congressional approval for many of his goals, Watt could become the ideal member of the administration to take on those interests and individuals hostile to the administration. As a result, the secretary had little incentive to control his caustic tongue during his first year in office.

Watt's tenure as interior secretary seems to fall into three distinct phases, each phase corresponding to about a year. He devoted 1981 to implementing a variety of administrative actions designed to redefine the conservation consensus and stimulate greater public land development. During confirmation hearings, Watt maintained that he wanted no major changes in laws, funding, or manpower; instead, he planned to fine tune policy with his vast administrative powers.[11]

In 1982, the secretary endorsed one of the goals of the dying Sagebrush Rebellion – the transfer of large tracts of federal land to private control. Rather than federal agencies simply transferring the title of the land to the state governments, as rebels envisioned, the secretary planned direct sales to private citizens. In addition, Watt pushed for several legislative reforms in 1982 to stimulate resource development. Because of numerous confrontations with environmentalists and congressional leaders, 1983 became Watt's year of reconciliation with his enemies and rebuilding support for public land development. Although his bizarre public comments eventually forced him from office, he pursued a strategy of reconciliation during most of 1983. Unable to muzzle himself in extemporaneous situations, however, the secretary's reactionary candor ultimately brought his resignation. To understand Watt's significance in the public lands debate, each phase of his tenure will be examined, focusing upon the political and rhetorical characteristics of each period.

After Ronald Reagan completed his first year as president, the *Los Angeles Times* asked him if James Watt represented a "political liability." The president answered, no, that "environmental extremists" had gone "beyond all bounds of reason" and that "Jim Watt . . . is going to restore some common sense."[12] No single phrase better summarizes Watt's first year in office, a political crusade to apply old-fashioned common sense to the nation's resource policy. Although Watt provoked strong and continuous opposition during 1981, he systematically worked to alter the prevailing conservation ethic. After only one month in office, the secretary instituted his first change. He planned to permit oil and gas exploration on 1.3 million acres off the California coast. One week later, he announced a moratorium on further federal land purchases and eliminated three major park purchase programs to the states. More important, six weeks into his term, Watt severed working relations with major environmental groups. Claiming that he had been "lied about, misrepresented and undermined at every turn by environmentalist groups" who had "poisoned the press" against him, Watt announced that they now had a "heavy burden to carry" in making their positions to his office.[13] By May, the secretary made it clear that he had no reason to work with, or even speak to, environmental leaders. He attacked the "hired guns" of the movement and argued that their true political agenda consisted of "membership, dollars, and headlines." Watt's chief spokesman, Ray Arnett, told environmental leaders that meeting with the secretary was out of the question and that only a "positive, constructive change of attitudes" on their part could allow a "meaningful dialogue to begin."[14]

By summer Watt appeared to be in deep trouble. The National Wildlife Federation, with more than 4 million members, asked the president to fire the secretary. A Harris poll in California found growing levels of public disapproval for Watt's policies. In fact, the chairman of the California Republicans warned Watt that offshore drilling disputes could severely harm party interests in 1982. In August, Watt found himself battling with the head of the House Interior Committee, Representative Morris Udall. Although the two men had often verbally sparred, they had maintained a working relationship in public meetings. Tired of hostile questions from committee members, Watt told Udall that such questions "drained" his batteries. As a result, he could not think about "things like the Tucson water aqueduct," an important project in Udall's home district. With apparent sarcasm, the secretary concluded: "I'm not asking you to do anything, because anything I mentioned would be blackmail. It is just that until I get my personal energies rebuilt, I can't do anything about the Tucson aqueduct, and I don't know how long that will take."[15]

Information released by the Republican National Party in October, 1981, confirmed Watt's polarizing effect upon the public. In September and October, the secretary raised more than $400,000 and was labeled by one official as a "tremendous draw, one of our top requests from office seekers." Appearing in Idaho, Utah, and Montana, Watt added 15 to 20 percent to expected contributions. On the other hand, the secretary ended the year embroiled in numerous conflicts. For example, following White House orders, he refused congressional requests for documents related to Interior Department negotiations with Canada. Although administration officials had ordered him to invoke the doctrine of executive privilege, it was his name that blanketed the nation's newspapers for refusing to comply with the Congress. In addition, his offhand remark, "I never use the words Republicans and Democrats. . . . It's liberals and Americans," was widely reported in November. Although Watt attempted to explain the remark as joking, many Democrats were outraged. To top off 1981, government auditors ordered the secretary to reimburse the government $4,000 for two private Christmas parties that he hosted using National Park facilities. Angry at continued public attacks from environmentalists, Watt ordered his senior staff to avoid contact with the "national representatives of environmental groups," observing that government employees were not being paid to listen to special-interest lobbyists.[16]

Watt went on a rhetorical rampage in 1981, giving speeches and press conferences throughout the United States. Preaching Reaganism like a backwoods minister, Watt used resource policy to symbolize the New Right ideology in operation. Because the secretary sought no major legislative changes during 1981, and because of his role as the administration's true believer, Watt could invite confrontation in the public forum. He used public land development to illustrate the change from Jimmy Carter's agenda of conservation and limited growth to Ronald Reagan's vision of abundant energy and economic growth. As result, natural resource development symbolized the New Right quest for free enterprise, energy independence, and enhanced national security. A closer look at Watt's remarks makes such overt symbolism evident.

In his first speech as secretary of the interior, Watt described the "four cornerstones of the Reagan conservation policy" to a wildlife conservation organization. Significantly, each cornerstone called for a radical departure from the conservation consensus: "America must have a sound economy" to be a good steward of the land; America must have "orderly development" of resources to prevent the ravages of "crisis development"; America's resources are for the "enjoyment" of all people, not only the "elitist groups"; and much of the nation's expertise in land management exists in the private and local sector, not the federal bureaucracy. In combination, these four goals emphatically rejected Aldo Leopold's ecological conscience and land ethic as the guiding standards for public land management and instead committed the United States to a systematic plan of resource development. Over twenty years of success in shaping resource policy appeared to end with Watt's rejection of the conservation consensus. With a decentralized public lands policy, the federal government's century-long role as the nation's primary landlord seemed in peril.

Watt made public land development part of the administration's overall plan to reduce the size of big government. Like Reagan's campaign linking of energy production, national security, and economic growth with natural resource development, Watt's comments tended to be simple, radical, and optimistic. Examining the texts of twelve speeches he presented in 1981 illuminates his rhetorical style.

Watt proposed a human-centered management philosophy that placed people at the top of a resource-use hierarchy. Implementing this notion may have been the single most revolutionary change made at the Interior Department. Attacking the rise of environmentalism in the 1960s and 1970s, Watt charged that the previous administrations had written "people out of the equation" in determining land use. By putting people back into the forefront, he planned to restore balance to the system. The "vast majority of Americans" are not "rugged young backpackers," the secretary observed. Instead, most Americans wanted parks and wildlife refuges that provided "easy access" and "safe shelter."[17]

To justify specific executive decisions, Watt articulated this human-centered view of resource use time and again during 1981. For example, his decision to halt purchases of new national park lands infuriated many environmentalists. The secretary argued that the existing parks needed "roads, campgrounds, latrines," and other facilities to serve visitor needs. With user needs being paramount, Watt found little reason to buy more park land until existing parks were upgraded. Calling programs to acquire more park land the "park a month club" and "park barrel legislation," Watt reasoned that the government was obliged to share existing "resources with the American people."[18] Significantly, the secretary's vision of sharing focused not on mountains, rivers, and wildlife, but instead upon the civilized wilderness: roads, lodges, food services, and structured campsites. Summarizing his plans for the public lands, Watt announced that hunters and fishers would receive "new keys of access" to the wilderness from the Reagan administration. "The past privileged position of the select few has been terminated," the secretary told a group of outdoor writers. "Access is available to all Americans."[19]

Suggesting that economic vitality and national security were inherently linked with the future of the public lands, Watt argued that the key to national economic recovery lay in sustained and orderly development of the nation's natural resources. He told one audience that a "healthy mining industry is essential to America's national security, to a strong economy, and to our environment." Indeed, the secretary maintained that environmental quality could not be separated from economic health: "To be a good steward of our natural resources – to protect the environment – we must have a strong economy. Poor nations make poor stewards."[20] In each speech Watt presented in his first year at Interior, he juxtaposed the shared goals of environmental quality, national security, and economic recovery with specific changes in public land policy he hoped to undertake.

Reflecting the New Right's goal of government decentralization, Watt drew attention to administration efforts to reduce, and in some cases dismantle, the federal bureaucracy. The "high tide of centralized government," claimed Watt, "is being pushed back" by the Reagan administration. Describing his reorganization of the Office of Surface Mining, Watt observed, "We do not need an army of more than 1,000 bureaucrats or a cumbersome network of 42 offices" to implement and enforce federal mining laws. In line with giving the private sector greater freedom, Watt advised the National Petroleum Council that the Interior Department had "dropped cookbook style, lock step regulation" of the resources in favor of a "creative entrepreneurial spirit."[21]

The secretary also argued that the federal government had to limit its everyday functions as well as its goals. Claiming that "national parks should be limited to areas of national significance," Watt suggested that urban parks be turned over to state or local governments for management. Americans do not want a "federally dictated recreation system," he announced. "They want a local system based on a mix of their own resources, services they buy when they want them, and a modest and responsive local, state, and Federal public recreation system for those things they cannot provide or purchase themselves." Ideally, parks and recreation should become the responsibility of local governments and the private sector, concluded Watt, and should not be a "primary responsibility of the Federal government."[22]

Watt's stormy relations with environmental groups was evident in oratory as well. Believing that the leading organizations were biased against the administration, he felt little incentive to build relations with them. He told the readers of *Field and Stream* that environmental lobbyists were losers: "They're not only single losers, they've lost repeatedly." Challenging his opponents to debate him on an "intellectual level," he asked, "Why don't they take Watt on substance rather than his personality, and his bald head, his thick glasses, his religion, and his friends?" The secretary told the National Recreation and Park Association that by attacking him personally, environmentalists had used the press to "raise dollars for their special interests and have kept the public from being informed on the *issues.*" Speaking to a group of newspaper editors, Watt characterized his opponents as "hounds in full cry" with himself as the prey, and complained that many newspapers had joined the "pack seeking to nail my pelt to the wall."[23]

Watt hoped to make 1982 a banner year for resource development by instituting even greater changes at Interior. Although some observers thought that he could go no further, the nation learned of significant new proposals to encourage more development of the public lands. Watt suggested that his first year in office had been devoted to changing societal attitudes toward the wilderness and that 1982 would be devoted to instituting new policies based upon those changed attitudes. Hoping to prevent the "ecological conscience" from guiding future public land decisions, the secretary tried to reinstill a utilitarian view of conservation, providing that natural resources be widely used to benefit humans and not held in preservation for spiritual or moral reasons. Just as Gifford Pinchot had rejected John Muir's quasireligious perception of the wilderness, so too did Watt reject the ecological views of Muir's modern descendants, the 10 million members of the organized environmental movement. But Watt faced growing constraints, as a review of the numerous elements surrounding the wilderness debate will show.

During his first year as interior secretary, Watt used his vast administrative power to spur natural resource development. By 1982, how-

ever, he envisioned more fundamental changes in the public land policy. In February, the administration announced plans to sell 35 million
acres of federally owned wilderness. Through such sales, popularly
known as "privatization," the administration planned to reduce federal management costs and yield $17 billion to help reduce the national
debt. Although Watt denied that the "asset management program"
involved any national park land, the general public seemed suspicious.
Part of this perception may have stemmed from leaked federal documents which suggested that all federal holdings, including parts of the
National Forest system, the National Park system, and the Wildlife
Refuge system, would be reviewed for possible sale. Although this internal memorandum never reached policy stage, it reflected the possible impact of "privatization" if taken to its fullest extent.[24]

Watt and Reagan proposed further changes in environmental statutes in 1982. In April, the president announced plans to open new
tracts of public land to development. The initiative would remove more
land from the status of wilderness protection and allow mineral exploration and mining. With "40 to 68 percent of the public lands
closed," declared Reagan, America's dependence on foreign energy
appeared excessive. In line with his campaign promises, Reagan maintained that his plan would help "diminish America's minerals vulner-
ability by allowing private enterprise to preserve and expand our minerals and materials economy."[25]

Later in 1982, Watt proposed new guidelines to "ease regulatory
burdens" on coal exploration. The proposal was greeted with immediate hostility because it could grant strip mining privileges in national parks and wildlife refuges. Although Watt pledged to exempt
the parks from any mining, environmentalists charged that with strip
mining near the parks, pressures to move inside the park boundaries
would someday become too great. He lobbied for other extensive
reforms to complement earlier administrative actions. Calling federal
coal mining regulations too restrictive, Watt asked Congress to relax
environmental rules in order to rectify the "huge abuse" that government had imposed upon the private sector.[26] Stretching his administrative power to its fullest limit, Watt approved the "most extensive
offshore oil and gas leasing program in the nation's history." He told
reporters that the new leases would "enhance national security, provide jobs, and protect the environment." In raw numbers alone, the
plan staggered observers. Between 1955 and 1982, about 3 percent of
the *total* continental shelf surrounding the United States had been

leased for oil exploration. In a single executive action, Watt opened almost the entire shelf.[27]

Watt's public land revolution gained even more national attention in a July cover story in *Time* magazine. The cover illustration reflected the public's growing disdain for Watt. In front of the slogan, "GOING, GOING . . . ! Land Sale of the Century," a sneering portrait of Watt looked at the reader. This article and growing attention toward Watt's behavior may have been the turning point in the secretary's effort to make radical changes in federal land policy. The negative backlash resulting from the privatization scheme continued to haunt Watt until he withdrew the plan one year later. The scope of the land sale, reported *Time*, is "enormous." In five years, 35 million acres of public land, or about 5 percent of all federal holdings, could be sold. In more graphic terms, the lands to be auctioned off equaled the size of Maine, New Hampshire, Vermont, and Massachusetts combined. Reflecting the polarized rhetoric of the conservation debate, the article concluded that the plan had "raised fundamental questions about how America should manage its land, and it has touched off a bitter battle between two rival and possibly irreconcilable forces."[28]

Although the secretary had envisioned significant legislative changes in 1982, the year evolved into a time of political fighting and partisan turmoil. The ongoing confrontation between Watt and leading environmental groups escalated, giving the public ample opportunity to sample the secretary's caustic style. Indeed, Watt's combative manner brought disfavor even from conservative Republicans. Reviewing his numerous political problems in 1982 helps explain why his personality became a central issue in the public lands controversy.

Congress cited Watt for contempt in February for refusing to turn over selected documents to a House panel. Although he maintained he was only following orders from the president, he found his name in negative headlines throughout the country once again. In the same month, the National Wildlife Federation sued Watt for illegal revisions of coal mining standards. The lawsuit charged that proposed changes would lead to "increased water pollution, flooding, soil erosion and destruction of fish and wildlife habitat."[29] The National Wildlife Federation's moderate reputation made the lawsuit particularly noteworthy. By angering such a group, Watt had alienated an organization of more than 4 million members, over 60 percent of whom had voted for Reagan in 1980. February concluded with more bad news regarding Watt's two Christmas parties. Auditors rejected his appeal and ordered the secretary to reimburse the government for the illegal functions. Although the Republican Party agreed to pay the costs, the negative publicity fueled nagging public doubts about Watt's integrity.[30]

Watt's infamous "Jewish threat" letter appeared in July, placing the secretary in a national controversy for yet another full week. In this case, however, leaders outside the environmental realm were involved. In a letter to Israeli Ambassador Moshe Arens, Watt warned that American support for Israel could be jeopardized if "liberals in the Jewish community join with other liberals" in opposing the Reagan administration's public land policies. Numerous leaders called the letter both threatening and bigoted. Representative Benjamin Rosenthal and Senator Daniel Patrick Moynihan urged the president to fire Watt. Under heavy pressure from the administration, Watt went before a Jewish group a week later and publicly apologized.[31]

Although embroiled in various political conflicts, Watt continued to push for greater wilderness development. By the summer of 1982, however, even diehard conservatives were backing away from the secretary. As the year progressed, Watt lost valuable support and faced new legal restrictions from an angry Congress.

Nationally syndicated political writer George Will blasted Watt's huge land sales program. Selling a chunk of America the size of Iowa, Will charged, "seems careless" in an economic recession. It is "economically improvident to dump tracts onto a depressed market," explained Will, "it is environmentally rash to do so at a pace likely to overwhelm the capacity for supervision."

More significant, however, was the loss of two allies, Senators Alan Simpson and Malcom Wallop of Wyoming. The two New Right regulars cosponsored legislation to "bar all oil and gas exploration in their state's wilderness areas." Why would two conservative, western politicians, turn their backs on Watt? "Constituent pressure," responded a Simpson aide. "They [Wallop and Simpson] are quite aware that a great many people in Wyoming want those wilderness areas left as they are." One week later, Senator Henry Jackson of Washington announced that fifty-one senators had agreed to cosponsor legislation to prevent oil and gas drilling on millions of acres of national wilderness. The bill already had received wide approval in the House by a margin of 340–58. When the Republican-controlled Senate bottled up Jackson's bill in committee, the Senate Appropriations Committee responded by eliminating the federal funds needed to process oil and gas leases in wilderness areas. If the senators could not restrict Watt's ability to make leases, they could at least control his ability to pay for them. The secretary's political base seemed to be crumbling as the 1982 general elections approached.[32]

The secretary's vaunted good neighbor program came under attack as well. Watt promised to defuse the Sagebrush Rebellion by treating western states with respect and seeking their input on relevant public land questions. Ironically, some observers criticized the Reagan administration for being just as autocratic as previous administrations in determining wilderness policy. Nine western governors charged that Interior's coal-leasing plan moved to "once again centralize on the Potomac critical decisions affecting western states." The governors, seven Democrats and two Republicans, demanded that Watt seek greater state participation in setting policy. They complained that of the 175 changes in federal mining regulations they had recommended, Interior had rejected 159 of them. At their annual meeting, the governors unanimously passed a resolution highly critical of the administration's land sales program. They argued that each state ought to be involved in determining how much and which tracts of federal land should be sold.[33]

By the end of 1982, the administration had suffered considerably from environmentalist criticism. The *Washington Post* reported that the political climate had significantly altered the Interior Department's strategy. After the 1982 general elections, Watt had planned to announce an initiative to develop millions of wilderness acres under federal protection. By Thanksgiving, however, department officials changed their plans, delaying them indefinitely. One official explained: "You can imagine what would happen if some liberal Democrats got ahold of something like the wilderness changes."[34] Watt's reputation had sunk so low that even after the fall elections, administration leaders feared the fallout that might accompany any large-scale development program. Prior to the 1982 campaign, Watt canceled a series of speeches in California at the administration's request. The secretary's negative image was "hindering his effectiveness" reported the *Washington Post*, "subjecting his every move to intense scrutiny."[35] By the end of the year, Watt's strategy of fighting in the public forum had given way to withdrawal and reconsideration of further plans to develop America's public lands.

Watt's speeches in 1982 confirm that he initially planned to take his case to the voters. He continued to justify public land development,

defend the Reagan administration in general, and encourage continued support from activists in the New Right. Firmly entrenched among
the New Right leadership, Watt became the administration's primary
link to the movement. As some conservative leaders became increasingly disenchanted with the president's moderation on issues such as
abortion and school prayer, Watt's ability to placate them became in-
valuable. Speaking to the Conservative Forum, Watt demonstrated
his role as the administration's ambassador to the conservatives. He
repeated his goal of finding energy wealth and protecting national security and noted that in a "war" to protect "liberty and freedom," conservatives had to fight enemies such as the Equal Rights Amendment,
abortion, and the "Left." The secretary also used this opportunity to
chastise fellow conservatives for not understanding the "global and
national picture," namely those issues targeted for presidential support.
He lashed out at those conservatives who were "carping, criticizing
and demeaning others because we think that some agenda item is more
important" than the president's agenda. Emphasizing his commitment
to the movement, Watt described his personal sacrifice for the New
Right: "I enjoy the fight with those liberals, even though it sometimes hurts. It takes your energy. It takes your strength." He closed
by asking members of the audience to help the president: "No conservative should have to look around to see if someone is going to
shoot him in the back."[36]

This presentation typifies the secretary's strength and weakness as
an administration advocate. On the one hand, his ideological purity
kept disgruntled conservatives happy with a part of the Reagan crusade. Although the president remained personally popular with the
New Right, the refrain of "Let Reagan Be Reagan" implied that the
president had lost his ability to lead. On the other hand, Watt's fundamentalist, black-and-white worldview frustrated and alienated many
individuals who could have been supporters of increased public land
development. Indeed, some conservative leaders believed that the secretary's inability to separate questions of morality from public policy
created a backlash against development interests.[37]

Initially, Watt assumed an offensive rhetorical strategy in 1982. Less
concerned with reiterating the broad goals of Reaganism, he concentrated on the specific policies he hoped to implement and on refuting
arguments advanced against his plans. As a result, he took several different turns in 1982, changing as political conditions changed. Seeking
momentum for his agenda, Watt stepped up criticism of previous ad-

ministrations. For example, he delivered a harsh attack on Jimmy Carter, charging that the "excessive preservationism worshipped by the previous administration, was bad for the economy, bad for environment, bad for freedom."[38]

The secretary also criticized members of his own department. Justifying major changes in personnel at Interior, he announced that a housecleaning was necessary when he assumed office: "Gone from the Department are those people who believed that the Federal lands should be reserved for the pursuits of the privileged few. Gone are those bureaucrats intent on strangling private enterprise with excessive red tape. Gone are those who believed that the Federal Government's prime objective should be to acquire ever more land to lock away from the American people." The secretary continued this line of argument in Dallas, claiming that the policies he inherited were "skewed heavily toward blind preservation of resources – the buying of land and resources by the Federal Government and the locking away of these resources." During the Carter years, charged Watt, the Interior Department was "jerked around by people who were committed to use every possible device to keep industry" from developing the public lands.[39]

Watt attempted to separate friend from foe during 1982 in order to get a bearing on public consensus for his policies. Realizing the difficulty in rebuilding relations with environmental groups, he sought support from the original conservationists, America's hunters and fishers. Conversely, he tried to dissociate himself from the "preservationists," those environmentalists who opposed wilderness development. Speaking in Reno, Watt attached the "Johnnies-come-lately" who confuse "preservation" with true conservation: "They think that the only way to protect the environment is to lock away the land so that it cannot be used – except by those with the time, money and good health to trample the wilderness in expensive hiking boots."[40] In Virginia, Watt claimed that the "anti-hunting forces" would split the conservation movement in two. "Hunting is going to be a big issue," he predicted. "The hunting versus anti-hunting forces will be a crucial factor in [the 1982] election." Noting that he found pro-Watt bumperstickers on old Ford pickup trucks with rifle racks and anti-Watt bumperstickers on "snazzy Subarus or Volvos," Watt caustically concluded that he would rather be "allied with the owners of Fords and Chevy pickups than the Volvo owners of America."[41]

The secretary's strategy revealed itself in a candid remark to *Field and Stream:* "In a conflict between the preservationists and the sportsmen, we're going to the sportsmen. We've sent the signals, so if there's to be a wedge driven between the conservation community, we'll help drive the wedge."[42] Intent upon making a prohunting statement prior to the elections, Watt attended an antelope hunting contest in Lander, Wyoming, that September. The *Washington Post* characterized the trip as the secretary's chance to modify his "image as a deskbound, development advocate." Wire service photos featured Watt aiming a hunting rifle and holding up a dead antelope. Ironically, Watt, who had not hunted in over twenty years, had to borrow a rifle to participate.[43]

Watt also employed more New Right phraseology in his 1982 speeches. Using such expressions as "widen the economic pie" and the "opportunity society," Watt linked public land policy with the larger mission of Reaganism. By using a commonplace often associated with the president, Watt made Interior policy an exemplar of the New Right agenda. Speaking to the American Association of Blacks in Energy, Watt aptly titled his address, "Economic Emancipation." President Carter's massive energy program, he claimed, worked to destroy the "backbone of the private enterprise system upon which our liberty is based." If the government could only "enlarge the economic pie," women and minorities would have greater opportunities, the secretary argued. "This is the road to economic emancipation." In another address, Watt proclaimed that Reaganism would "enlarge the economic pie so that we can meet our commitments to the underprivileged, to the young, to the elderly, to the sick and handicapped." The panacea of economic growth pervaded his oratory. Unlocking America's natural resources by "giving industry the green light to move ahead" would create 24 million new jobs by the turn of the century.[44]

As the elections neared in 1982, the secretary attempted to minimize the growing political disfavor created by the land sales program. Although privatization had many supporters among conservatives, the general public seemed either indifferent or hostile toward the idea. By endorsing the sales program, Watt found himself being attacked with the same arguments used against the Sagebrush Rebellion. After six months of negative publicity, the secretary responded to the criticisms of privatization. He announced that a large misunderstanding had emerged: "It is an *asset management* program. It is not a privatization program." Calling his plan "small potatoes" compared with other land sales in American history, he argued that he would sell only the public lands that did not serve "legitimate public purposes." Watt concluded that the sales were reasonable: "If you had a pickup truck you no longer needed for your ranch, you would not just park it. You would sell it once you had identified the truck as surplus to your needs."[45] Although environmentalists would reject such an analogy as faulty, it typified the administration's appeal to common sense.

From July to December, 1982, Watt increasingly kept his opinions to himself. Following advice from administration officials, he significantly reduced his speaking schedule and waited for the fall elections to calm Republican anxieties. He had begun 1982 on the offensive, calling for massive new development and attacking his opponents in the media and among the various environmental groups, but the year ended quietly, pragmatic politics dictating his silence. In addition, the secretary's efforts to reform public land policy through offshore oil leases, greater coal leasing in the West, and public land sales found few public supporters as the elections neared. As a result, it seemed the Reagan Revolution was on hold until 1983.

The secretary's public communication in 1983 showed an almost schizophrenic quality in attempting to reconcile his antagonists while remaining ideologically pure. As the secretary apologized to various groups, he also became more strident in his extemporaneous remarks. Significantly, his gaffes were candid statements reflecting his particular worldview, not slip-of-the-tongue errors. He began the year with a pair of blunders. Speaking on a national news program, Watt observed that if anyone wanted to witness the failures of socialism, "don't go to Russia. Come to America and go to the Indian reservations." The comment drew sharp reaction. The nation's two largest Indian organizations demanded his resignation while nationally syndicated writer William Raspberry suggested that as the person in charge of the reservations, Watt ought to hold his tongue. One ought not draw "attention to embarrassing problems," maintained Raspberry, "unless you seriously intend to do something about them."[46] Two days later, Watt told *Business Week* that "centralized planning and control of society" represented the main objective of the nation's environmental community. "Look what happened to Germany in the 1930s," the secretary warned. "The dignity of man was subordinated to the powers of Nazism." Reaction to the comments was again swift. Suggesting that Watt had finally gone bonkers, Gaylord Nelson of the Wilderness Society advised, "It's time the white-coat people took him away." Michael McCloskey, executive secretary of the Sierra Club, charged that only Watt could fail to see the difference "between Hermann Goering and John Muir."[47]

Watt exacerbated the situation two months later when he replaced the Beach Boys musical group with singer Wayne Newton at the annual Washington, D.C., Fourth of July celebration. As the official in charge of the Washington Mall, Watt controlled most aspects of the event. He announced that he wanted to bring "wholesomeness" to the holiday, that he wanted the celebration to stand for the "family and for solid, clean American lives. We're not going to encourage drug abuse or alcoholism as was done in the past. . . . It's going to be the military people with their patriotism and Wayne Newton."[48] Watt found himself embroiled in the greatest controversy of his short tenure. Richard Cohen criticized Watt for attempting to make a political point by mandating a self-defined "American music." Numerous people spoke out against the secretary, many arguing that the selection of Newton seemed the ultimate contradiction: How does the living symbol of Las Vegas conjure up images of patriotism and wholesomeness?[49] The political heat was so great from this decision that President Reagan gave the secretary a plaster foot with a hole in it to poke fun at Watt for shooting himself in the foot.[50]

Each of the gaffes appeared on the surface unrelated to the public lands debate. The comments, however, show how the public shaped its perception of Watt. The secretary's extreme views placed him at the public forefront, especially since his comments had at various times offended environmentalists, Democrats, Jews, American Indians, and followers of popular music. Significantly, his characterizations were intentional remarks designed to explain administration values and policies. Although he clarified each controversial statement by enlarging the context, Watt never denied his opinions.

As the year progressed, more of Watt's political decisions came back to haunt him. In March, the press learned that he had removed half of the scientists on a federal oil exploration advisory committee because they were deemed "politically unacceptable" by the Republican National Committee. Responding to this charge on the CBS News program, "Face the Nation," Watt claimed that he had intended only to "clean up the advisory groups. Let's get good advisors that want us to be successful." To justify his decision, Watt suggested that some scientists had given Jimmy Carter poor advice that had ultimately "hurt the country's parks and energy development." More negative publicity emerged when an Interior Department attorney noted in a legal memorandum that Watt had no authority to relax environmental standards on the public lands in order to stimulate resource development. After the memorandum appeared, the attorney was transferred and department employees ordered to destroy or return all copies.[51]

More bad news plagued Watt in April when the results of an eight-month-long investigation of the Interior Department's coal-leasing program were revealed. The House Appropriations Committee concluded that the secretary's efforts to lease vast tracts of western land had employed "fire sale" prices and allowed private interests to reap "windfall profits." The report claimed that confidential sales data had been leaked to the coal industry one month prior to the bids. Although some department officials sought to postpone the sales because of the information leak, they were overruled by an assistant interior secretary. The Government Accounting Office found that the resulting coal bids cost the federal government over $100 million. Responding to the controversy, the House Interior Committee ordered Watt to halt all coal leasing in the disputed areas.[52]

Reagan administration officials recognized the precarious results of Watt's controversial actions and attitudes. Although his style remained popular with many conservatives, it continued to make him increasingly less popular with the general public. Some feared that Watt's tarnished image might rub off on Reagan during the 1984 presidential campaign. Recognizing this problem, the president's staff took several steps to minimize potential damage. The administration announced that Reagan would deliver a speech to "comprehensively define his environmental policies" for the first time in his administration. Lou Cannon observed that Reagan's speech was part of the administration's counteroffensive to convince the American people and Congress that the president was "neither hostile nor indifferent to environmental concerns." Cannon noted that Watt had also taken steps, including weekly luncheon meetings with the press, to help correct the "distorted" presentation of his policies. Armed with charts, graphs, and slick sheets, Watt launched his "truth campaign" to provide an accurate account of his record. According to the *Washington Post,* the secretary "blitzed the talk-show circuit to tell millions of viewers that he is, in fact, a conservationist whose record has been distorted by malicious foes."[53]

Watt took his truth campaign to Denver in May, speaking to a national meeting of newspaper editors. Claiming to be on a "campaign to introduce the real Jim Watt to America," he contended that the "eastern press corps" did not understand a westerner such as himself, one who speaks the same in public as in private. He characterized his agenda as part of the Reagan Revolution, which he called a great new "political science experiment" in public land management. "If I failed in the experiment," he observed sarcastically, "I equalled the record of my predecessors." The newspaper editors challenged Watt to cite specific cases of the press being manipulated by the environmental movement, a frequent allegation in his "truth campaign." Refusing to list specific examples, the secretary told the editors to "just read the papers" to find distorted reporting of Interior policy.[54]

Although Watt continued to justify administration policies throughout the year, he also began attempting to placate various interests. He appeared at the last minute before the National Congress of American Indians. Although a lower-level Interior official had been scheduled to speak, the secretary felt he should apologize to the Indians he had "insulted" several days earlier. He used the address to build goodwill ("I was the first" secretary to visit the nation's largest reservation) and apologize for any offensive remarks that he might have made ("And if my words have caused hurt. . . . I apologize for that hurt."). Using a commonplace employed by Reagan several times, Watt maintained that he had been abused by the liberal news media representatives who refused to report his side of the story. Moreover, he told the Indians that he had merely tried to focus public attention on reservation problems, but because of the "unprofessional press conduct it was blown out of shape, lied about."[55]

Watt also increased his efforts to divide sports enthusiasts from the environmental movement. Calling for continued "scientific game management," the secretary praised hunting as a "legitimate tool" in game management. "The hunting instinct is healthy," he continued; "we believe the recreational values of hunting are substantial and should be encouraged rather than condemned." To impress his point, Watt contrasted the typical American hunter with opponents of game management who wanted an "all-powerful central government that dictates to people in every nook and cranny of America." Such individuals hoped to close the public lands to "hunting and other access by the American people." If it was unclear who these unnamed forces were, Watt clarified that in his conclusion. He charged that some special interest groups "who oppose or ignore consideration of man

in the environmental equation" would concentrate all authority in a
"dictatorial government that would deny individual freedoms and liberties."[56] In such an appeal, the secretary linked his opponents in the
environmental community with the larger enemy of the New Right—
liberals who sought centralized decision making in the United States.

Watt also used ceremonial occasions to help build public trust in
his agenda. Speaking to commemorate the fiftieth anniversary of the
Grand Coulee Dam, he praised the "courage" of those who constructed
the dam. Building such a dam, he observed, created strong opposition in the 1930s, just as his development policies created an unfavor-
able response fifty years later. Calling for a human-centered view of
natural resources, the secretary claimed that the spirit of those who
built the dam commands us to "aim high, to assure future generations
the means to improve their standard of living, and the means to maintain their freedom."[57] Ironically, the dam was a symbol of Franklin D.
Roosevelt's New Deal, a point the secretary glossed over in his formal
speech.

Under growing pressure from the Congress and leading environmental organizations, Watt decided to take his "truth campaign" on
the road during the summer of 1983, making two trips to Montana
in less than three weeks. Examining Watt's communication during
these two trips provides insight into the secretary's advocacy and altered rhetorical strategy, as well as illustrating western reaction to his
policy making. His first speech, to the Western Governors' Conference, addressed a key group in the secretary's good neighbor program.
Earlier in his term, he had labeled the Sagebrush Rebellion a moot
issue because, by working with the western states, the federal government would become a responsible landlord. In 1982, however, the
western governors officially denounced Watt's leadership. The second
speaking occasion was another ceremonial speech, celebrating the fiftieth anniversary of Glacier Park's "Going to the Sun" highway. Two
themes dominated the secretary's speeches during his Montana trips.
First, he emphasized the balanced and reasonable nature of his public
land policy. Rather than stressing the need to develop the natural resources, he presented himself as the moderate alternative to either
blind preservation or total development of the lands. Second, and
more important, he admitted making mistakes as interior secretary
and even called public attention to his past errors.

Speaking to the western governors in Kalispell, Watt proclaimed
his public land reforms a success. Prior to his speech, Democratic poll-

ster Peter Hart had told the governors that Watt was the "least popular figure in public opinion surveys in the Western states." In fact, 80 percent of those Hart polled considered Watt too "pro-development to be an effective steward of the public lands."[58] As a result, the secretary faced an already hostile audience armed with fresh evidence.

With the national press corps waiting for a public confrontation with the governors, Watt's altered style served him well. He told the governors that a new philosophy, "taking care of what we own," had been implemented, and he adamantly observed that no one was "selling national parks or wildlife areas." More important, he demonstrated humility, concluding that he had done a "miserable job" of setting up the public land sales of 1982. Announcing that there would be no wholesale "sell-off of the lands," the secretary advised the governors that they would have an "active voice in saying what is sold." During his first two years as secretary of the interior, noted Watt, he had to wrench the department from an extreme position back into the "mainstream of the conservation movement." Because 90 to 95 percent of his reforms had now been implemented, Watt claimed, Interior policy would show even more balance between "preservation and development in the months ahead." Apologizing for his apparent indifference toward the governors in establishing the "asset management program," he asked, "Do I do everything right the first time? No." According to a news account of the speech, the secretary labeled his plan to sell 35 million acres of federal land as stupid. "We did a miserable job in 1982," he said. "Have I been harsh enough on myself for 1982? I want to be harsh."[59]

The first Montana trip witnessed the typical political protests that had accompanied Watt throughout his tenure. While he spoke to the governors, a crowd of two hundred gathered to protest administration environmental policies. Adopting a variety of attention gimmicks, the protesters called attention to Watt's various calamities. Bags of coal were auctioned off for three and one-half cents per ton, in a parody of the coal leasing program under Government Accounting Office investigation. The protesters also auctioned off pieces of a Montana-shaped cake—to the *lowest* bidder—while a Wayne Newton impersonator serenaded the crowd. At the same protest meeting, a Watt impersonator jumped in the back of a pickup truck and proclaimed that God had given him a sign that morning—a "For Sale" sign. When someone offered a dollar for a piece of cake, the Watt impersonator shouted, "Do I hear less?"[60]

The western governors had mixed reactions to Watt's speech. Governor Toney Anaya of New Mexico called the presentation a sample of the "big lie," while the governors of South Dakota and North Dakota had praise for Watt. Governor Ted Schwinden of Montana called Watt the "second best communicator in the country," trailing only President Reagan. Listening to the secretary given a speech, claimed Schwinden, was like going to a faith healer. "You get the feeling walking out of there that you're not going to limp anymore. But a half block later, you're limping again."[61]

In mid-July, Watt returned, for the fiftieth anniversary of Glacier National Park's "Going to the Sun" highway. Local news coverage of this trip provided more evidence of Watt's altered style. Speaking in a less confrontational tone and attempting to defuse the lingering hostility of many in the West, Watt praised humanity's victory over nature. Commemorating the rugged, dangerous project that literally carved roads through high mountain passes, Watt employed the highway as a meaningful and necessary symbol of human development in the wilderness.

Praising those who built the highway, Watt argued that since 1917, "there's been warfare going on" over whether national parks should be "the playground or the preserves of America." The "Going to the Sun" highway proved the benefit of developing the parks for human consumption. Millions of people had seen the "beauty and grandeur of this area because there were men and women with enough courage and strength of character to build a highway." Indeed, Watt challenged the ecological notion that a true wilderness area lacks any signs of human activity. This road "intruded, crowded, changed habitat, brought pollution, it brought people. . . . But some people had enough courage to build a highway into a virgin area so people could enjoy it. It altered life." The secretary also used the occasion to chastise his opposition. Insisting on the moderate nature of his public land policy, he concluded, "I want to take care of people. I want to have jobs and better housing and health care . . . that requires economic activity as well as preservation activity."[62]

Watt also made himself available to the local news media during the trip. Asked about recent criticism by William Turnage of the Wilderness Society, the secretary called Turnage America's best public relations man because he "doesn't care what he says and he gets people like you and manipulates you to do whatever he wants to do." Watt also used the trip to announce several long-term goals, pledging to

request "hundreds of millions of dollars" in the next few years to acquire new national park lands. Because of the sluggish national economy, he observed, such a request would not come in 1984 or 1985.
In making such a promise, Watt hoped to dampen one of his lingering problems—the policy that stopped the purchase of additional park
land in favor of developing existing sites.[63]

The secretary also used the trip to bypass channels and appeal directly to Interior Department employees. He advised workers at
Glacier National Park that if he had read everything printed, "I
wouldn't like the Secretary of the Interior." As a result, he concluded,
"You folks deserve a better Secretary of the Interior than has been
portrayed. And you have one. What the press has been saying about
the Secretary of the Interior has been terrible." The national attention
that Watt brought to Montana intrigued the local media. One reporter noted that the secretary was being followed around Glacier National Park by *Newsweek,* the Associated Press, and newspapers from
Missoula, Spokane, Kalispell, and most television and radio stations
in the state.[64]

Less than two weeks after his second trip to Montana, Watt stunned
many observers by pulling the Interior Department out of the administration's asset management program. According to the Associated
Press, the land sales program had come under great "criticism from
Western ranchers concerned that they might lose valuable grazing rights
on millions of acres of federal land and from environmentalists who
believed that land would be sold for development." The report also
noted that the Reagan administration was under growing pressure from
western congressional delegates who wanted to "scuttle the program"
before it became an issue in the 1984 election. A Watt aide suggested
that the secretary closed the privatization program "because he regards
it as a political liability to President Reagan." After announcing the
Interior Department had pulled out of the land sales program, Watt
sent a letter to the western governors noting that the "mistakes of 1982"
involving the land sales "are not being, and will not be, repeated."[65]

James Watt's fall from power happened with exceptional speed. He
always maintained that he would resign if he became a liability to Reagan. In early 1983, the *Washington Times* reported that Watt would resign before 1984 in order to increase Reagan's reelection chances. If
Reagan declined to run, the paper suggested, Watt would not resign
his position.[66]

The immediate cause of Watt's resignation was an off-the-cuff remark made before two hundred Chamber of Commerce lobbyists. The secretary probably felt comfortable speaking to this group given his two-year position as a Chamber lobbyist in the mid-1960s. Ridiculing affirmative action guidelines, Watt recalled that an Interior Department advisory committee had every kind of "mix you can have. I have a black, I have a woman, two Jews, and a cripple. And we have talent." Surprisingly, the *Washington Post* reported, "Watt's remark drew laughter from the audience." As with his other gaffes, immediate public reaction was harsh. In this case, however, calls for Watt's resignation escalated as the days progressed after his comment. Significantly, Republican Senators Robert Dole and Howard Baker called for the secretary's resignation while the president's daughter, Maureen Reagan, declared that Watt would leave office if he were "truly loyal to the president." Reagan, who initially stood by Watt, attempted to downplay the comment after the secretary's public apology. By 1 October, Watt's western base of support was crumbling. Of the eighteen Republican senators in the western states, eight either demanded his resignation or refused to support him publicly. Possibly most significant of all, Reagan's close friend and Watt's first champion, Sen. Paul Laxalt, remained silent. On 10 October, nearly three weeks after the comment, the secretary resigned.[67]

Watt left office with a substantial record. Reviewing his achievements, Philip Shabecoff noted that Watt had opened up record amounts of public land for oil and coal development. Additionally, the status of the national parks changed under Watt, with less money for new land but significantly more money for development of existing parks. Most important, Watt restructured the Interior Department to assure that policy changes would be "institutionalized through new guidelines."[68] As an efficient federal bureaucrat, Watt knew how to leave his program intact for future administrations. He boasted that he had added more land to the federal holdings than any secretary since William Seward had purchased Alaska—"an all-time record in modern history." Characteristically, Watt did not mention that, when one subtracted the public lands either sold or exchanged during his tenure, the total size of the federal holdings remained unchanged.[69]

In nearly three years as secretary of the interior, Watt accomplished the near impossible: he moved national public land management from an ecological/preservationist perspective to a human-centered/development orientation. As a devout Christian fundamentalist and a committed New Right conservative, he openly preached the good news of Reaganism. Perceiving a clear link between his oratory and his policy making, many Americans held Watt accountable at both levels. The secretary's public communications, however, seemed to generate greater public interest than his numerous administrative reforms. As a result, Watt's rhetoric both helped and hindered the aims of the administration, depending on one's perspective. Although his remarks often placed him in the forefront of attack, he continued to challenge accepted notions of public land management. The aesthetic qualities of wilderness preservation seemed a foolhardy criterion for assessing national wilderness policy. Instead, Watt urged that human needs guide future resource decisions: visits per park; trends in coal and oil demand; and increased exploration for strategic minerals. From Watt's perspective, unused land was unproductive, and unproductive land was wasted land. Significantly, the secretary found many receptive forums.

Although he left the administration under public pressure, Watt accomplished much of his original agenda. Understanding the means of redirecting the movement of a vast bureaucracy, he successfully changed the course of the Interior Department. "He was a consummate bureaucrat," noted a former colleague. "He knew how to make a big, sprawling agency do what he wanted."[70] The conservation consensus, hammered out by individuals such as Aldo Leopold, Wallace Stegner, Bernard DeVoto, and Stewart Udall would have to reassert itself after its heavyweight brawl with Watt and his supporters. Preservation of the wilderness had lost some of its luster and altruism in the conservation debate.

Ironically, Watt may have inadvertently saved the environmental movement from a dangerous hibernation. Enormously successful for two decades, environmentalism had become increasingly complacent in the late 1970s. The rise of the New Right, the election of Ronald Reagan, and the zeal of James Watt, generated the issues, headlines, and membership drives that the movement needed. In this manner, Watt's administration may have been a mixed blessing for the environmental community.

Environmentalist Bil Gilbert summarized Watt's place in the history of American conservation. Recalling his thirty-five years of experience with public land issues, Gilbert concluded that three individuals have made the greatest impact on how Americans view nature: Aldo Leopold, Rachel Carson, and James Watt. "The last name," noted Gilbert, "is listed with absolutely no ironic or sarcastic intent."[71] Whether historians will accept Gilbert's conclusion remains to be seen. In any event, the legacy of James Watt will certainly be a topic of consideration in any discussion of the public lands in the Reagan era.

6. Selling the Public Lands

LOCK, STOCK, AND BARREL

The rise of the Sagebrush Rebellion, coupled with Ronald Reagan's electoral mandate in 1980, suggested that radical changes in the management of the nation's public lands were forthcoming. Although Reagan and his lieutenant, James Watt, backed away from giving the lands to the individual states, both men pledged to use the public resources more productively than previous administrations. However, a second prodevelopment philosophy, privatization, entered the national public lands debate in 1980, seeking the same goals as the Sagebrush Rebellion but employing a fundamentally different strategy. Rather than transferring the title of federally owned land to state management as the sagebrush rebels envisioned, advocates of privatization urged massive land auctions to help reduce the national debt and eliminate the sustained cost of federal management.

Led by a small group of vocal economists, the privatization movement appeared as a natural extension of the New Right. With funding and political status conferred by various private research foundations, privatization advocates sought to generate public support for the land sales. In developing arguments for their cause, the economists presented an intellectual analysis of public land use that the Sagebrush Rebellion sorely lacked. As a result, proponents of privatization stressed a philosophical rationale for their plan based upon free-market economy principles. Rhetorically, advocates aimed their message at academic audiences, special interest groups, and the general public through the national and local news media. Moreover, several privatization advocates received appointments in the Reagan administration and could work for their plan within the confines of the federal bureaucracy. The movement was a significant departure from the Sagebrush Rebellion debate because the economists presented an extensive alternative that attacked the pragmatic benefits and the ideological assumptions that guided the conservation consensus. In this manner, privatization opponents appeared better prepared to debate environmentalists than the rebels ever were.

To assess the role of privatization in the larger conservation debate, the connection between the New Right and privatization will be explored. Additionally, leading advocates as well as their rhetorical characteristics will be identified and analyzed. Considering these topics will help explain why a movement enriched with political opportunity failed to gain much public support. Although some observers associated the privatization campaign with James Watt, in fact the connection between the two was weak. Watt's land sales program seemed minuscule when compared with privatization's extreme goals. While he considered selling about 5 percent of the public lands, privatizationists urged the eventual sale of *all* of them.

Leaders of the New Right borrowed tactics from the liberals in activating political conservatism in the mid-1970s. Probably the most striking success of the New Right has been in the rise of the conservative research foundation. The most prominent, the Heritage Foundation, funds scholarly research, books, journals, lobbyists, and lectures, all designed to take the conservative message to relevant audiences.[1] The privatization movement took shape in such foundations and has its strongest backing there.

Privatization garnered public attention largely because of the financial and scholarly support of various research foundations, especially the Political Economy Research Center (PERC), located in Bozeman, Montana. Founded by Montana State University economists in 1976, the center grew rapidly. It left the confines of the university in 1983, and director John Baden resigned his faculty position to devote full time to the center. An introductory document released in 1983 described PERC's goals. Working with scholars, business leaders, and government officials throughout the United States, the center provided research grants, published books and monographs, sponsored conferences, and distributed guest editorials to national and local newspapers. PERC's major goal, to "develop constructive alternatives to increased government control over our economy and our lives,"[2] aptly reflects the free-market faith of the New Right. The center issued research findings that supported the contention that private industry and market forces were inherently superior to centralized economic planning. The only legitimate function of government, argued

Baden, is to provide national defense and police protection. "There's
no reason for the Postal Service," he noted. "It's dumb, silly."[3]

Although PERC's funding originated with a grant of $20,000 from
Montana State University, the center became self-supporting almost immediately with grants from private sources. PERC raised over $400,000
its first two years, with the largest single donation ($120,000) coming
from another conservative group, the Liberty Foundation. The 1983
budget of $250,000 came from a variety of "medium sized founda-
tions" and companies including Amax Coal, as well as the Heritage
Foundation, the Cato Institute, and several endowments.[4] Funds
helped pay salaries for seven full-time staff members as well as numerous associates and a variety of public communication efforts.

Three conferences sponsored by PERC in 1980, for example, cost
between $31,000 and $80,000 each. In addition, PERC paid "prominent scholars to write papers on topics suggested by the Center."
With conferences often held in Montana resorts, most were well attended. The center picked up the cost for many participants with
only one restriction: those individuals who failed to attend sessions
were later billed for room and board. The center has published ten
books and sponsored many conferences in its short history. With leading economists and media representatives attending seminars, PERC
offered a free-market alternative to prevailing intellectual theories of
natural resource management. The center had a clear mission. "We're
engaged in building the intellectual foundation for a system of natural
resource management," Baden observed, "that will be more environmentally sensitive, more equitably and more economically efficient
than a system of management by bureaucracies."[5] Hoping to convince
the nation's opinion leaders that the marketplace should guide land-
use decisions, Baden characterized the center's efforts as "The New
Resource Economics."[6]

Other conservative groups supported PERC's efforts to alter the
direction of federal natural resource policy. The Heritage Foundation
published *Earth Day Revisited,* a volume of prodevelopment writings.
Edited by Baden, the book advanced numerous criticisms of federal
land management and offered various plans for decentralizing federal
public land policy. In 1982 the Heritage Foundation and the Pacific
Institute for Public Policy Research cosponsored a conference on the
public lands that included politicians, academics, and journalists. The
conference proceedings were published the next year under the title

Private Lands and Public Lands. The Heritage Foundation also sponsored the work of Steven Hanke, a leading advocate of privatization who left the Reagan administration in 1982 to pursue public land reform in the private sector. With foundation funding, Hanke published a plethora of essays and editorials extolling the concept of privatization. Another research group, the Manhattan Institute for Policy Research, also lent intellectual status to the privatization movement. In 1982 it brought leading advocates together for a national conference and distributed the conference proceedings in pamphlet form to "policymakers, concerned citizens and educators."[7]

Although privatization was led by only a few individuals, each achieved national stature in the conservation debate. Given prominent attention in numerous publications and newspapers, privatizationists articulated an intellectual justification for the Reagan administration's plan to sell 35 million acres of public land in 1982.[8] Observing the various leaders more carefully should illuminate the rhetorical and political choices that guided privatization in the national public lands debate.

Holding a Ph.D. in economics from Indiana University, Baden taught at several colleges before ending up at Montana State University in 1970. A logger and sheep rancher as well as a professor, he often cited personal experiences to demonstrate the flaws of federally owned public lands. For example, he recalled a friend who wanted to subdivide his land for individual lot sales. Opposing the project because it threatened deer feeding areas, environmentalists blocked the intended subdivision. Baden was shocked to learn that "deer had acquired property rights to wildlife habitat on private lands," a seemingly inefficient result of Aldo Leopold's ecological conscience. In another case, Baden pointed to a fellow sheep rancher, Dave Flitner of Greybull, Wyoming, who went out of business because eagles and coyotes killed hundreds of his lambs. Unable to manage the predators because of federal restrictions, he saw his seventy-five-year-old ranching operation go bankrupt.[9] Wildlife and wilderness values appeared to have priority over economic considerations, an aberration to many in the New Right who advocated a human-centered system of resource allocation. Indeed, Baden claimed, "The genius of our system lies in its tendency to encourage people to do good while doing well."[10]

Unlike Baden, Hanke had little experience with the day-to-day problems of western ranchers, miners, and loggers. Rather, he favored pri-

vatization because of an abiding commitment to the free-market ideology of the New Right. Hanke joined the President's Council of
Economic Advisors in 1981 and told Reagan that the Sagebrush Rebellion "isn't going to solve the problem. It just moves the bureaucratic processes from Washington to the state capitals." Angry with
the administration's failure to act in a truly conservative manner,
Hanke resigned his position in June, 1982. Noting that taxes and federal spending actually increased in Reagan's first eighteen months as
president, the economist concluded, "There's a massive gap between
rhetoric and reality."[11]

Through speeches, interviews, and essays, he became the most vocal
figure in the privatization debate. Reflecting the extreme notions of
other free-market purists, Hanke opposed all government activities except for defense concerns. After leaving the Reagan administration,
he published a flurry of articles supporting federal land sales. Arguing
that privatization would be won or lost "depending whether or not
people come forward to make the case," Hanke decided to step forward. "You have to literally get out in the field," he observed, "and
make people aware of these arguments so they can put pressure on
people in office."[12] Hanke became so displeased with the administration's failure to carry out the New Right agenda, that he authored
a stinging editorial, "Would the Real Mr. Reagan Please Stand Up?"
which concluded, "This pattern of double talk and policy flipflops now
appears to be a hallmark of the Reagan administration."[13]

Another privatization advocate, William Tucker, analyzed the public lands debate as a class conflict, in which environmentalists were
characterized as anti–blue collar, antiprogress aristocrats. In his book
Progress and Privilege, Tucker endeared himself to forces in the New
Right by advancing an intellectual and historical indictment of the
environmental movement. Although not directly concerned with the
economics of a free-market resource policy, Tucker attended various
privatization conferences to offer his observations on the public land
question.

An examination of the specific privatization arguments demonstrates the intellectual framework that advocates developed. Privatizationists rejected the Reagan administration's good neighbor program
of working more closely with the states in determining how the public lands should be used. Committed to an absolute free-market economy, proponents advocated one solution: sale of the public lands to
the private sector. Unlike Watt's asset management program which

stressed the sale of unwanted and unused lands, the privatizationists wanted *all* land targeted for eventual sale. Moreover, the economists saw little merit in supporting the Sagebrush Rebellion. Hanke argued that a successful Sagebrush Rebellion, transferring federal lands to state governments, was flawed because it merely substituted one form of public ownership for another. The rebellion therefore offered little hope to adherents of privatization. While still a member of the Reagan administration, Hanke delivered a "message to Sagebrush Rebels," charging that all politicians and bureaucrats, whether federal, state, or local, are never "directly responsible for the consequences of their decisions." With the Reagan administration in office, he continued, some bureaucrats "pronounce the rebellion dead" because the so-called "right" people are in power. On the contrary, it made no difference who controlled land policy, since "the *only* way to improve productivity and efficiency of public lands is to privatize them." Pleading with rebels to accept the "one fundamental principle" of America's founders – the notion of limited government – Hanke concluded, "Until we begin to privatize the public lands, we will not have accomplished anything of real economic or moral value."[14]

Privatizationists articulated a fundamentally different view of the world than that of environmentalists. Arguing from an ecological perspective, environmentalists endorsed ongoing government efforts to protect all creatures in the ecosystem. Quality-of-life arguments, lacking economic precision, were at the center of environmental rhetoric. The goal of multiple use with permanent federal ownership and management seeks to balance competing demands upon the land. Although multiple use may be economically inefficient, environmentalists accepted this as a necessary price for a healthy ecosystem. On the other hand, privatizationists viewed the world from an economic perspective, promoting policies that would foster economic freedom. Because of this vantage, they demanded that humans be placed at the top of any hierarchy of values. As a result, advocates of privatization soundly rejected the ecological conscience as a useful framework for making public land policy. In *Earth Day Revisited,* Baden delineated the economists' reasons for rejecting environmentalism. He disputed the belief that any culture can change individuals in such a way that "public interest *becomes* self-interest." In other words, an environmental ethic based upon altruism rested upon a false interpretation of human behavior. Instead, argued Baden, all people choose purposefully, selecting "options they expect to benefit from the most." Humans therefore respond to rewards and costs, not abstract values: "If an action is made more costly, it will be taken less frequently; if rewarded more, it will be taken more frequently. Incentives matter." In Baden's ideal state, the free market provided the superior means of determining use of the natural resources. "In a private setting," he observed, "we need not count on the goodwill or morality of decisions-makers; their greed will suffice."[15]

Baden attacked the perception that environmentalists were "self-sacrificing defenders of the public interest." Because they have no apparent profit motive, "we are to assume that their motives are pure." On the contrary, asserted Baden, public ownership of the western lands leads to either overproductive (and environmentally damaging) use or underproductive (and economically wasteful) use. Higher energy costs and increased unemployment represented the spillover effects of America's underused public lands.[16]

Another economist, Bruce Johnson, stressed the difference between the cost and the price of public land ownership. Noting that government can artificially set the price of wilderness at zero, he claimed that the actual cost to society was much higher. Why? If a "commercially viable forest is set aside for aesthetic purposes," the cost of preservation results in higher timber prices and lower taxes and employment rates.[17] Because the public naively believes that wilderness costs nothing, they predictably want more, according to the economic worldview. To demonstrate the true cost of preservation, Johnson suggested a user fee that would reflect the actual cost be placed on all government services. Under this plan, only those people who actually visited Yellowstone National Park, for example, would have to pay for the park's services. Johnson observed that Americans are too concerned with results rather than processes. Perceiving injustice and inequality, they typically rush to fix the problem without reviewing the process. As a result, Americans typically enact laws to regulate levels of employment, inflation, energy use, and so forth. Such good intentions, however, do not always produce good results. Not only are processes important, argued Johnson, "they are critical to producing desired results," with the private sector better able to handle concerns for environmental protection.[18]

Calling ecology a subversive science, Tucker maintained that environmentalism offered a conservative social doctrine based upon the belief that "nature must be preserved and human activity minimized." To counter such extremism, he suggested a new ecological ethic. "We should extend our moral concerns to plants, trees, and animals," he claimed, *"but not at the expense of human beings.* Our first obligation is to humanity."[19]

Other privatizationists also demanded a human-centered view of nature be used in making public policy. Terry Anderson of PERC argued that wilderness should not have any right to exist; if a tree "has rights, I have no idea how to measure a tree's value as a tree would perceive its value." Asked if it is sinful for humans to destroy another species of life, Anderson replied, "Not necessarily. At least not from my property rights perspective." Baden qualified his answer to the same question, noting that destruction of another species is a heinous crime from a moral perspective. But he definitely opposed any governmental intervention to save an endangered species. Instead, society should allow some private individual or group to "pay something" to save the threatened life-form. Asked to clarify his position, Baden noted that if a person owns a mountain with rare forms of plants or animals, from a free-market vantage that person enjoys the right to destroy the species.[20] Since the 1960s, the ecological conscience and the land ethic had justified government intervention to protect plants, animals, rivers, and mountains. Applying the economist's bottom-line perspective to land policy, the privatization movement challenged the notion that nonhuman forms of life had inherent rights to exist. Although they often couched their appeals in less dramatic language, privatizationists agreed that humans should be placed at the top of any wilderness-use hierarchy.

Selling the federal lands made economic sense, advocates argued, because the sales would lead to more productive use of the nation's natural resources. In a variety of publications, Hanke observed that privatization benefited the nation in four different ways: the productivity of western ranches would be enhanced; a tax base would be transferred from the federal government to the state and local governments; federal revenues would be raised from the sales; and federal management costs would be significantly curtailed.[21] In nearly every speech, interview, and essay Hanke presented, he reiterated these four benefits. He told the nation's sheep ranchers, for example, that virtually any comparison "between publicly and privately owned land indicates greater productivity on private land."[22] Although environmentalists called such comparisons unfair, from the economist's perspective, privatizationists could easily substantiate the efficiency of the private sector. As the conservation debate often illustrated, prodevelopment rhetoric gained currency through its apparent quantitative accuracy. Hanke's four benefits were probably inviting to many Americans wearied by the combined inflation and recession of the late 1970s. To prove the federal government's inefficiency, advocates often detailed specific cases of public land mismanagement. Tucker repeated the case in which environmentalists blocked a dam from completion because an endangered species, the snail darter, would become extinct. Because of their success in the Tellico Dam controversy, claimed Tucker, environmentalists were "prancing through the country turning up endangered species almost anywhere that a Federally funded developer was putting a shovel." Tucker criticized guidelines that based land-use decisions upon noneconomic factors such as endangered species. Calling competition among earth's creatures unavoidable, he suggested that extinction is the "common fate of all individuals, of nearly all species to date." If humans must "assume guilt for the destruction of other creatures while pursuing our interests," concluded Tucker, "then that may be the price of our existence."[23]

Why would well-intentioned federal bureaucrats become inefficient and insensitive directors of the public lands? Attacking any governmental intrusion into the economic sector, privatizationists maintained that various institutional features of government prevented efficient and productive use of the nation's resources. Federal bureaucrats hoard land, argued Hanke, in order to maintain their positions of power. If the public lands were sold, many bureaucrats would "significantly reduce their employment opportunities and growth potentials," since the BLM and the Forest Service's "raison d 'etre is to manage federal land."[24] More important, argued Tucker, the rules of land management were so complicated that only the bureaucracy could understand them, making such managers "indispensable to the workings of everyday life."[25] Calling government land management simplistic, Baden charged that self-interest always thwarted the best of intentions. In reality, bureaucrats are "primarily concerned with their careers, their personal well-being, the respect of their professional colleagues, and the perquisites of their office."[26] Even though federal officials claimed to act in the best interests of society, privatizationists countered that personal gains inherently overshadowed economic efficiency and resource productivity.

From the perspective of the New Right, the process of centralized decision making corrupted even the best intentioned public land managers. Baden and Laura Rosen suggested that bureaucrats have distorted incentives because they "cannot directly claim the benefits" that would result from effective resource decisions. Moreover, because of their short terms in government service, it becomes "rational for bureaucrats and congressmen to weigh the personal, political, short-run advantages of their decisions more heavily than the long-run general advantages."[27] In the private sector, however, wasteful practices are "quickly separated from control of productive resources: they go bankrupt." With no means of distinguishing between efficient and inefficient federal land managers, concluded Baden, the government "can engage in the environmentally destructive and economically irrational practices that it does."[28]

Baden and Richard Stroup, a Reagan appointee in the Interior Department, suggested that economic principles help to illuminate why politicians make poor wilderness managers. Government officials do not seek to help future generations because "wise husbanding of resources is not likely to help the politician get elected or reelected today." Private landowners, on the other hand, must always consider the future wants and needs of a consumer-oriented society. As a result, politicians can always blame someone else for policy decisions while private owners "alone will suffer the losses of inefficient decisions or benefit from wise ones."[29] In applying a cost-benefit analysis to human motivation, the privatizationists rejected both the multiple-use goal of public land management as well as the notion of altruism as a guide to managerial actions.

Criticizing the conservation consensus of the 1960s and 1970s, supporters of privatization portrayed environmentalists as a group of irresponsible elitists. Although Tucker made the most detailed case against environmentalism, other advocates supported his contentions. Hanke, for example, charged that environmentalists "want to control the use of these lands, without bearing the responsibility and costs of ownership." Responding to attacks upon the Reagan administration's asset management program, Hanke asserted that leading environmental groups "have been busy producing analytical nonsense, and, as a result, a number of myths about privatization have gained currency."[30]

Moreover, advocates charged that environmentalists often disguised their true political agenda in public debate. Some cited the Audubon Society's Rainey Reserve, a privately owned wildlife refuge in Louisiana, as a typical example of the movement' double standard. When oil was discovered on this property, noted Baden, the Audubon Society "pumped the oil under very carefully monitored conditions. Everybody won." In contrast, he continued, when the Interior Department proposed oil exploration in the Bob Marshall Wilderness Area of Montana, the Audubon Society claimed that "it's the ultimate desecration to even think about exploring it for oil."[31] The Rainey Reserve, observed Hanke, illustrated that what "generates conflict, confrontation, and controversy on public lands produces harmony on privately owned land." Any reasonable person, he maintained, would conclude that if "private property works to benefit society in this way, the Government ought to 'privatize' some of its land." Repeating this same argument in the *Wall Street Journal*, Hanke noted that the Rainey Reserve proved that "private ownership and free markets are the institutions that best guarantee the protection of the environment and the protection of consumers' needs."[32]

Committed to a free-market economy, Baden and Stroup proclaimed that "people willing to vote for environmental quality should also be willing to buy it for themselves to use and hold as an investment." If environmentalists wanted portions of the public domain preserved, then the Sierra Club or the Wilderness Society ought to buy the land and manage it as they saw fit. Responding to the charge that land sales would allow only the wealthy the opportunity to enjoy the wilderness, Baden and Stroup repeated their faith in the marketplace to allocate scarce commodities. Elegant restaurants, fast-food chains, Broadway theaters cater to "all tastes and income levels." "Rich people," they argued, "tend to get more, but in the private sectors they must pay for it."[33] In other words, some people inherently get more and some get less in a true, free-market society. In contrast, argued Baden, environmentalists often took wealth away from members of the working class. This theft occurred whenever environmentalists joined forces with bureaucrats and politicians to "generate programs that produce wealth for a select few, and many of these programs are economically inefficient and environmentally destructive."[34] From this vantage, environmentalists did not ultimately help disadvantaged Americans enjoy the wilderness, because such individuals lacked adequate finances to spend time pursuing recreational activities.

Tucker advanced the most definitive attack upon the contemporary environmental movement. His thesis was simple: The idea of progress, in which each generation attempts to make life better for itself than for previous generations, is stifled by privilege. In an attempt to preserve the status quo (and their privileged position), aristocrats natu-

rally opposed any movement toward progress. The rise of the environmental movement, claimed Tucker, "represented a withdrawal of upper-
middle-class attention from the interests of the poor." As a *privileged*
minority," environmentalists opposed any economic growth that might
endanger their unrestricted use of the public lands. Accordingly, environmentalists opposed oil exploration, coal mining, dams, resort facilities, and other forms of development as an invasion of their public
playgrounds. How can preserving sections of wilderness be analogous
to the economic privilege of aristocrats in previous generations? Tucker
explained this in several ways. At a psychological level, environmentalism reflected a "backward-looking effort to recapture a sense of America's lost innocence." Saving the public lands, he observed, represented
a futile effort to "reopen the American frontier." From a more pragmatic perspective, wilderness areas and national parks served as "parks
for the upper-middle-class,"[35] preserving their insulation from society's lower classes. Because environmentalists lacked the economic resources to become an economic aristocracy, argued Tucker, they acted
as an "aristocracy in the political realm, which is more effective than
the economic realm these days."[36]

Environmentalism also retained some of its popularity from the
1960s, when a new sense of social awareness had emerged in the United
States. In a time of shifting political values and attitudes, environmentalism offered the perfect political crusade for the neoliberal generation of the 1980s. It gave adherents of the 1960s counterculture an alternative which still satisfied their psychological need to rebel but
preserved their high degree of societal privilege. In this manner, environmentalism appeared to give supporters the opportunity to have
their cake and eat it too.

Privatizationists portrayed conservation issues in the emotional language of extreme alternatives often typical in the public lands debate.
Even though many advocates claimed scholarly detachment, the emotional connotation of their rhetoric demonstrated their obvious commitment to the ideological foundations of the New Right. Some advocates, for example, dichotomized land policy as either capitalistic
(and prodevelopment) or socialistic (and propreservation). Baden
claimed that environmentalism had been guided by a "collective political philosophy that has nothing to do with conservation." The problem with the "collectivist idea (as with socialism)," wrote Baden, "is
that when the public owns something, the government usually runs
it, and everyone suffers the consequences."[37] The real choice in the

privatization debate, concluded Hanke, is between "private property and individual freedom versus public ownership and serfdom." Demonstrating that debate's emotional language, Hanke argued that opponents of privatization "are outright socialists, and they will have to show their true colors. It's such a clean, pure, perfect issue. Either you do want property rights or you want public, collectivized arrangements. There's no middle of the road."[38] Inviting cattle ranchers to join the movement, Hanke maintained that wilderness ownership can "determine whether an economic system is socialist or capitalist." In light of this nation's founding principles, concluded Hanke, America's "socialized lands are truly an anomaly."[39]

Supporters of privatization rejected multiple use as a reasonable alternative to private ownership. Some writers, in fact, claimed that government efforts to balance land use among competing groups actually served to harm the lands. Baden and Rosen asserted that government aid to farmers had promoted the destruction of wildlife habitat and federal grazing lands. As a result, multiple use may have fostered environmental degradation in the name of wise management. Contrary to popular belief, noted Baden, the "market system has not despoiled the environment. Public control, subsidies and the absence of clearly defined, well-enforced, and transferable property rights have led to virtually all of the major ecological disasters in America."[40] In reality, private landowners, observed Hanke, often practiced a true form of multiple use. Because "it's usually an all or nothing decision" regarding public land use, multiple use is "largely a myth of the public lands." In contrast, he pointed to Maine. Although 98 percent privately owned, the state had significant multiple use with private roads, hunting, and fishing open to the public.[41] Tucker believed that federal laws declaring wilderness to be a valid alternative in multiple-use designation thwarted legitimate use of the public lands. By giving wilderness comparable status with mining, logging, and ranching, the government provided environmental groups "an all purpose tool for stopping economic activity."[42]

As privatizationists made their case in speeches, periodicals, and conferences, several constraints confronted supporters. In line with the movement's intellectual character, advocates articulated specific plans to implement privatization as national policy. Unlike the Sagebrush Rebellion, which eschewed concern about specific points, privatizationists presented a well-defined course of action. Such detail, however, opened up greater attacks from the opposition. In addition, privatizationists became increasingly frustrated with the Reagan administration's effort to downplay the scope of its asset management program. Although many New Right leaders endorsed privatization of the public lands, both Reagan and Watt seemed reluctant to embrace the plan fully. Examining these constraints will help explain the movement's inability to affect significantly the public lands policy during Reagan's first term as president.

Baden and Stroup offered the public a systematic and detailed plan designed to satisfy all interests: business, government, environmental groups, and the general public. To begin the process of privatization, all lands currently designated as wilderness areas would be placed in the hands of qualified environmental groups such as the Audubon Society and the Sierra Club. In exchange, the groups would agree that no future wilderness areas could be created and that the wilderness areas could be developed or preserved as the groups saw fit. As a result, the environmentalists would be forced to decide if any mining, logging, or grazing could be done on their lands. The remainder of the vast federal holdings would be either sold or leased to private citizens. Such a divestiture, the two economists concluded, "could yield enormous social benefits. With land in private hands, all parties concerned become much more constructive in their thinking and language."[43]

Hanke refuted the public perception that privatization would result in western ranchers losing valuable grazing lands to wealthy, out-of-state land investors. Unlike the Sagebrush Rebellion, which seemed popular with the ranching community, privatization offered no clear indications that ranchers would have access to the land for grazing. Hanke outlined his privatization plan in the *National Woolgrower*. Any parcel of land not earning a 10 percent real rate profit would be declared surplus and put up for sale. The government would act like a private business manager, noted Hanke, by eliminating "low yielding items in his portfolio and [selling] them." For the many ranchers who rented federal lands for grazing, Hanke would extend credits for past fees and offer these ranchers a "first refusal option . . . no one else could purchase it before they had a right to exercise their option." If the rancher did not buy the land, then it would be made available for public auction. Asked if the government should help ranchers raise purchase funds through a loan program, Hanke replied, "Absolutely not." From his vantage, getting the government out of the process would set the free market loose.[44] This plan of action failed to generate much support in the ranching community. According to one source, "not a single major commodity sector supported privatization: livestock, mining, oil and gas, coal, or timber."[45]

As Watt distanced the Interior Department from the privatization movement, many advocates became angry with the administration's moderation on land issues. In an editorial published in the *Los Angeles Times*, Baden claimed that both Watt and Reagan had failed to reform public land policy adequately. Part of the problem, he observed, was the "emotional atmosphere surrounding nearly every political decision Watt made." Had the secretary "fostered a more reasonable and tolerant atmosphere," continued Baden, he might have been successful in implementing the administration's limited version of privatization. Writing in the *Chicago Tribune*, Baden concluded that privatization "is now associated almost solely with Watt, to the detriment of the concept." Watt's tenure had generated "more analyses of the Beach Boys controversy than of the federal land sales question."[46]

Hanke's bitterness toward the Reagan administration became evident in a November, 1982, interview in which he called it "just a typical, traditional Republican administration." "It's basically the Nixon-Ford administration without either Nixon or Ford," he charged. "If you have strong preferences like I do, there's really nothing for you to do." Hanke ridiculed the administration's failure to support privatization fully. "Faced with questions and criticisms about privatization," he declared, "the administration has remained tongue-tied." If only Reagan would have taken action to "untie some tongues," this would have gone a "long way toward a more balanced airing of this important concept in the media."[47]

In the summer of 1983, Hanke directed specific criticism at Watt. Noting that liberals often called the secretary a failure, Hanke charged, "When judged by authentic conservative standards, Secretary Watt has also been a failure." For example, the national park system cost the nation's taxpayers about $500 million per year to maintain. By increasing user fees by 2000 percent, Hanke pointed out, the parks could become self-sufficient. Hanke also challenged Watt to sell some of the park land, an "authentically conservative way" of approaching federal resource management.[48] When the secretary ended the Interior Department's participation in the administration's privatization program, Hanke responded angrily. Watt never fully supported the concept, he wrote. "Watt has been opposed to the president's land-sales program from the beginning." As early as May, 1982, maintained

Hanke, Watt had attempted to downplay privatization, fearing that western ranchers might oppose the plan. Additionally, Watt sabotaged the plan by giving supporters of privatization little support and by inflaming environmentalists with his extreme visions of the land sales. Hanke also complained that the secretary had ordered his staff not to use the term privatization when discussing the administration's asset management program.[49]

Foes of privatization responded with their own scholarly analysis of "The New Resource Economics." Calling privatization "appealing in its simplicity," C. Ford Runge, an economist at the University of Minnesota, charged that the "premise of privatization does not confront real problems of information, imperfectly competitive markets, externalities or the existing structure of property rights." Runge noted that while the private sector may be more efficient in a technical sense, this assumption is based upon a system that has correct information and foresight, no monopoly power, and no external complexities. "Unfortunately," he observed, "the real world is full of these complexities, all of which interfere with . . . efficient private decision making." To bolster his critique of privatization, Runge pointed to the transfer of government land to the railroads during the late nineteenth century. Claiming that such lands were used inefficiently in many cases, he concluded that failure to consider "real world" complications was a fundamental flaw in the case for privatization. Those advocates who cited the original Homestead Act to support privatization relied upon an "erroneous historical analogy." According to Runge, that act "was designed to overcome a problem of excess supplies of land, not to conserve resources like wilderness lands."[50]

Another environmentalist, M. Rupert Cutler of the National Audubon Society also rejected many of the privatizationist claims. Cutler noted that the oil and gas exploration on the society's Rainey Reserve, often cited as a perfect example of privatization, was atypical. Development of the reserve funded improvements in wildlife habitat necessary to increase the reserve's carrying capacity for wildfowl. Moreover, no mineral development noted Cutler, "occurs on any other part of Audubon's eight-unit national sanctuary system." Cutler attacked the underlying premise of privatization, the assignment of economic values to wilderness, arguing that alternative values should receive equal consideration. Baden "doesn't mention our concerns regarding ecological diversity," claimed Cutler, as well as the "distributional question involving traditional access to the out-of-doors by all citizens."

But in terms of economic value, environmentalists believed that privatization would also be costly. Significant development on the public lands, such as the construction of hotels and resorts, could destroy western watersheds. The result of such action, Cutler concluded, "could well be a repeat of what our nation went through fifty years ago – flooding, the bankruptcy of communities, the wasting of people and resources, until the land is repurchased by the government and restored to ecological health at great public expense."[51]

In 1981 some environmentalists formed their own research foundation, Carrying Capacity, Inc., to combat privatization. A representative of the group, Judith Jacobsen, argued that the free-market approach failed to assign economic values to clean air, water, and ecological diversity. Refuting the notion that the private sector inherently makes the best resource decisions, Jacobsen concluded, "Property rights haven't stopped the deterioration of farmlands" throughout the United States. Arguing that overgrazing on the federal lands was contributing to the "desertification" of the area, Carrying Capacity endorsed "more governmental control in the form of environmental regulations."[52] Leaders in the mainstream environmental movement also attacked privatization, often in their efforts to oppose the administration's overall public land agenda. From their vantage point, there appeared to be little difference between Reagan and Watt's asset management program and the free-market economists and their privatization crusade.

Why did privatization fail to arouse western ranchers, miners, farmers, and loggers? From its inception, the movement seemed to emerge in an opportune time. They had a sympathetic president, support from many members of the U.S. Senate, researchers at well-funded think tanks, and a strongly documented political and philosophical agenda. More important, advocates portrayed their plan in the appealing guise of the free market, private property, and the founding fathers. Several factors help to explain why privatization failed to gain any lasting public support during Reagan's first term. Leaders in the movement did not recognize the amount of public sentiment against such sales. The notion of selling large tracts of wilderness seemed extreme even to many conservatives in the West. Additionally, the administration's good neighbor program satisfied regional demands for more development of the public lands. Although privatization seemed consistent with a free-market economy, the concept engendered little enthusiasm. Moreover, as public reaction mounted against the Reagan administration's prodevelopment policies, Watt moved the Interior Department away from land sales. As Watt revealed in 1983, pressure from western members of congress led him to eliminate his asset management program. Ironically, privatization had become too conservative a doctrine for even Ronald Reagan and James Watt.

In addition, privatizationists were rhetorically inept in several areas. According to Christopher K. Leman, the proponents of privatization, including many economists, overextended the economic efficiency argument. Noting that Steven Hanke's land sales plan imposed a "stricter test on the public lands" than on the private sector, Leman concluded that the free-market economists "managed to sour many people by insisting on an often sloppy and one-sided interpretation of what efficiency recommends."[53] In addition, many privatizationists were disdainful of alternative values in the conservation debate. When discussing issues such as endangered species, clear air, and national parks, the free-market economists were unable to entertain other values that might motivate many members of their audience.

Privatizationists brought an economic perspective to the national conservation debate that claimed superiority over the ecological views of the conservation community. They offered economic efficiency and a free market as the guiding paradigm for the public lands debate. In contrast, the Sagebrush Rebellion relied upon an antibureaucratic, antieastern brand of conservatism. Although the rebellion and the privatization movement shared important goals, the rebellion seemed to have wider public support. This perception may be misleading, however. As a campaign to gain attention for western grievances, the rebellion relied on several vague generalizations and emotive symbols. On the other hand, privatizationists offered a legislative agenda with a detailed intellectual and philosophical justification. Because of this specificity, advocates of privatization faced more systematic constraints in the public debate than did the rebels.

Most significant in their failure to win support, privatization advocates faced a reinvigorated environmental movement that had grown significantly stronger in the ongoing battles with James Watt. The bottom line for privatization rests in the movement's failure to mobilize any sustained and widespread support in the West. While scholars held at least sixteen conferences between 1980 and 1983 debating the need to sell the public lands,[54] calls for such sales received a cold response in the West, the region which gave the Sagebrush Rebellion life in 1979. Without the support of this region, the privatization crusade had little chance of changing federal land policies. By the beginning of 1984, privatization appeared to be silenced as a viable movement for foreseeable generations.

7. Rebuilding the Consensus

ENVIRONMENTAL RHETORIC, 1981–84

Invigorated by their brief, successful skirmish with the sagebrush rebels, environmentalists were prepared to oppose any effort to significantly alter prevailing public land policy. Interior Secretary James Watt's zealous campaign to unlock the wilderness for development aroused fears among environmentalists that the conservation consensus was no longer politically secure. Flexing their strength at the national and local levels, environmentalists fought nearly every action proposed or adopted by the Reagan administration. They mobilized their own constitutency and attempted to persuade the general public to reject calls for public land development. To illuminate the environmental role in the conservation debate, this chapter examines leading advocates in the movement and the rhetorical strategies and themes they employed.

Environmentalists relied greatly upon the writings of Aldo Leopold in presenting a philosophical rationale for wilderness preservation. Although they also invoked the names of John Muir, Bob Marshall, Theodore Roosevelt, and Gifford Pinchot, Leopold's land ethic and ecological conscience served as the foundation of most environmental discourse. Because of Leopold's influence on those who shaped and maintained the conservation consensus, it was appropriate that his legacy would reemerge in the public lands debate of the 1980s.[1]

Leopold presented a qualitative scale to guide public resource decisions, based on a deep love of nature as well as a commitment to scientific objectivity. The land ethic simply enlarged the "boundaries of the community to include soils, waters, plants, and animals" and changed humanity's role from the "conqueror of the land-community to plain member and citizen of it."[2] At a pragmatic level, such an awareness could help humans recognize the ecosystem's inherent interdependence and in turn minimize potentially devastating resource policies. At a philosophical level, wilderness yields values inherently unavailable in an urban-industrial society. By experiencing a wilderness similar to that which their ancestors knew, contemporary Americans might better understand their "distinctive national origins and evolution" and become "culturally prepared to face the dark and bloody realities of the present."[3]

Most important, wrote Leopold, human interaction with the wilderness should remind "us of our dependency on the soil-plant-animal-man food chain." Modern civilization had "cluttered this elemental man-earth relation with gadgets and middlemen," making an ecological awareness increasingly difficult to foster.[4] Publicly recognizing the value of wilderness reflected a genuine intellectual humility so often lacking in the shallow-minded modern. Those able to perceive the land ethic also realized that "raw wilderness gives definition and meaning to the human enterprise." Acknowledging the criticism leveled by some critics that wilderness catered to an elitist element of society, Leopold charged that the basic error with this position "is that it applies the philosophy of mass-production to what is intended to counteract mass-production." In reality, the ultimate value of outdoor recreation comes from the "degree to which it *differs from* and *contrasts* with workday life."[5] As a result, the greater the wilderness experience, the higher the value of the activity, no matter how few individuals actually gained the experience.

Environmentalists constructed their appeals based upon Leopold's philosophical perspectives. Many advocates cited the land ethic with no acknowledgment or definition, demonstrating how ingrained the concept had become within the conservation community. Speaking at Yale University, William Turnage of the Wilderness Society credited Leopold, the "philosopher laureate for the American Conservation Movement," for advocating wilderness management dictated "not just by what is expedient and profitable, but what is moral and right."[6] Serving as an ethical yardstick, the land ethic became a model principle for human behavior in the wilderness. People must recognize that wilderness can "shrink but not grow," Leopold had observed. They may retain wilderness for recreation, wildlife, or science, "but the creation of new wilderness in the full sense of the word is impossible."[7]

Most significant for the 1980s conservation debate, Leopold rejected a public lands policy based on economic motives because "most members of the land community have no economic value." Of the 22,000 plants and animals native to Wisconsin, for example, less than 5 percent can be "sold, fed, eaten, or otherwise put to economic use." In fact, a lack of economic value characterizes "entire biotic communities" such as marshes, bogs, and deserts. Relying upon economic self-interest to achieve fair public land use was hopelessly lopsided, he wrote, because it ignored those elements in the ecosystem without commercial value but "essential to its healthy functioning."[8] Although Leopold died in 1949, his discourse foreshadowed the central dilemma in the most current conservation debate: how does a society balance economic demands with ecological needs and keep all factions pleased with the outcome?

An important measure of Leopold's influence appeared in the work of two contemporary advocates of conservation, Edward Abbey and Wallace Stegner. Both writers found the advent of the Reagan era an ideal time to reiterate the ideas Leopold had expressed years earlier. Noting that wilderness "complements and completes civilization," Abbey argued that a completely human-made environment would not be a "civilization at all but merely another kind of culture." He challenged humans to acknowledge the rights of all living and non-living things, even boulders and mountains. "It is not enough to understand the natural world," observed Abbey, "the point is to preserve it. Let Being be."[9] The growing popularity of wilderness recreation in recent years reflected an "elemental impulse" that still survives in the hearts of modern men and women, an impulse pushing humans to rediscover "our ancient, preagricultural, preindustrial freedom." Echoing Leopold's praise of the frontier, Abbey claimed that freedom to experience the wilderness offered a lesson often missing in modern America: the open, available, and democratic walk in the woods. Suggesting that such a freedom was interdependent with other freedoms, Abbey concluded, "It is my fear that if we allow the freedom of the hills to be taken from us, then the very idea of freedom may die with it."[10]

In a speech aptly titled "The Gift of Wilderness," Stegner noted that when humans lose touch with the natural earth, they also lose touch with their humanity. Those sensitive to the land ethic, the "philosophers of the garden" in Stegner's words, "conceive America to be an intricate organism of which man is not an irresponsible beneficiary but a living part, a participant who suffers and perhaps perishes if he mishandles too roughly the land, water, and air by which we live."[11]

Believing that nature can make better individuals, Stegner observed that love of wilderness teaches civilized responsibility.[12] Many Americans, even devout Christians, he concluded, have learned to leave behind the "Judeo-Christian tradition which puts man at the center of the universe and gives him dominion over the beasts of the field and the fowls of the air." Yet he remained cautious in predicting the future. Until humans "arrive at a land ethic that unites science, religion, and human feelings," the potential for destroying the wilderness remained possible.[13]

Environmental rhetoric took shape among three different groups: the grass-roots protest, the organized environmental movement, and the radical amateurs.[14] Although the groups sometimes shared members and overlapped in their efforts, significant differences existed. As a rule, radical amateurs such as Abbey, Stegner, Ansel Adams, and Cecil Andrus found media outlets available to them because of their standing in earlier conservation affairs. As a result, they were considered newsworthy when responding to Watt's public lands agenda. Although environmental groups could gain public attention, their audiences were generally more limited in scope: their own group members, resource conferences, legislative hearings, and newspaper editorials. The grass-roots protest, often consisting of local environmentalists, often gained media coverage in areas targeted for public land development. Reviewing their response to the Reagan administration's public lands agenda reveals common rhetorical and political strategies.

Six months after Watt's confirmation as the secretary of the interior, many environmental groups demanded his resignation. By July, 1981, the National Wildlife Federation, the Sierra Club, the Audubon Society, the Friends of the Earth, the Wilderness Society, and the Izaak Walton League wanted Watt fired. Among environmentalists, the secretary symbolized the antithesis of the conservation consensus. The Izaak Walton League, a moderate conservation group that did not oppose Watt's nomination, had a typical reaction to the Reagan administration. After the president's first three months in office, the league charged that "it is clear that piece by piece, acre by acre, principle by principle, our natural resource legacy is being eaten away" and that the nation's numerous conservation achievements "either have been dismantled or are being considered for such." At the league's annual convention, delegates voted unanimously to ask Reagan to fire Watt because his actions "ignore the principles of thoughtful environmental stewardship advocated by the Izaak Walton League, threaten the conservation accomplishments of generations of Americans, and jeopardize America's position of world leadership in resource management, wilderness, and parks." Stressing the league's moderate membership, a spokesperson concluded, "The IWLA is mainstream America. It is grass roots, and the word from the grass roots is: GET JAMES WATT OUT!"[15]

To help force Watt's dismissal, the Wilderness Society published *The Watt Book* in 1981. Circulated to members of the media and Congress, it detailed forty-three actions or proposed actions by Watt "that run counter to federal law or clearly established public sentiment."[16] Other groups mobilized to fight administration plans as well. The Friends of the Earth initiated a monthly "Watt Watch" column in their official journal to give members the latest news on the secretary. The Audubon Society distributed a newsletter called "Audubon Action" updating legislative hearings and proposed changes in federal conservation policy. Audubon leaders started a Citizen Mobilization Campaign in twenty cities, and asked each of the 470 local chapters of the society to sponsor workshops to "discuss ways and means of dealing with the current threats."[17] Such efforts, combined with public support for wilderness preservation, helped many environmental groups reverse the trend of falling memberships that had plagued many organizations in the late 1970s.[18]

Representing between 6 and 10 million Americans, major environmental organizations have made themselves the key overseers of the nation's natural resources. Watt's challenge to unlock the public lands provoked considerable resistance from them. With the financial resources, the research capabilities, and the personnel to counter administration claims, the organized environmental movement waged a rhetorical war against Reagan and Watt's prodevelopment agenda.

Environmentalists denounced administration resource policies as extremist and insisted that wilderness preservation was approved by most Americans. Hoping to counter New Right charges that the movement consisted of wealthy elitists who did not care about the welfare of the working class, environmentalists pointed to the "radical" views espoused by some members of the administration. Noting that every aspect of the "Audubon cause has been repudiated" by the Reagan administration, Russell Peterson announced that the "plume hunters are back in business." Referring to the birth of the Audubon Society to protect birds from destruction for their feathers, Peterson linked the current debate with the group's tradition of opposing exploitation of nature. The modern plume hunters were dangerous, he claimed, because that mentality "is being institutionalized in the executive branch of our government."[19]

Other advocates joined Peterson in seeing an attempt to return to the values of the Gilded Age. At the Yale School of Forestry and Environmental Studies, Turnage described the Reagan administration as a horde of "New Barbarians," bureaucrats who would "return us to a barbarous age—a time of Robber Barons and Economic Royalists." Arguing that Reagan appointees held "almost life or death power over the future of our public lands and the quality of our environment," Turnage charged that such bureaucrats had imposed their will through the "force of their arrogance, devious strangulation of the budget and the systematic intimidation of dedicated career professionals" of the National Park Service, the Forest Service, and the Fish and Wildlife Service.[20] Employing a different historical parallel, Turnage claimed that Watt had "done more to try to dismantle the long-standing conservation laws and to repudiate sound public policy than any other person to ever hold his office." Watt was the first secretary since the Teapot Dome scandal to so "arrogantly violate the integrity of his office. Albert Fall stole from the present. James Watt would rob the future and bankrupt the nation's crown jewels."[21]

In contrast to members of the Reagan administration, environmentalists claimed that their goals upheld mainstream American values. Brock Evans of the Audubon Society noted that public opinion polls had consistently endorsed preservationist ideals for more than fifteen years. As a "people's movement," environmentalism represented a genuine cross-section of the nation: young and old, male and female, all levels of income, and liberal and conservative voters. Peterson refuted Watt's claim that only the "hired guns" (lobbyists) of environmental groups opposed the Reagan administration. The Audubon Society, he observed, made policy from the bottom up; leaders represented the views of members who determined policy within the local chapters. Evans cited the success of an Audubon fund-raising letter to show the public's disapproval of the administration's plans. Asking for contributions to oppose Secretary Watt in 1981, the group found eight times more members giving nine times as much money as in any other previous fund-raising attempt.[22]

Environmentalists portrayed Reagan and Watt as the pawns of big business and the New Right. Turnage claimed that Watt "sought the advice and counsel of every major industry which takes its profits from the land–oil, gas, mining, timber." The American Petroleum Institute gave Watt a wish list, for example, and within six months, the "administration had acted favorably on almost every item."[23] Peterson maintained that the "groundwork was laid for Interior initiatives . . . by the Heritage Foundation in their transition report . . . in which mineral exploration was recommended as a 'dominant use' of the public lands, including wilderness areas."[24] Speaking to members of the Montana Wildlife Federation, Gaylord Nelson of the Wilderness Society characterized members of the Reagan administration as ideologues who came to Washington with "their little prefabricated cubicles, and they intend to squeeze the world inside them whether it fits or not." Watt had a simple objective according to Nelson: "strip away or compromise most developmental guidelines, eliminate or compromise the use of environmental impact statements, significantly compromise the Surface Mining Act, junk wilderness review procedures and open maximum amount of land for maximum development immediately with very little concern for any competing values."[25]

Many environmentalists claimed that other values besides economic ones ought to be considered in determining public land use. Broadening the common definition of natural resources, Evans asserted that the phrase meant much more than wood, minerals, oil, and gas. Rather, natural resources should also include "wildlife and wildlife habitat, scenic vistas, pure streams, clean air, undisturbed natural places, wild places, national parks, places which maintain the amentities of life as well as the commodities of life." To reinforce his point, Evans also redefined access to the resources as the "right of those who treasure these resources always to be able to count upon their existence–in substantial measure–on our public lands."[26]

This argument, which is typical, illustrates the quality-of-life theme employed to counter economic appeals. While advocates of development cited the need for more strategic minerals, timber products, and oil exploration, environmentalists suggested that less quantifiable measures be used to assess value. Indeed, the *High Country News* warned readers that the conservation movement had been put on the defensive in attempting to "match the talk about 'cost effectiveness'" which had allowed Watt and other Reaganites to set the ground rules of the public lands debate. By returning to their original values, the editorial concluded, environmentalists could win public support for their cause: "The public can tell the difference between Watt's rhetorical effluent and a clear statement of values. The important thing is that bureaucrats, activists, and politicians lift themselves out of the muck and start saying what they really believe in."²⁷ Agreeing that multiple use provided a reasonable method of determining public land use, environmentalists argued that the lands would not be locked up when many uses such as mining and grazing could be accommodated with recreation and preservation.

The clash between economic needs and quality-of-life considerations were clearly articulated in Nelson's speech to a public lands conference in Oregon. Responding to calls for privatization, he claimed that the movement "is strangely devoid of any serious discussion or concern for that enormous heritage of nonmarket cultural, social and resource values on the public lands." Instead, administration advocates centered their visions on "short term, purely economic-and-commodity-specific issues" with maximum production, full utilization of resources, and profitability serving as the sole guidelines for public land management. Charging that the privatization movement had no "constituency within or outside the Congress," Nelson concluded that the anti-Watt resolutions passed by the Western Governors' Conference revealed little ground swell for land sales in the Rocky Mountain states.²⁸

Nelson also challenged the argument that private ownership of the land would lead to more environmentally sound resource decisions than federal management. On the contrary, the "cut-and-run forestry" practiced on private forests, especially in the East, had "left behind eroded watersheds, floods, polluted streams and years of slash burning fires fought at public expense." To further substantiate the irresponsible management of private owners, Nelson added that the "only major stands of old-growth timber left in the lower forty-eight states are found on public lands that were never privatized." Privatization's inherent flaw was the belief that money represented the only effective motivation for humans. Nelson listed other values that also explained human behavior: "We can leave our children and future generations a better country and, at the same time, live in a better country ourselves. That reality has proven down through history to be a powerful motivating force." Drawing attention to the pragmatic, everyday uses of the public lands, Nelson observed that advocates of privatization ignored nonmarket values, especially that of outdoor recreation. If the public lands were auctioned, the "private owners would not and could not accommodate the 288 million 12 hour recreation visits per year that now occur annually on National Forest and BLM lands."²⁹

Environmentalists devoted considerable attention to the claim that the public lands were somehow locked up to resource development. They feared that continued economic uncertainties, especially in energy production, would make the lock-up appeal attractive to many. Speaking to the Commonwealth Club of San Francisco, Nelson termed Watt's claim of a massive lock up of the public lands a gross exaggeration. Nelson's fear of the political consequences of the argument was clear: "If Mr. Watt and his supporters can convince the public there is a significant and unjustifiable 'lockup' of vital resources on public lands, they may very well achieve a substantial measure of success. . . . If he prevails, we will witness a significant and tragic degradation of a portion of America's magnificent and irreplaceable heritage." Calling Watt's statistics misleading, he suggested that even in the best light, the secretary's arguments "represent just about one-half of a half truth, or less." Nelson cited numerous examples of Watt's faulty reasoning to disprove the lock-up contention.³⁰

Influential private citizens used their standing in the community to attack the Reagan administration's concerted effort to develop the public lands. Former secretaries of the interior Stewart Udall and Cecil Andrus found Watt's criticism of previous administrations too much to take silently. Writers Abbey and Stegner joined with photographer Ansel Adams in denouncing administration plans for resource development. In so doing, they reiterated the values of preserving the wilderness for a larger audience than environmentalists and helped take the conservation message beyond those already sympathetic to the cause. Because their persuasiveness relied to a great degree upon their public reputations and not their technical expertise, the radical amateurs attacked the philosophy of wilderness development, not simply its specific policies. In this manner, the radical amateurs defended the intangible values of wilderness as well as its more obvious values such as hunting, fishing, grazing, and logging. They expanded the conservation debate to the general public and effectively countered arguments advanced by members of the administration and conservative research foundations. As a result, the topic of wilderness preservation versus development found audiences in newspapers, on television and radio programs, and at public events.

In 1981, Adams traveled to the nation's capital to criticize the public land policy of the Reagan administration. After meeting with

Senators Howard Baker and Alan Cranston, he told reporters that he had never seen a secretary of the interior "so arrogant and intractable toward the land and natural beauty" as Watt. In an effort to prevent further development of the public lands, Adams helped devise a letter-writing campaign to Congress, personally called upon congressional leaders, and granted interviews to such diverse publications as *Playboy, People,* and *Saturday Review.* Reflecting a common concern among environmentalists, he told one interviewer that Reagan and "his anti-environmentalists don't have any interest in the future. To them it's a matter of making the biggest profit in their generation." Adams asserted that he had been forced to speak out: "I'm using whatever influence I have. I write articles and give interviews and let my photographs be used. . . . I write letters everyday, and try to get other people to write . . . to be a living petition."[31]

Stegner was also angry enough to participate actively in the conservation debate. Asked if he enjoyed speaking and writing in favor of wilderness preservation, he responded, "Not really, no. But I feel obligated, since I think I know something about it, to say how I think it is, because so often people speaking for the other side are misleading. . . . If you know anything at all, it's your obligation to try to keep the record straight." Downplaying his status as an environmental advocate, Stegner concluded that he could publish some essays and make some speeches: "I can toss my pebbles onto what I wish were an avalanche of protest." Writing essays for the *Washington Post* and *Living Wilderness* and making speeches in Utah, California, and Wyoming, Stegner noted, "Any time I get a chance to open my mouth, I air that topic [conservation]." Arguing that it was proper for government to own and manage the public lands, he advised Americans to keep the bureaucrats "under citizen surveillance" because many agencies "have been known to endanger the very things they ought to protect." Americans must "renounce short-term profit, and practice working for the renewable health of our earth." Sounding like a latter-day Leopold, he maintained that although the wilderness may serve as a playground, a schoolroom, and a laboratory, above all else the wilderness serves as a shrine in which "we can learn to know both the natural world and ourselves, and be at least half reconciled to what we see."[32]

Speaking in favor of the national park system, Stegner argued that the parks "are a cure for cynicism, an exhilarating rest from the competitive avarice we call the American Way." "Absolutely American, absolutely democratic," the parks "reflect us at our best rather than our worst," he asserted. "Without them, millions of American lives, including mine, would have been poorer." Watt's effort to give park concessionaires greater control in park management disturbed Stegner. By viewing parks as tourist resorts and not sanctuaries, Watt appeared to endorse public use of the wilderness only "if it is profitable to someone." The secretary's refusal to expand the national park system led Stegner to conclude that the parks are "truly an occupied country, and their worst enemy is the administration of the department created to be their protector."[33]

Another radical amateur, Edward Abbey, has achieved national recognition as both a novelist and a self-identified environmental journalist. Besides fiction, he has written essays for such diverse publications as *Harper's, Playboy, Reader's Digest, Rolling Stone,* and the *New York Times Magazine,* as well as many conservation journals such as *Audubon* and *Outside.* Abbey has avoided identification with environmental groups.

He sprinkles his public discourse with hyperbole and sarcasm. Speaking to a rally in Wyoming, he proclaimed: "Emotionalism is bad. When people get angry, they sometimes do crazy things like standing up for their rights." Urging greater grass-roots activism, he admonished the audience to "take part, be a citizen, don't be like a tick on a dog, ornamental but useless. Earth First! Grizzly bears, second. People, third. J. Paul Getty, last."[34] Speaking to a national audience through his essays, Abbey served the conservation campaign by refuting New Right charges that environmentalism was designed to serve an elitist, upper-class constituency. Calling a journey into the wilderness "the freest, cheapest, most non-privileged of pleasures," he observed that a person needs only two legs and a $17.95 pair of army surplus boots to enjoy the wild places of the United States. "Any poor slob with enough cash in his jeans to buy a ghetto blaster," he continued, "can buy instead a backpack, a sleeping bag and a bus ticket to Yellowstone."[35]

Like Leopold and Stegner, Abbey characterized the wilderness as an essential ingredient in American democracy. Without wilderness, he feared, the United States would become as congested and disheartening as Europe. "Open space," argued Abbey, "was the fundamental heritage of America; the freedom of wilderness may well be the central purpose of our national adventure." He defended the expansion of wilderness and praised federal restrictions placed upon the "Jeeps,

Blazers, Broncos, and Winnebagoes" that infiltrated the pristine forests and mountains. With America's public lands lying "under the massive assault of industrial armies of Government and Greed," Abbey begged his readers for more brave deeds and fewer words.[36] What made Abbey particularly potent as an advocate was his ability to articulate familiar conservation concepts, such as the land ethic, to the general public. Employing both fiction and essays to further the cause of wilderness preservation, Abbey found a larger and more culturally diverse audience than most other advocates.

Abbey's most popular novel, *The Monkey Wrench Gang*, was published in 1975 and generated a great deal of controversy among environmentalists. The novel's characters rejected political decision making and instead waged war against the engines of progress, justifying their "ecotage" as the final stage in preserving the wilderness.[37] In the late 1970s, a radical environmental group called Earth First! was founded and based much of its philosophy on Abbey's novel. Members of Earth First! advocated "civil disobedience to protect the environment, but not the destruction of property" according to a founding member, Howie Wolke.[38] Although Abbey was not a formal member of the group and refused to endorse sabotage, he publicly identified with Earth First!, speaking to several rallies sponsored in the West to oppose the Reagan administration. Speaking to members at the Glen Canyon Dam, a site destroyed by Abbey's characters in the novel, the author announced: "Oppose the destruction of our homeland by those alien forces from Houston, Tokyo, Manhattan, D.C. and the Pentagon. And if opposition is not enough, we must resist. And if resistance is not enough, then subvert, delay, until the empire begins to fall."[39] Although most major environmental groups repudiated Earth First! tactics, the small group brought a great deal of attention to environmental issues in general and to Abbey's discourse more specifically. Most important, Abbey succeeded in forcing environmentalists to consider how far they might go in protecting the wilderness from further development.

Abbey, Adams, and Stegner represented the activist private citizen in the conservation debate. The radical amateurs provided an articulate, eloquent, and passionate response to calls for greater resource development. Undaunted by the empiricism rampant in the debate, such as economic growth projections, strategic mineral assessments, and board feet of timber needed for export, these advocates persuaded their particular audiences by their passion. In public forums the radical amateurs helped legitimize the discontent of the environmental community. If a Pulitzer Prize–winning novelist such as Stegner could ignore his writing or a world-renowned photographer such as Adams could put aside his art for the cause of wilderness, that act in itself *symbolically* affirmed the values of preserving the public lands. Although Abbey, Adams, and Stegner are not household personalities, they have served as opinion leaders in the true sense of the phrase. They have addressed an educated and powerful segment of American society and in so doing have taken the environmental message to the avenues of political power in the United States.

Two other private citizens gained considerable public attention in the public lands debate, Stewart Udall and Cecil Andrus. Considered environmentally sensitive secretaries of the interior, both men had played central roles in the development of the conservation consensus. Although they were associated in some measure with environmental groups after leaving office, both men spoke as private citizens, personally angered by Watt's comments and policies. Believing that Watt and Reagan had misled the public, Andrus and Udall spoke out to provide their account of conservation's true history. Both men concentrated on the bipartisan development of the consensus in direct contrast with the politicization of the Reagan administration. While faulting Watt for various factual misstatements, Andrus and Udall concentrated on the long-term consequences of Reagan's public lands policy if successfully implemented. The institutionalization of a pro-development ethic in federal land management appeared far more dangerous than any specific damage Watt could accomplish during his tenure.

After leaving office in 1981, Andrus refused to comment publicly upon Watt's performance. He imposed a six-month silence on himself to give Watt an opportunity to establish himself. Although he eventually did criticize some administration actions in 1981, Andrus left the daily conservation debate for a private business in Idaho. Nearly two years later, he broke his silence to comment specifically on Watt's policies. Andrus expressed some dissatisfaction with the Reagan administration in a 1981 interview with the *High Country News*. He rejected the argument that oil and mineral exploration must be allowed in wilderness areas if feasible. "Now the law *permitted* it [drilling] but it did not *mandate* it, and it has been the view of all administrations—from 1964 on through 1980, Republican and Democrat alike, elephants and donkeys, that you just don't do it."[40]

Andrus found the ideal audience to make his first major statement on Watt in a meeting of the American Society of Newspaper Editors in May, 1983. Although Andrus and Watt were scheduled to appear back to back on the convention program, Watt altered the speaking schedule. Presenting his address several hours earlier than planned, Watt left Denver before Andrus arrived, thereby eliminating the face-to-face confrontation many observers had anticipated. Reporting that he found a tape recording of Watt's speech, Andrus noted that he changed his prepared remarks and "if anybody thinks it's unfair, why I'm not the one who changed the schedule."

Acknowledging his many months of silence, Andrus claimed, "I've turned the other cheek until frankly I'm out of checks." Among interior secretaries, he continued, "it was kind of an unwritten, gentlemen's agreement" that when one assumed office, "we didn't castigate the ones that came behind us." To set the record straight, he reviewed his policies during the Carter administration and systematically criticized Watt's plan to lease coal reserves in Wyoming and Montana, to increase offshore oil leasing, and to radically alter the direction of national park management. Watt's frequent charge that the parks were dumping raw sewage into lakes and streams when he assumed office particularly outraged Andrus. To refute the claim, he cited congressional testimony by the superintendent of the National Park System that no instances of the dumping could be found. Attacking the Reagan administration's antiecological policies, Andrus charged that both Reagan and Watt believed, "if you can't dig it up or cut it down, it has no value at all."

Andrus was concerned by the growing partisanship surrounding environmental policy. Recalling that America's public lands policy had never been dictated by "donkeys and elephants," he argued that Watt had shattered decades of bipartisan cooperation in setting policy. The "thing that really bothers me," reported Andrus, was that Watt did not accept the "entrusted role of stewardship" that ensures a "good legacy for those that follow." To understand the competing perspectives that humans have regarding the public resources, Andrus suggested that answering a single question could reveal our attitudes toward nature: "Did we inherit this land from our forefathers or did we borrow it from our children?"[41] As a confirmed ecologist, Andrus believed that Americans must look to the future, not to the past, in determining public land use.

Stewart Udall also spoke out against the Reagan administration.

Considered by many an elder statesman in the environmental movement, Udall had implemented many acts of the conservation consensus as the secretary of the interior from 1961 to 1969. His popular history of the public lands in America, *The Quiet Crisis,* had made him
one of the best known conservationists of the 1960s. In that book,
he called for a land ethic to guide future policy decisions. Speaking
to the Institute of the American West, he discussed the historical
foundations of conservation, crediting Leopold with beginning the
wilderness concept among Forest Service leaders in the 1920s. Noting
that there exists a "confusion about our history," Udall presented his
account of the nation's public lands. Emphasizing the need to understand one's historical roots, he pointed out that much of the conservation legislation of the 1960s would never pass in the 1980s. Because
energy seemed abundant in the 1960s, conservationists seized an ideal
opportunity to institutionalize the goal of wilderness preservation.
Outlining the major topics he intended to cover in the speech, Udall
suggested that as an individual, Watt was not all that important, but
that the anticonservation attitude manifested by the New Right, Ronald Reagan, and others could have profound implications for future
generations.[42]

Insisting that conservation must be recognized as an American institution, Udall observed that Americans were the pioneers and cre-
ators of conservation's seminal ideas and that the concept of a national
park was "an American idea. It's imitated all over the world." Ironically, even historians appeared to forget conservation's historical impact. "I remember chiding Arthur Schlesinger, Jr.," recalled Udall, that
the "New Deal program was a resource program, a conservation program." Building dams, replanting forests, and developing soil erosion
programs helped heal America during the Great Depression. In the
1930s, "we in effect went back to the land to start over again." Americans must always remember, warned Udall, that conservation is "deeply
embedded in our history."[43]

Udall also was disturbed by the explicit partisanship of the Reagan
administration. America's public lands policy had always been hammered out through discussion and argument at the local, state, and
federal levels. "That's why it's so appalling for me," he stressed, to witness the administration's "latest and newest sneaky policy" to sell the
public lands. "I never expected in my lifetime" he concluded, "to see
a Secretary of the Interior propose a land sales program." Recalling
the bipartisan heritage of the conservation consensus, Udall pointed

to Richard Nixon and Gerald Ford's continuation of the Kennedy and Johnson agenda. The worst feature of Watt's tenure, claimed Udall, was "the breaking of the national bipartisan consensus that developed over environment and ecology." Even with the great assault upon conservation, Udall found the consensus to be holding its own. Wyoming's congressional delegation, for example, consisting of three conservative Republicans, "got together and passed a Wyoming wilderness bill and we heard no peep from Mr. Watt." Recalling the central belief of the land ethic, that all creatures exist in a complex and interdependent world, Udall noted that most Americans believe that "environmental concern is crucial to life itself," because humans are capable of "poisoning and destroying life and the fabric of life." End ing on a note of optimism, he predicted that with eternal vigilance, conservationists could prevent the intrusive and harmful development that threatened the West.[44]

Observing the public lands debate at the state and local levels confirms that the conservation consensus retained broad public support during Watt's term as interior secretary. Examining the debate in two different states, Utah and Montana, indicates that the rhetorical characteristics of national environmentalism also permeated the state and local debates. The administration's failure to engage any significant western interest in public land development seemed to diminish congressional efforts as well. As Rocky Mountain residents resisted calls for privatization or leasing the wilderness areas, western politicians had little incentive to endorse such politically volatile policies. Without the support of congressional leaders such as Barry Goldwater, James McClure, Paul Laxalt, Alan Simpson, or Jake Garn, the advocates of development lacked a national legislative base. Surprisingly, westerners rejected a central assumption of privatization—that residents of the various states wanted to own the public lands in their area. Indeed, the primary goal of the conservation consensus, permanent federal ownership of the lands combined with multiple use management, seemed firmly rooted among westerners.

Although Utah may be one of the most conservative states in the nation, residents respect the intangible values of wilderness as well as the economic values. As a result, Utahns presented a political anomaly: conservative environmentalists. Part of this sentiment certainly must stem from the state's valuable tourist industry.[45] Moreover, Utah is primarily an urban state, and many Utahns perceive wilderness in terms of recreation and not employment opportunities. With almost

80 percent of the state's population residing in urban locations along the Wasatch Front, few residents were directly tied to the public lands for their livelihood.

During the public lands debate, Utahns fought to define which tracts within the state should be federally designated wilderness areas with limited and stringent safeguards placed on resource development. Differences of opinion among the various interest groups was striking. While the State Wilderness Commission recommended 480,000 acres for possible wilderness status, environmental groups asked for more than 1.6 million acres. A leading newspaper editorialized that the state ought to "err on the side of land" in selecting study areas. "It's easier to take land out of wilderness," the editorial noted, "than put it in once development has begun." If such a proposal sounded ambitious, readers were asked to keep in mind that many states with a fraction of Utah's public lands had already designated much larger tracts of land as wilderness. Another editorial pointed out that wilderness yielded many values besides backpacking, watersheds, animal habitat, cattle grazing, recreation, and tourism. Moreover, the editorial dismissed charges that wilderness status locks up the land, observing that both mining and grazing were allowed under certain conditions.[46]

A writer for the *Deseret News* also stressed the less tangible benefits of wilderness. Calling the commission's recommendation of 480,000 acres "infuriatingly shortsighted," Joseph Bauman claimed that few "nature lovers will support the hacking up of their favorite hiking, camping, hunting, and photography areas of southern Utah." He appealed for public comments to the commission, demanding that more land be included in the review process. An increasingly urbanized Utah, he concluded, needed the multiple benefits offered by wilderness areas.[47]

Significantly, the urban-rural division in Utah affected how residents viewed the purpose and use of public land. In a statewide public opinion poll, the *Deseret News* found a "heavy plurality of Utahns" favored wilderness designation for over 2.6 million acres of federal land within the state. The paper concluded that environmentalists had correctly claimed that "wilderness has much support in the populous counties." The poll also found that urban residents were more likely to favor wilderness than rural residents, so the heavy prowilderness majority was partly a reflection of the state's declining rural population. The poll also revealed that non-Mormons were more likely to favor wilderness designation than Mormons. Of all those affiliated with a religious organization, Mormons were the least likely to endorse wilderness preservation.[48]

Throughout 1983 the wilderness debate raged in Utah with environmentalists mobilizing to testify at congressional hearings held in various parts of the state. In several cases, the state's congressional delegation encountered heated sentiment during the public hearings. A newspaper debate between the director of the Utah BLM, Roland Robison, and the director of the Utah Wilderness Association, Richard Carter, demonstrated the rhetorical strategies of the environmental movement. As an official of the Reagan administration, Robison argued that wilderness must be seen in the eye of the beholder, one person's wilderness being "another's ore deposit, or still another's favorite off-road vehicle recreation area." In contrast, Carter advised readers that public land development must be undertaken with great caution. Echoing Leopold, he noted that once valuable watershed and wildlife habitat had vanished it could never be replaced. He refuted the lock-up argument, observing that wilderness status created a savings account that would remain "undisturbed for future generations, if ever needed." In the tradition of Leopold, Stegner, and Abbey, Carter stressed the inherent values of a frontier experience that could not be measured in economic terms: "Wilderness represents the last stand of humanness. We measure ourselves against wilderness and as long as it exists, we will not be be a nation in despair and abandoned to mediocrity."[49]

In a guest editorial that appeared during congressional hearings, Carter expanded several arguments. In terms of total wilderness, he judged Utah to be sorely out of step with other western states. While Idaho had 4 million acres of wilderness and Montana 3 million, Utah's 29,000 acres was even smaller than areas in North Carolina, South Carolina, or even New Hampshire. In addition, Carter claimed that the lock-up argument did not follow logically because oil, gas, and minerals were virtually nonexistent in potential wilderness areas. Even so, he claimed that wilderness designation offered "classic multiple use" of the lands: hunting, hiking, horseback riding, trail maintenance, and outfitting were all allowed in wilderness areas.[50]

During congressional hearings within the state, environmentalists pressured Utah legislators to increase the number of acres designated for study as potential wilderness. Over two hundred people attended a hearing in Salt Lake City with the state's entire delegation present. According to published reports, citizens who spoke at the hearing were three to one in favor of increasing the wilderness acreage, even though many who wanted to testify were unable to because of time constraints. One observer reported that environmentalist comments "ranged from polite disagreement to a caustic denunciation of the delegation." The fervor of some environmentalists unnerved the hearing chairman, Sen. Jake Garn. He argued with some speakers who testified, tried to restrain audience applause when prowilderness statements were given, and when one person laughed, he demanded to know what was funny. To minimize the impact of environmental speakers, Garn called upon prodevelopment advocates out of turn. As a result, about forty-five of the scheduled seventy-five speakers were unable to testify. Frustrated by the affair, Garn lectured the audience not to be sure they were "so damn right" regarding the amount of wilderness needed. The senator's behavior angered Cecil Garland, a rancher from Juab County who jumped up and held out his "rough, sunburned hands, saying he was a hard-working rancher who supported wilderness, and now look at all these soft-handed folks who are against it."[51] Besides Garland, teachers, ranchers, senior citizens, and members of the Utah Association of Neighborhoods joined with environmentalists in supporting greater amounts of wilderness for Utah.

In all, four legislative hearings were held in the state during the summer of 1983. The long process of political give and take ended with a compromise victory for environmentalists. The state wilderness commission recommended approximately 700,000 acres for wilderness study, a significant increase from the original amount. More important, environmentalists were able to gain wilderness classification for several valuable tracts not included in the original study. Apparently the pressure environmentalists placed on legislators succeeded in changing some minds. Utah's representative of the National Parks and Conservation Assocation called the final recommendation a positive step, which showed a "positive response to the overwhelming endorsement for wilderness recommendations that we saw at the public hearings in August."[52]

In Montana, a state with large tracts of federally designated wilderness, the Reagan administration encountered great local opposition to efforts to develop such areas. Environmentalists initially fought administration plans to lease the Bob Marshall Wilderness Area for oil and gas exploration. Later, when Secretary Watt announced specific tracts of public land slated for privatization, many Montanan's reacted angrily. In both cases, environmentalists employed a systematic campaign of public communication to help generate citizen support for preserving the wilderness. Although some groups, such as the Montana Cattlemen, generally favored administration policy, most grassroots groups rejected Watt's attempt to alter the fundamental elements of the conservation consensus.

The Wilderness Act of 1964 created a system of wilderness areas that protected large sections of public lands from any significant human intrusion. The act granted mineral companies twenty years to make claims upon the public lands, and by 1984, those tracts without claims would be closed to any future exploration. The Interior Department, however, had issued only a handful of oil and gas leases through 1980. Faced with the approaching deadline, Watt planned to substantially increase leasing in order to establish sites for future mineral exploration. One of the primary areas targeted for leasing, the Bob Marshall Wilderness Area in central Montana, became the focus of a national issue during Watt's first year in office.

Almost 1 million acres in size, the Bob Marshall is the second largest wilderness area in the continental United States. When the government announced plans for oil and gas leasing in the area in 1980, several hundred protesters demonstrated in Missoula. Environmentalists issued press releases, sent letters to newspapers, and consolidated various local conservation organizations to help prevent any mineral exploration in the area. Emphasizing the importance of the land ethic, they argued that the Bob Marshall was necessary to help increase the nation's fragile grizzly bear population, to serve as a key area in reintroducing the Rocky Mountain wolf, and to provide wildlife habitat for elk, deer, mountain goats, and numerous other forms of wildlife. Additionally, the Bob Marshall served as home to significant varieties of wild plant life, some found only in Montana. Environmentalists also maintained that the area provided important uses for humans which would suffer under extensive mineral development. Over 237,000 visits occur annually in the Bob Marshall, with 25 to 30 percent from hunters in the fall of the year.[53]

Roland Cheek, an outfitter from Columbia Falls, Montana, represented a typical opponent of wilderness development. Calling himself a "fiscal conservative with strong environmental tendencies," he published a semiannual newsletter to stimulate public support for preserving the Bob Marshall. Because local residents "don't have the political muscle" to save the area by themselves, Cheek attempted to engage more widespread support with a book of photographs and de-

scriptions of the local mountain ranges, rivers, trails, and valleys. Supporters of the Bob Marshall "have got to interest people in the country, or they're going to lose," he insisted. Opposed to any oil and gas
exploration in the wilderness area, Cheek described himself as "maybe
. . . a Teddy Roosevelt Republican." Writing in 1982, he suggested
that the best thing for the Bob Marshall "would be for the Republicans to take a beating next election for environmental purposes."
Hoping that his book might help save the wilderness from development, Cheek concluded, "I like the Bob Marshall the way it is." Significantly, Cheek's wish that Republicans might suffer at the ballot
box in 1982 came true. Representative Tony Coehlo of California concluded that environmentalists "organized at the grass roots, where there
has been a vacuum recently. The environmentalists picked up on that,
and it turned out very effective." In fact, environmentalists were so
effective in the 1982 general elections that 80 percent of the candidates
backed by the Sierra Club were elected, and of the sixty-six candidates
endorsed by the League of Conservation Voters, forty-seven won.[54]

Environmentalists used the Bob Marshall controversy to prevent
Watt from increasing the number of leases in the nation's numerous
wilderness areas. With the secretary's immense executive power, he
could offer such leases without congressional authorization. According to Stewart Udall, Watt could not repeal any laws but "the secretary is free to make policy on such things as park acquisition or oil
drilling in wilderness."[55] In May, 1981, the House Interior Committee
prohibited any leasing in the Bob Marshall area. Using an obscure
legal provision giving the Congress the right to withdraw lands under
emergency conditions, the House stopped any leasing of the Bob
Marshall. Although Watt called the action unconstitutional, he agreed
to desist. However, his former employer, the Mountain States Legal
Foundation, challenged the committee's action in court. Federal Judge
W. J. Jameson ruled that the congressional action was constitutional,
but that the committee could not stipulate how long the wilderness
must be withdrawn from leasing. When Congress moved to prohibit
leasing in all wilderness areas, Watt accepted the moratorium. Representative Pat Williams of Montana, who led the fight in Congress,
believed that Watt "was responding to what was obvious public demand: that he get his hands off of these fragile and beautiful places."
Noting the national significance of the Bob Marshall decision, Williams concluded, "Montana led the way in protecting the nation's remaining wild places."[56]

Nowhere in the country did opposition to privatization develop more strongly than in Montana. Grass-roots activism helped reinforce the growing distrust of sales throughout the western region. As the Interior Department and the Forest Service announced specific tracts of land slated for auction, local citizens recognized the impact of privatization. Calls to increase local control of the public land and enhance private property gained few adherents among westerners raised with federal lands surrounding their hometowns, farms, and ranches.

Although the administration's asset management program, better known as privatization, was announced in February, 1982, it took over a year for the specific sites to be selected. When tracts were made public, an immediate outcry resulted. The decision to study 872,000 acres in Montana for possible privatization angered Montana's Sen. John Melcher, who charged that the Reagan administration had "bitten off a wad they will never chew." In fanciful frontier imagery, Melcher promised that a "full bore of both barrels of Montanans who use national forest [will] have their chance to fire their shots." The announcement also drew an angry response from environmentalists. "They're selling off the birthright of every American citizen for a quick buck," said Bill Cunningham of the Montana Wilderness Association. "We're going to fight 'em every step of the way."[57]

Not only did environmentalists oppose the land sales, but both houses of the Montana legislature passed resolutions condemning privatization. Representative Williams claimed that the people of the West would not tolerate such sales: "They would march on the Capitol if it became clear that such sales were to go ahead."[58] In a lengthy anti-privatization editorial, the *Great Falls Tribune* used photographs of signs on fenceposts to illustrate the potential impact of privatization in Montana. The signs carried numerous warnings to anyone who crossed the fence: "Everyone stay out"; "No hunting, survivors will be prosecuted"; and "Private Property, No Trespassing, Violators Assume All Risks." The editorial charged that the Reagan administration tried to sell privatization with inflammatory comments about those people who regularly used the public lands. "That doesn't sit well in Montana," the editorial responded, "where national forests and Bureau of Land Management acreage are used by a wide variety of people—from ranchers leasing land for grazing to recreationists. The simple fact around here is that the public lands are appreciated and used by the public."[59]

The targeted sale of one popular tract, the seventy-five-mile-long

Crazy Mountain range in central Montana, brought vocal opposition
from local residents who feared that the land might be sold to out-
siders or people with no concern for the land. The notion of using
the profits of privatization to retire the national debt seemed simplistic to many Montanans. Tom McGuane, who owns a ranch near the
mountains, argued, "It's crazy to sell the Crazies just to support the
Treasury for 20 to 30 minutes." Moreover, area residents feared the dire
economic consequences that privatization might bring. Bonnie Swan-
dal, a local rancher, stressed that most ranchers could not afford to
buy the lands if auctioned to the highest bidder. The mayor of Liv-
ingston, Montana, agreed, noting that out-of-state interests would
swallow up the land: "The natives can't afford it. A lot of the land
has been fenced off. When I was a boy you could fish anywhere. People don't let you on the river anymore. I'm against it [privatization]."
Other residents claimed that the sales might threaten family well-being
in the immediate area. Dennis Brandon, a trapper, pointed out that
the Crazy Mountains kept his family fed through the winter months:
"In this country, a lot of folks don't work in winter so you got to lay
in meat," meaning deer, elk, and moose. Although federally owned
and managed, the Crazies provided wide use for local residents, including recreation and hunting, as well as logging, firewood cutting,
and cattle grazing.[60]

Roger Johnson, a Forest Service official in Missoula, reported that
about 80 to 85 percent of the people he talked with were opposed to
privatization. Many Montanans remained in the state because of the
availability of the public lands. "If the lands are lost," he concluded,
"it will definitely affect their lifestyle." Ranchers in western Montana
expressed their disapproval of the potential sales as well. John Ham
said that he could not afford to graze his cattle on private land at prevailing rates and Pearl D'Ewart argued that privatization would bankrupt many ranchers already in a tight financial bind. Others expressed
a common feeling that large tracts of wilderness represented an inherent part of the American West. D'Ewart, who started her cattle ranch
in 1937, claimed that the public lands were essential: "I think that's
part of what makes our West what the West is." Scott Damby, who
circulated antiprivatization petitions near the Crazy Mountains, echoed
a similar feeling: "It's our land. It's not some politician in Washington's land to sell. It's yours and mine to use."[61] Ironically, the same
appeal that guided the Sagebrush Rebellion – the claim that the rights

of westerners ought to be respected by the federal government–was expressed by antiprivatization advocates.

When the specific tracts to be privatized were identified, local environmentalists intensified their opposition. Chuck Griffith of the National Wildlife Federation's regional office argued that privatization invited disaster. Some areas listed for sale included "critical wintering ranges for deer, and year round ranges for antelope." He warned that privatization of grazing lands in eastern Montana might lead to another Dust Bowl. Once the lands were developed for agriculture, erosion would threaten the state once again. Griffith claimed that, in any event, the sale of public lands would pay "just one-half of 1 percent of the interest on the national debt for one year."[62] He also encouraged sportsmen to oppose the sale because it could destroy the habitat for thousands of elk, deer, and hundreds of bighorn sheep. Claiming that the government should never use a solely economic justification as a rationale for land sales, Griffith suggested that other values ought to be considered when making such consequential decisions. To demonstrate such ecological values, he presented a tract-by-tract list of the benefits of the areas proposed for privatization. For example, one tract was used by 130 bighorn sheep; another tract, which would be subdivided if sold provided winter cover for 200 elk; and another, adjacent to a winter game range, gave 1,700 elk winter habitat.[63]

Showing environmentalist commitment to the land ethic, Dan Heinz, a retired range management specialist with the Forest Service, argued that bureaucrats often ignored "high public values" in assessing public land use. Although extremely isolated tracts of land seemed like logical parcels to sell, Heinz noted that closer examination revealed important ecological values that deserved protection. For example, an isolated tract in southwestern Montana listed for privatization, also served as home for geese, trumpeter swans, and other waterfowl. The long-range impact of such sales disturbed Heinz. In most cases, he charged, privatization would lead to one result: subdivision of the lands for resale to numerous buyers. According to the Montana Wildlife Federation, subdivisions "stress private recreational opportunities and second homes damage public values of any area, almost without exception."[64]

Adverse public response to the sales program forced administration officials to alter their goals. Mike Penfold, director of the BLM's Mon-

tana office, admitted that public reaction indicated "there is not a mood
in the state for a major land sale, although many favor land exchanges."
Because such exchanges allowed the federal government to increase
wilderness areas by adding nearby parcels of private land, some observers endorsed such trades. Penfold sounded more like an environmentalist than a member of the Reagan administration in evaluating the
asset management program. Through the use of exchanges, he noted,
the direction "we intend to take it toward [is] favoring wildlife and
recreation values and [improving] river access."[65] Many environmentalists agreed with employing land exchanges in place of outright privatization. Griffith argued that BLM plans for nine central counties
in the state emphasized producing saleable commodities at the expense
of outdoors enthusiasts and wildlife. A better alternative, he suggested,
would be exchanges, especially those tracts with low public values for
land with higher public values.[66]

Calling the federal land sales program a failure, the *Bozeman Daily
Chronicle* editorialized that privatization "is going over as well as second-
home lots on Mount St. Helens." Projecting the first-year impact of
privatization, the Montana BLM office had predicted that it would
sell between 13,00 and 17,000 acres of public land in 1983. By October,
only 1,693 acres had been sold. Acknowledging a soft real-estate market, the editorial claimed that the principal reason for the failure of
privatization was the public and political opposition. The *Chronicle*
concluded, "Most Montanans don't want to see huge chunks of public land sold off, fearing that large, out-of-state corporations would
outbid them for the land and then close it off to public use for hunting, firewood cutting and other activities."[67]

Comfortable with millions of acres of land under federal control,
Montanans appeared representative of most westerners. Federal ownership and management of the public lands seemed practical, fair, and
proper to those who lived near the wilderness. From their vantage,
all Americans have rights on the public lands, rights that would be
severely diminished through wide-scale development or privatization. Pressure from western interests succeeded in stopping privatization. When Secretary Watt withdrew Interior's participation in the
administration's overall privatization plan in August, 1983, environmentalists achieved a major victory in preserving America's conservation consensus.[68]

Environmentalists succeeded in preventing any lasting ground swell
of public support for the administration's public land reform. Mobi-

lizing thousands of advocates nationwide, they persuaded many citizens that ecological values demanded continued federal protection. Although Watt changed the direction of Interior policy and brought a human-centered view of nature back to the conservation debate, environmentalists prevented or restricted many of the specific policy changes attempted by the Reagan administration. Watt may have changed attitudes at the Interior Department, but his specific policies needed greater support from the public and the Congress.

Moreover, environmentalists emerged from the public lands debate with a new sense of enthusiasm and direction. "The environmental movement is enjoying an unanticipated resurgence," reported the *Wall Street Journal*, "and it can thank President Reagan." Indeed, the movement hired economists, engineers, biologists, and other professionals in order to enhance its ability to engage in political decision making. The president of Shell Oil, John Bookout told the newspaper that the environmental movement was "more determined . . . more active and better funded" than at any time he could recall, including the 1960s and 1970s.[69] Moreover, many groups acknowledged the need to redesign their management style in order to compete effectively in the public lands debate. The *Los Angeles Times* reported a major transformation of leadership in the environmental movement in the post-Watt era. The Sierra Club, for example, announced a search for a professional leader who was "very strong in finance and budgets, who has a track record in management, who can offer entrepreneurial leadership, who is alert to changes in the marketplace." The break in the tradition of leadership from within the organization resulted from the rapid growth and the great demands placed upon the various environmental groups. "In a way, environmental leaders have become victims of their own success," reported Michael McCloskey of the Sierra Club. "We have grown so rapidly that executives have become preoccupied with management and finance."[70]

After James Watt's resignation from the Interior Department in October, 1983, the public lands debate left the nation's front pages. Although the departure of Watt soothed many critics, two other factors put natural resource issues on hold. First, Watt's successor, Judge William P. Clark, attempted to reconcile environmentalists and changed the tone at Interior when dealing with critics. Second, the political system went into its election-year hibernation, with members of the administration backing away from controversial policies as the 1984 presidential campaign neared.

Clark worked to reduce tension between the Interior Department and the environmental community and drew attention to the bipartisan tradition of the nation's conservation consensus. Speaking to the National Wildlife Federation less than two months after Watt's departure from office, Clark promised that environmentalists would have both information and access when dealing with the department. In the tradition of bipartisanship endorsed by earlier Interior Secretaries Udall and Andrus, Clark asked the audience, "Should not partisanship likewise stop at the forest's edge, the desert's edge and the river's edge?"[71] By the end of January, 1984, Clark had made several major changes in policy. According to one national publication, Clark had agreed to consult with environmentalists and state governments on issues such as offshore oil drilling, to buy more land for the national park system, and to carefully review Watt's plan to increase coal mining on the public lands.[72]

Although the administration proposed no significant changes in public land policy as the presidential campaign neared, the president defended his record and reaffirmed his belief that a human-centered view of the natural resources should prevail. Pledging to preserve endangered species and to protect wilderness areas, Reagan also proclaimed that "quality of life means more than protection and preservation." Quality of life also meant, concluded the president, "a good job, accommodation for a growing population, and the continued economic and technological development essential to our standard of living."[73] Environmental groups, however, saw little hope for positive change and continued to oppose the administration's overall environmental policy throughout 1984.[74]

From a rhetorical perspective, environmentalists kept the administration on the defensive during most of Watt's tenure. They exploited his numerous gaffes as clear manifestations of his true personality and linked his agenda with the extreme elements of the New Right. More important, environmentalists at all levels returned to their intellectual heritage in the public lands debate. Unlike other political groups, they found no reason to reassess the land ethic and the ecological conscience that had transformed utilitarian conservation into the contemporary environmental movement in earlier decades. Confidence in their crusade certainly carried over to the movement's campaign of public communication. Throughout their battle with the Reagan administration, environmentalists continued to characterize their movement as one of public interest rather than special interest. As a public interest, explained Brock Evans, there "is no economic gain for us in the policies and programs we advocate for the public lands. Creation of new parks, wilderness areas, wildlife refuges . . . does not return any specific gain to our treasuries. We work on them, fight for them, care about these issues because we believe in them, and because we truly think it is best for the country that we love."[75] No phrase better summarizes the sense of mission that guided environmentalists during the public lands debate.

8. The New Right versus the New Deal

COMPETING VISIONS OF PROGRESS

IN THE CONSERVATION DEBATE

In 1978 the director of the Mountain States Legal Foundation criticized the pervasive influence of environmental groups in determining public land policy. Calling the environmentalist a "zealot for his cause," James Watt implied that some groups hoped to weaken the United States. He termed environmental impact statements, wilderness-use restrictions, and "frivolous" law suits as the paralysis by analysis agenda of the environmental extremists. Little known before the election of Ronald Reagan, Watt advanced the New Right's growing disdain for preservation of the nation's public lands. Like other advocates in the New Right, Watt employed his cause, wilderness development, to symbolize the larger struggle between liberals and conservatives, the New Deal versus the New Right.[1]

Rhetorically, the conservation debate centered upon competing visions of growth and progress. Environmentalists perceived unchecked growth as a cancer out of control, an evil that demanded strict regulation. Economic and industrial growth presented numerous problems: pollution of the air and water; waste of precious natural resources; and unabated overpopulation. In contrast, political conservatives viewed growth as a panacea, a means of increasing economic prosperity for the entire nation. Much of the rhetoric focused on determining the place of economic growth in setting national resource policy.

The notion of progress, wrote Sheldon Wolin, has been the "driving force, the defining *Geist*" of most Western societies for nearly three centuries. Representing expanded benefits for a society as a whole, "the idea of progress functioned as a political critique directed against the power-wielding institutions of monarchy, aristocracy, and church."[2] However, the American experience seemed to transform the meaning of progress in guiding behavior. "As defined in Europe by generations of intellectuals," noted Arthur Ekirch, the concept of progress "came to be treated as a purely philosophical idea. However, in America, the unique experience and concrete achievements of the people helped to give the concept a dynamic reality." Significantly, Americans believed that progress could be either "impeded or accelerated by human will and effort." As a result, progress was a goal within the reach of the individual and not restricted by the status of one's birth.[3]

In the United States, observed Wolin, progress somehow became the "personal property of liberalism, even though there was no necessary connection between the two." As liberalism embraced and refined the New Deal, the New Frontier, and the Great Society, a subtle yet substantive change was evolving in American politics. As a result, observed Wolin, the "left's historic monopoly on change is being successfully challenged and conservatism is emerging as the party of progress."[4] By focusing on the public lands debate between 1979 and 1984, one may see how conservatives staked a claim on the idea of progress in the debate over natural resources.

In the twentieth century, the federal government had become the manager, as well as the owner, of millions of acres of land. In the 1960s, America's conservation movement was fundamentally altered by the philosophical precepts of ecology. Until that decade, advocates of development *and* advocates of preservation had based their ideology upon a human-centered view of nature. The decision either to preserve or develop the wilderness was based on the potential benefits to humans, either spiritual or economic.[5] Basing their worldview on the writings of Aldo Leopold, who by then had gained a popular following, and Rachel Carson, ecologists viewed humans as being in an interdependent and complex relationship with other creatures in the ecosystem. Rather than seeking wilderness preservation for its spiritual and cultural benefits, ecologists argued that preservation was a superior philosophy from two different perspectives. Scientifically, ecology made good sense because it would keep humans from destroying their planet with pollution and overpopulation. Morally, ecology made good sense because it extended rights to all creatures, teaching a standard of humility that should characterize civilized cultures. The series of federal laws passed in the 1960s and 1970s, collectively known as the conservation consensus, helped institutionalize Leopold's land ethic and ecological conscience, central tenets of ecology. Having mandated permanent federal ownership of the public lands, multiple use of the nation's resources, and strict standards for resource development, the United States seemed firmly committed to an ecological perspective.[6] Spoiled by two decades of legislative success, environmentalists were shocked to learn in 1980 that their fundamental assumptions were under attack by the New Right, an attack reinforced by members of the Sagebrush Rebellion and by the presidential campaign of Ronald Reagan.

Writing in 1985, Linda Medcalf and Kenneth Dolbeare called the New Right the "most significant new force in American politics in half a century." Rather than defending the status quo like the Old Right, those in the New Right demanded a change in the existing power structure. Arguing that true conservatives could not be complacent and simply hold the line against further change, Paul Weyrich announced, "We have to take a turn in the other direction. The New Right does not want to conserve, we want to change–we *are* the forces of change."[7] The 1980 levels of wilderness were unacceptable to members of the New Right; the conservation consensus needed to be dismantled to promote necessary economic development.

Although seeking major changes in tax policy and defense spending, the movement especially emphasized plans to fight abortion, school prayer, and the Equal Rights Amendment. While committed to reducing the intrusion of the government into the private lives of citizens, the New Right rejected the libertarian leanings of some conservatives. "Free enterprise is not absolute," wrote one advocate. "It is a means, not an end."[8] Reflecting the movement's activist approach, one writer concluded, "When men and women are free to choose their own 'life styles,' and to decide what image of humanity they wish to represent, their children must be left increasingly to the protection of the state."[9] Such claims indicated the sense of mission that America's new conservatives brought to the political debate. With a large national fund-raising network and the intellectual support of private research foundations, the New Right planned to replace New Deal liberalism as the guiding force in American politics. In doing so, they hoped to begin by unlocking the nation's public lands.

Related to how a society perceives and encourages progress is the notion of growth, a convenient measure of the amount and direction of progress. Progress had largely been "identified in economic terms," observed Richard Slotkin, "an increase of productive capacity, levels of consumption from year to year and decade to decade."[10] But progress was more than economic gain; the notion of progress also included measureable growth in the pursuit of knowledge, in science, and in

other advances of society.[11] Liberals had fastened on economic growth
as a prerequisite for equalizing opportunity for competing groups in
society. If opportunities were equalized, liberals assumed, then all
classes could achieve a better qualify of life. The advent of the ecology
movement in the 1960s, however, cast doubt on liberal assumptions
about growth and provided an alternative view of progress.

Ecologists argued that growth-oriented measures of progress were
doomed in an age of shrinking resources after decades of material over-
indulgence. Hoping to reform American culture as well as preserve
its wilderness, environmentalists attacked the economic impulse that
motivated human behavior. They emphasized that limited growth and
a "small is beautiful" life-style had to replace the nation's commitment
to material growth. While America's economic standard of living had
become the envy of the world, Interior Secretary Stewart Udall observed in 1963, "we are not better prepared to inherit the earth or to
carry on the pursuit of happiness." Echoing Aldo Leopold, Udall
called for a land ethic that would "stress the oneness of our resources
and the live-and-help-live logic of the great chain of life."[12]

Writing in 1967, Robert Rienow and Leona Train Rienow presented
a typical ecological interpretation of growth. "Untrammeled growth
in any species consumes its environment to its own death," they concluded. "To talk, therefore, about a forever-expanding economy is
preposterous. There is an end. But first we invite a shambles of our
surroundings." Placing faith in an ever-expanding economy, they
charged, was to "try and conceive of infinity, a rather hopeless thrust
by men who are something less." Another ecologist, Paul Sears, observed that it was "disturbing to hear the current glib emphasis on
economic 'growth' as the solution to all ills. Growth, in all biological
experience, is a determinate process. Out of control . . . it becomes
pathological giantism and by no means is the same thing as health."
In a popular book that drew considerable attention to ecology, Barry
Commoner attacked the panacea of growth, maintaining that there
must be some "limit to the growth of total capital, and the productive
system must eventually reach a 'no-growth' condition." Noting that
progress had become "synonymous with quantitative growth," the
Science Action Coalition observed that material growth may have in-
hibited the human experience. "Increased consumer goods do not
guarantee higher quality of life," they concluded, "but instead may
even lead to deterioration through increased wastes and resource de-
pletion."[13] This limited-growth, ecological view of nature affected the

attitudes toward wilderness policy. Rather than seeking maximum economic return on the public lands, ecologically minded land managers recognized wilderness preservation as a legitimate goal in determining land use.

In contrast to the ecological belief that growth should be checked and regulated, the New Right envisioned an expanding, growth-oriented economy. Various advocates presented economic growth as the key to emancipating the nation from the excesses of liberalism. Placing faith in market forces instead of government regulation has been a commonplace for conservatives for many years, but New Right advocates presented a somewhat different conception of the marketplace. Although the movement shared many values with the Old Right, David Broder noted, there had been an "infusion of new doctrine—particularly in the area of economics."[14] Samuel T. Francis, a proponent of the movement, claimed that the central focus of the New Right political economy "is likely to be economic growth, a value often confused with, sometimes encompassing, but not identical with the free market." In defining this difference, Francis observed that "economic growth involves the lifting of most legal and administrative restraints on enterprise—the demise of environmentalist legislation and OSHA, the sale of federally owned land in the Far West, etc." Francis argued that in place of the free market of the Old Right, "or the 'stabilization' of the present elite, the New Right should center its economic aspirations on the concept of economic growth." Although growth required decentralization of federal fiscal and environmental policies, "this reorientation toward a freer economic climate is incidental to the central idea of economic growth, expansion, and dynamism."[15]

During the 1980 presidential campaign, Ronald Reagan emphasized the need for economic growth, especially through greater development of the nation's public lands. Reagan strengthened his link to the New Right by advancing campaign promises consistent with the movement's developing political theory. Moreover, Reagan's platform meshed comfortably with the New Right's notion that government had locked up the public lands, thereby stifling economic growth and fueling inflation and unemployment. America "doesn't have to be in the shape that it is in," Reagan declared when he debated Jimmy Carter. "We do not have to go on sharing in scarcity with the country getting worse off, unemployment growing . . . all of this can be cured and all of it can be solved."[16] Progress, it appeared, was firmly entrenched in the conservative, not the liberal, worldview.

Why are progress and growth rhetorically engaging values for American audiences? Several factors help explain this. Visions of progress may be tied to varied cultural and philosophical foundations, with the Judeo-Christian tradition and the Enlightenment offered as possible origins for America's predilection for progress and growth.[17] Although such historical connections may be identified, the rhetorical power of these values probably emerges from a more intrinsic American myth. Driven to find a better life for themselves and for their children, Americans have been motivated historically by the pursuit of progress. Significantly, Americans believed that they could bring progress by their own efforts. Noting that the frontier allowed "each man to believe that he could improve his condition and make his fortune by his own efforts," Russel B. Nye concluded that by the end of the eighteenth century the idea of progress had become a "national principle."[18]

The vehicle to achieve progress has been growth, expansion, the development of the wilderness, and later, the rise of industry. In this light, notions of a Manifest Destiny and Social Darwinism justified unrestricted growth.[19] Although several scholars have identified a connection between Reagan's rhetorical success and his use of the western myth, this link emphasizes the symbolic dimensions of the popular American western.[20] In employing the growth analogy, Reagan (and advocates in the New Right) was exploiting a more fundamental cultural symbol than the western. Viewing sustained growth as an essential component in the maintenance of democracy, New Right conservatives adopted a worldview that originated with the discovery of the New World.

While the British political and economic world centered on the command of the sea, the early colonists, who had been raised in this tradition, shifted their attention to the frontier. The magnetic attraction of this untouched natural resource, observed Henry Nash Smith, "interfered with the conception of an empire based on maritime commerce by suggesting the quite different vision of a populous, agricultural society, largely self-contained, in the Mississippi Valley."[21] Knowledge of the frontier helped settlers justify breaking the traditions of Europe in their quest to improve their life-style. In this manner, wrote Slotkin, "Progress itself was to be asserted as a positive good against the aristocratic and peasant traditions that emphasized stasis and permanence in productive techniques and social relations."[22]

Sacvan Bercovitch identified the cultural roots of the progress argument in his study of the "Puritan errand," the colonial migration to

America. The errand meant more than a change of geography; it symbolized movement from a "depraved Old World to a New Canaan."
It was central to the Puritan consensus to view "migration as a function of prophecy, and prophecy as an unlimited license to expand."
Employing the rhetoric of the errand to justify their expansion into
the wilderness, the Puritans gave birth to a uniquely American conception of nature. In this new culture, the meaning of frontier changed
from that of a "barrier" to progress to that of a "threshold" of progress.[23] In this manner, westward expansion was ordained as a religious,
as well as an economic and social, act. Noting that the direction of
expansion is always progressive, Slotkin concluded, "as each new frontier is met and conquered, it in turn becomes a Metropolis, and as
such the base for a new and deeper foray into the Wilderness."[24]

The Puritans perceived migration as synonymous with progress,
both spiritually and materially. Wilderness served as a "mirror of prophecy" for the Puritans. They saw in the American frontier a "chosen
nation in progress—a New Israel whose constituency was as numerous, potentially, as the entire people of God, and potentially as vast
as America."[25] For the scholar of rhetoric, the importance of the Puritan errand lies in its persistence throughout American history. The
Puritans left an important cultural legacy for future generations, wrote
Bercovitch, bequeathing their descendants "a system of sacred-secular
symbols (New Israel, American Jerusalem) for a people intent on progress; a set of rituals of anxiety and control that could at once encourage and confine the energies of free enterprise; a rhetoric of mission
so broad in its implications, and so specifically American in its appli-
cation, that it could facilitate the transition from Puritan to Yankee,
and from errand to manifest destiny and the dream."[26]

Reagan's portrayal of the United States as a "city on the hill," spe-
cially selected by God, relied on a vision of progress even more culturally ingrained than the western myth. Although Reagan and advocates in the New Right discussed the public lands primarily in
relation to economic treasures, such as oil, strategic minerals, and
employment, an underlying moral assumption was also present that
by using God's gift of nature, America could remain productive and
strong. In contrast, preservation of the wilderness appeared to be an
unproductive and wasteful philosophy.

From a rhetorical perspective, the conservation debate centered on
two distinct views of nature. The vision of a chosen people, a nation
intent on progress, relied on a worldview of growth and expansion.

The New Right's view of the public lands tapped this collective vision of a nation on an errand. Perceiving nature as a commodity to be used to benefit society, advocates of development reaffirmed the Puritan view of prophecy. The ecological worldview, dominant in policy-making decisions in the 1960s and 1970s, had little appeal for many Americans tired of calls for restraint, conservation of resources, and limited growth in the early 1980s. Seeking to dismantle the big government of New Deal liberalism, Ronald Reagan and his followers offered a human-centered view of nature, proposing that wilderness ought to serve humanity, rather than humanity serving wilderness. In this sense, appeals to economic growth as a measure of progress were rhetorically engaging within the larger political debate.

Preservation or development remains the great dilemma in determining how best to use the American public lands. The conservation debate illuminated an inherent tension between the ecological and economic conception of nature. With advocates from various political factions working to determine the appropriate levels of growth and progress, the debate seems destined to continue for decades to come. The apparent consensus for an ecological policy was challenged as the national economy stagnated in the late 1970s. As a result, environmentalists were forced to justify more specifically the economic consequences of wilderness preservation. The scientific and moral benefits of an ecological conscience had to be redefined for a public wary of environmental extremists. On the other hand, the New Right's human-centered view of nature appeared to be politically popular, but not necessarily among those people who used the public lands on a regular basis. While many in the West acknowledged an interest in economic development, they were also committed to some degree of wilderness preservation.

The conservation debate of the early 1980s advanced the question that has generated controversy in the United States for two centuries: how should the wealth of the public lands be used and distributed? Because answers to this question must always emerge in political dialogue, the future of the wilderness seems ultimately linked to the quality of the public debate on such issues. The great dialogue will certainly continue.

Notes

PREFACE

1. Henry Nash Smith, *Virgin Land* (Cambridge: Harvard University Press, 1950), p. 250.
2. Wendell Berry, *The Unsettling of America* (San Francisco: Sierra Club Books, 1977), p. 30.
3. Tom Arrandale, *The Battle for Natural Resources* (Washington, D.C.: Congressional Quarterly, 1983), pp. 1, 6.
4. Roderick Nash, *Wilderness and the American Mind*, 3rd ed. (New Haven: Yale University Press, 1982), p. 336; Arrandale, p. x.
5. Joseph Petulla, *American Environmentalism* (College Station: Texas A&M University Press, 1980), p. 98.

CHAPTER 1

1. Grant McConnell, "The Conservation Movement: Past and Present," *Western Political Science Quarterly* 7 (1954): 456.
2. McConnell, p. 471.
3. Samuel P. Hays, *Conservation and the Gospel of Efficiency* (Cambridge, Mass.: Harvard University Press, 1959), p. 175.
4. For an analysis of the Hetch Hetchy debate, see Nash, *Wilderness*, pp. 161–81.
5. Hays, p. 271.
6. See Nash, *Wilderness*, pp. 210–19.
7. For an account of the Echo Park debate, see Elmo Richardson, "The Interior Secretary as Conservation Villain: The Notorious Case of Douglas 'Giveaway' McKay," *Pacific Historical Review* 41 (1972): 333–45. See also Wallace Stegner and Richard Etulain, *Conversations with Wallace Stegner* (Salt Lake City: University of Utah Press, 1983), pp. 167–71.
8. Nash, *Wilderness*, p. 217.

9. Roderick Nash, "American Environmental History," *Pacific Historical Review* 41 (1972): 368. Aldo Leopold, *A Sand County Almanac* (New York: Oxford University Press, 1966), p. 240.

10. Stewart L. Udall, *The Quiet Crisis* (New York: Avon Books, 1963), p. 192.

11. Leopold, p. 258.

12. Ibid., p. 238; Nash, *Wilderness,* p. 197.

13. Stewart L. Udall, "To Save the Wonder of the Wilderness," *New York Times Magazine,* May 27, 1962, p. 40; Udall, *Quiet Crisis,* p. 202; Wallace Stegner, "Living on Our Principal," *Wilderness* (Spring, 1985), 15, 17. According to Stegner (p. 16): "It was Leopold's distinction that he combined and reconciled two strains of thought. He had no romantic revulsion against plowing, or cutting trees, or hunting birds and animals, or any of the things we do to make our living from the earth. He was only against the furious excess of our exploitation, our passion to live on our principal. It struck him as sad that unexploited land, land left alone, seemed actively to offend our continent-busters."

14. Arrandale, pp. 50, 51.

15. Ibid., p. 50

16. Roderick Nash, "Path to Preservation," *Wilderness* 48 (1984): 5; Arrandale, p. 54

17. Arrandale, pp. 55, 56.

18. Ibid., p. 57.

19. Stephen Fox, *John Muir and His Legacy* (Boston: Little Brown and Co., 1981), p. 329.

20. Richard D. Lamm and Michael McCarthy, *The Angry West* (Boston: Houghton Mifflin Co., 1982), p. 239.

21. Telegram from Ronald Reagan to Dean Rhodes, Nov. 20, 1980, in U.S. Congress, Subcommittee on Mines and Mining Oversight Hearings, *Sagebrush Rebellion: Impacts on Energy and Minerals,* 96th Cong., 2nd sess. (Washington, D.C.: Government Printing Office, 1980), p. 287.

CHAPTER 2

1. For example, see Frank J. Popper, "The Timely End of the Sagebrush Rebellion," *Public Interest* 76 (1984): 61–73; John G. Francis, "Environmental Values, Intergovernmental Politics, and the Sagebrush Rebellion," in *Western Public Lands: The Management of Natural Resources in a Time of Declining Federalism,* ed. John G. Francis and Richard Ganzel (Totowa, N.J.: Rowman and Allanheld, 1984), pp. 29–46; Sally K. Fairfax, "Beyond the Sagebrush Rebellion: The BLM as Neighbor and Manager in the Western States," in Francis and Ganzel, pp. 79–91.

2. Lawrence Rakestraw, "The West, States' Rights, and Conservation," *Pacific Northwest Quarterly* 48 (1957): 89–99.

3. William Rowley, *U.S. Forest Service Grazing and Rangelands: A History* (College Station: Texas A&M University Press, 1985), p. 176.

4. Brock's guest editorial appeared in the *Denver Post* Feb. 2, 1947, and is cited in William Voight, Jr., *Public Grazing Lands* (New Brunswick, N.J.: Rutgers University Press, 1976), p. 95.

5. See Bernard DeVoto, "The West Against Itself," *Harper's* 194 (Jan., 1947): 1–13, for the opposition arguments to the land transfer. Rowley (p. 207) points out that opposition also appeared in *Collier's, Sports Afield, Field and Stream, Outdoor Life, Outdoor America,* and the *Salt Lake Tribune.* See Rowley, pp. 222–24, for a discussion of the public lands in the early 1950s and the inability of ranchers to pass supportive legislation.

6. Lamm and McCarthy, p. 232.

7. Ibid., p. 233: "Under RARE, lands *considered* for wilderness designation were withdrawn from all commercial activity *during* the inventory; until final classifications were determined, these lands became *de facto* wilderness, subject to the same laws that governed *established* wilderness areas. Specifically the RARE process froze both mining and lumbering activities on those lands; ventures already begun were allowed to continue but nothing new was authorized."

8. Stegner and Etulain, p. 50.

9. Lamm and McCarthy, 320, 329. See also Peter J. Ognibene, "Sagebrush Senators," *Rocky Mountain Magazine* (July–Aug., 1981): 46: "Yet the myth of the totally independent, self-reliant westerner lives on despite the facts. Today, for instance, the Rocky Mountain states get $1.20 in federal spending for every dollar they pay in federal taxes. No region gets more, and some get considerably less. The Midwest gets the least: 79 cents for every dollar."

10. See George Melloan, "Rebellious Mood in West," *Wall Street Journal,* Aug. 16, 1979, p. 18; Bill Stall, "West's Sagebrush Rebellion a Lost Cause in Congress, Udall Says," *Los Angeles Times,* Sept. 6, 1979; Gladwin Hill, "Stakes Are High in the 'Sagebrush Rebellion,'" *New York Times,* Sept. 2, 1979, Sec. E, p. 5.

11. See Tom Beck, "The Angry West," *Newsweek* (Sept. 17, 1979): 35–39; "Sagebrush Rebellion Brushfires Scorch Feds," *High Country News* (Sept. 7, 1979): 13.

12. Popper, p. 68.

13. Johanna H. Wald and Elizabeth H. Temkin, "The Sagebrush Rebellion: The West Against Itself–Again," *UCLA Journal of Environmental Law and Policy* 2 (1982): 189–90. Wald and Temkin report that the rebels were led by "members of the public livestock industry. . . . The rebellious ranchers have been joined by miners, some energy companies, timber companies, developers and similar interests."

14. "Rebels Revel in New Power, Polish," *High Country News* (Dec. 12, 1980): 1; Montana Democratic Party Issue Brief No. 6, "The Sagebrush Rebellion," 1981, unpublished pamphlet obtained at the Carroll College Library, Helena, Montana.

15. Richard Starnes, "The Theft of the West," *Outdoor Life* (June, 1981): 95; "Cliff Young, "What's Behind the Sagebrush Rebellion?" *National Wildlife* (Aug.–Sept., 1981): 32. Harvey's speech came from the "Paul Harvey Western Lands Rally . . . [maybe] the largest political event ever put on in Idaho," according to the *Sagebrush Rebellion, Inc., Newsletter,* Summer, 1980. Copies of numerous SRI newsletters were made available by Twyla Bee Montano, Office Manager, Sagebrush Rebellion, Inc., Boise, Ida.

16. Lamm and McCarthy, p. 281.

17. Malcom Cawley, "The Sagebrush Rebellion," Ph.D. diss., Colorado State University, 1981, p. 149.

18. National Association of Counties Factsheet, published in U.S. Congress, House, *Sagebrush Rebellion: Impacts on Energy and Minerals,* 96th Cong., 2nd sess., H. Rept. 96-39, p. 259.

19. Vernon Ravenscroft, "Sagebrush Rebellion: A Look from the Inside," *Blackfoot* [Idaho] *Morning News,* July 8, 1980, p. 4.

20. For a discussion of the rebellion's fundamental logical appeals, see "There's More Rhetoric than Reality in the West's 'Sagebrush Rebellion,'" *National Journal* (Nov. 17, 1979): 1928–31. Also see Lamm and McCarthy, pp. 208–324.

21. Ravenscroft, "Sagebrush Rebellion," p. 4.

22. Sample speech, "Sagebrush Rebellion Presentation," prepared by the Nevada Legislature's Select Committee on Public Lands, Nov., 1980. The select committee, funded by state appropriations, acts as clearinghouse for Sagebrush Rebellion information. The committee provided a wide assortment of documents, including this sample speech.

23. House Hearings, *Sagebrush Rebellion,* testimony of John Harmer, p. 48.

24. *Sagebrush Rebellion, Inc., Newsletter,* Summer, 1980.

25. Ibid., Winter, 1981–82.

26. Ronald F. Reid, *The American Revolution and the Rhetoric of History* (Annandale, Va.: Speech Communication Association, 1978), p. 68.

27. Sagebrush Rebellion, Inc., pamphlet; *Sagebrush Rebellion, Inc., Newsletter,* Summer, 1980.

28. *Sagebrush Rebellion, Inc., Newsletter,* Summer, 1981; Vernon Ravenscroft, guest editorial, *Lewiston* [Idaho] *Morning Tribune,* Feb. 17, 1981.

29. Governor List quoted in Gary Turbak, "America's Sagebrush Rebellion," *Kiwanis Magazine* (Feb., 1981): 28; House Hearings, *Sagebrush Rebellion,* p. 27, testimony of Calvin Black; Paul Laxalt, "The Sagebrush Rebellion: A Backgrounder from Senator Paul Laxalt," Feb., 1980 (a copy of this article, intended for Senator Laxalt's constituents, was supplied by the senator's

staff); James McClure, Speech presented to the Western Colonies in Revolt Symposium, July, 1981, Sun Valley, Ida. (transcript of the speech at Montana State Library, Helena).

30. Harvey Merrill quoted in Cawley, pp. 146–50. Cawley bases his description of the celebration on a news report in the *Moab* [Utah] *Times Independent*, July 10, 1980. Merrill quoted in Craig Rayle, "July 4th Fireworks Misses Wilderness Study Area," *High Country News*, July 11, 1980, p. 3.

31. Senator Orrin Hatch, "A Second American Revolution," speech presented to the Western Coalition on Public Lands, Sept. 6, 1979, Reno, Nev. (transcript at Idaho State University Library, Pocatello).

32. Richard A. Viguerie, *The New Right: We're Ready to Lead* (Falls Church, Va.: Viguerie Co., 1981), p. 78.

33. John L. Dobra and George A. Uhimchuk, "Property Rights, Legal Efficiency, and the Political Economy of the Sagebrush Rebellion," *Nevada Review of Business and Economics* 5 (1982): 3.

34. See Janice Hocker Rushing, "The Rhetoric of the American Western Myth," *Communication Monographs* 50 (1983): 14–32.

35. The western myth seems more appropriate in environmentalist rhetoric. It better reflects the preservationist notion that wilderness needs protection for the intangible benefits it offers to humans. Aldo Leopold demonstrated that wilderness preservation could be linked to the individual qualities fostered by a frontier experience. On the other hand, sagebrush rebels had little rhetorical need to detail the spiritual and cultural benefits of the wilderness.

36. Charles D. Elder and Roger W. Cobb, *The Political Uses of Symbols* (New York: Longman, 1983), p. 54.

37. Reid, p. 37.

38. Alan Crawford, *Thunder on the Right* (New York: Pantheon, 1980), p. 82.

39. McClure, Sun Valley speech.

40. Hatch, Reno speech; Sen. Orrin Hatch, letter to the editor, *Washington Post*, Dec. 5, 1979, Sec. A, p. 26.

41. Ravenscroft, "Sagebrush Rebellion," p. 4.

42. Melloan, p. 18.

43. House Hearings, *Sagebrush Rebellion*, testimony of Sen. Richard E. Blakemore, p. 8.

44. Ibid., testimony of Jac Shaw, Nevada Division of Public Lands, p. 17.

45. Senator McClure quoted in Turbak, p. 28; Sen. Orrin Hatch, *Congressional Record–Senate* (Aug. 3, 1979): S 11666.

46. For a description of the rhetorical theory of "persuasive slogans," see Michael Calvin McGee, "The 'Ideograph': A Link between Rhetoric and Ideology," *Quarterly Journal of Speech* 66 (1980): 1–16.

47. Hatch, Reno speech.

48. House Hearings, *Sagebrush Rebellion,* testimony of Marlene Simmons, p. 108. Simmons closed her testimony with a plea that "development and motorized recreation are not dirty words, but excessive wilderness withdrawal and public land lock-up should be!"

49. Arrandale, p. 37.

50. Hatch, Senate speech.

51. Sample letter, Nevada Select Committee.

52. Sagebrush Rebellion, Inc., pamphlet; League for States' Equal Rights pamphlet (copy at Idaho State University Library, Pocatello).

53. Cobb and Elder, p. 99.

54. Hatch quoted in Ognibene, p. 46; Lynn Shepard quoted in Marsha and Roseanne Carter, "West Tangles with East in Sagebrush Rebellion," *Phoenix Magazine* (June, 1980): 75.

55. Sen. Orrin Hatch, "The Sagebrush Rebellion is Real! Utah for Utahns, Not the Washington Bureaucrats," newsletter to Hatch's constituents (copy at University of Utah Library, Salt Lake City).

CHAPTER 3

1. Writing essays for *Outdoor Life* and *Field and Stream,* Starnes and Trueblood have been major figures in the hunting and fishing community.

2. See "Environmentalists Oppose Land Transfer," *High Country News,* Nov. 2, 1979, p. 13.

3. Young, p. 33; Cecil Andrus, "The Attack on Federal Lands," *National Parks and Conservation* (Apr., 1980): 9; Donald Nelson, letter to the editor, *Idaho State Journal,* March 8, 1981.

4. House Hearings, *Sagebrush Rebellion,* testimony of James H. Pissot, p. 175.

5. Wald and Temkin, p. 194.

6. Wallace Stegner, "If the Sagebrush Rebels Win, Everybody Loses," *Living Wilderness* (Summer, 1981): 34.

7. Veto message to the Arizona State Senate, April 8, 1980 (copy from Gov. Bruce Babbitt); Andrus, "The Attack on Federal Lands," p. 10; Ted Trueblood, "They're Fixing to Steal Your Lands," *Field and Stream* (March, 1980): 167.

8. U.S. Department of Interior, *1980 Survey of Fishing, Hunting, and Wildlife Associated Recreation* (Washington, D.C.: Government Printing Office, 1982), p. 40.

9. "Institute Says States Neglect Public Lands," *Denver Post,* Feb. 6, 1981 (microform, published in *Newsbank,* ENV. 1981, 17: F2). "By law, the land departments of most states are required to manage state land for the highest possible monetary gain. The mandate appears in the constitutions of some

states and is why public use of lands gets second consideration or totally is ruled out, the report said."

10. Cecil Andrus, letter to the editor, *Washington Post*, Dec. 5, 1979, Sec. A, p. 26.

11. Bruce Babbitt, "Federalism and the Environment: An Intergovernmental Perspective of the Sagebrush Rebellion," *Environmental Law* 12 (1982): 850.

12. Andrus, "Attack on Federal Lands, p. 10; Wald and Temkin, p. 196.

13. Young, p. 34.

14. Babbitt, "Federalism and the Environment," p. 854; Frank Gregg, quoted in Montana Democratic Party, "The Sagebrush Rebellion."

15. House Hearings, *Sagebrush Rebellion*, testimony of Marlene Simmons, p. 14.

16. Trueblood, "They're Fixing to Steal Your Land," p. 41; Richard Starnes, "The Sagebrush Rebellion," *Outdoor Life* (March, 1980): 10; Editorial, *Outdoor Life* (April, 1981): 10; Ravenscroft, p. 4.

17. Montana Democratic Party, "The Sagebrush Rebellion."

18. Joan Nice, "Rebels Revel in New Power, Polish," *High Country News*, Dec. 12, 1980, p. 3.

19. Ted Trueblood, "The Sagebrush Ripoff," *Field and Stream* (Mar., 1981): 19.

20. Ken Robison, Speech presented to the Western Colonies in Revolt Symposium, July, 1981, Sun Valley, Ida. (transcript in Montana State Library, Helena). Senator Hatch was quoted in *The Sagebrush Ripoff*, Summer, 1981, newsletter published by the Utah Chapter of the Sierra Club, Salt Lake City (transcript in the University of Utah Library, Salt Lake City). Senator Hatch was also quoted in Maitland Sharpe, "The Sagebrush Rebellion," *Outdoor America* (Sept.–Oct., 1980): 26.

21. Andrus, letter to the editor.

22. See Trueblood, "The Sagebrush Ripoff."

23. Ted Trueblood, "Save Our Public Lands, Inc.," *Outdoor America* (Sept.–Oct., 1981): 7–9. Trueblood noted that by July, 1981, his organization had the names and addresses of over 22,000 Idahoans, a significant number considering Idaho's total population of just under 1 million at the time (Ken Robison, *The Sagebrush Rebellion: A Bid for Control* [Blackfoot, Ida.: D and S Publishing, 1981], copy in Idaho State University Library, Pocatello).

24. Surveys cited in David F. Salisbury, "Sagebrush Rebels See Open Range in Reagan's Victory," *Christian Science Monitor* Nov. 18, 1980, p. 1. The poll showing that 60 percent of the public opposed the rebellion was conducted by a Phoenix polling firm, Behavior Research Center. The poll asked 1,025 adults if they supported state seizure of the public lands in the West. Support for continued federal management "was high among older, middle-to-upper income white males who described themselves as political moderates or conservatives." See "Sagebrush Rising Rouses Few in West, According to New Poll," *High Country News*, Dec. 14, 1979, p. 13.

25. "Folks Like Land Idea Once They Learn of It," *Denver Post*, Dec. 28, 1980, p. 2. Cited in Cawley, p. 190.

26. Salisbury, p. 1.

27. John G. Francis, "Environmental Values, Intergovernmental Politics and the Sagebrush Rebellion," in Francis and Ganzel, p. 33.

28. Ibid., p. 36.

29. Senator Laxalt quoted in Young, p. 33; Attorney General Leroy quoted in "The Sagebrush Rebellion: Misdirected Dynamite," *High Country News*, Feb. 22, 1980, p. 2; Senator McClure quoted in Brad Bugger, "Sagebrush Rebellion Died, But What Were the Legacies?" [Pocatello] *Idaho State Journal*, Apr. 5, 1987, Sec. B, p. 1.

30. Ravenscroft, p. 4; "Question and Answer Factsheet" prepared by the Nevada Legislature's Select Committee on Public Lands (copy in the author's possession).

31. House Hearings, *Sagebrush Rebellion*, National Association of Counties Factsheet, p. 261.

32. Cited in Sharpe, "Sagebrush Rebellion," p. 6.

33. Andres Grose, letter to the author, Mar. 27, 1984.

34. House Hearings, *Sagebrush Rebellion*, testimony of James Haggard, p. 55.

35. Utah Foundation, "Utah and the Sagebrush Rebellion," Research Report No. 399, Jan., 1980 (transcript in the University of Utah Library, Salt Lake City).

36. Salisbury, p. 1; "West Senses Victory in Sagebrush Rebellion," p. 29.

37. U.S. Congress, Senate, *James G. Watt Nomination Hearings*, 97th Cong., 1st sess. S. Rept. 97-1, p. 461. (In response to several questions, Watt noted, "I believe in a 'good neighbor' policy under which the Department seeks to cooperate with local governments and citizens affected by Department actions."); Watt quoted in Young, p. 33.

38. Brad Knickerbocker, "Echoes of 'Sagebrush Rebellion' Resound in Washington Corridors," *Christian Science Monitor*, June 4, 1981, p. 1; Sen. James McClure, Interview with the *Idaho Falls Post-Register*, cited in "Unrest in the West: Who Owns This Land?" *Changing Times* (July, 1981): 32.

39. Sara Terry, "Sagebrush Rebellion Becomes the Newest Bad Guy Out West," *Christian Science Monitor*, Aug. 5, 1981, p. 1.

40. Michael Reese, "Watt Defuses a Rebellion," *Newsweek* (Sept. 21, 1981): 48.

41. William Endicott, "West Fights to Keep Sagebrush Rebellion Alive," *Los Angeles Times*, Aug. 31, 1981, Sec. I, p. 1.

42. Mark Lewis, "What Became of the Sagebrush Rebellion," *Great Falls* [Montana] *Tribune*, Sept. 26, 1983, Sec. B, p. 1.

43. Popper, p. 69.

44. Robert H. Nelson, "Why the Sagebrush Revolt Burned Out," *Regula-*

tion (May–June, 1984): 34. Nelson cited hearings in Utah in which rebel cattlemen, during October, 1981, voiced "fears that the state, as new landlord,
might not honor their present federal grazing permits."

45. Sen. Jake Garn quoted in Sanford J. Unger, "Washington: The 'New
Conservatives,'" *Atlantic Monthly* (Feb., 1979): 22.

46. Samuel P. Hays, "Conservation and the Structure of American Politics:
The Progressive Era," in *American Political History as Social History*, ed. Hays
(Knoxville: University of Tennessee Press, 1980), p. 243.

CHAPTER 4

1. Laurence I. Barrett, *Gambling with History* (New York: Penguin Books,
1983), p. 127.

2. Bureau of the Census, *Statistical Abstract of the United States: 1981* (Washington, D.C.: Government Printing Office, 1981). During the Carter administration, unemployment ranged from 14 percent in 1977 to 13 percent in 1980.
The consumer price index steadily increased from 1977 (6.5 percent) through
1980 (13.5 percent). During Carter's last year in office, spendable weekly earnings declined by 6.7 percent. For a full range of statistics, see p. 380 (unemployment), p. 405 (weekly earnings), and p. 459 (price index).

3. Barrett, p. 128.

4. Elizabeth Drew, *Portrait of an Election* (New York: Simon and Schuster,
1981), p. 108.

5. Barrett, p. 51.

6. See Robert Ivie, "Speaking 'Common Sense' About the Soviet Threat:
Reagan's Rhetorical Stance," *Western Journal of Speech Communication* 48 (Winter, 1984): 39–50. Carter's "malaise speech," presented in July, 1979, was os-
tensibly on the topic of energy, but according to two political commentators,
"the heart of his message was, in essence, an attempt to shift blame from himself to the people. There was, he said, a 'fundamental threat to American
democracy' in what he called a 'crisis in confidence . . . that strikes at the very
heart and soul of our national will.'" See Jack W. Germond and Jules Witcover, *Blue Smoke and Mirrors: How Reagan Won and Why Carter Lost the Election of 1980* (New York: Viking Press, 1981), p. 36.

7. Reagan quoted in Drew, p. 116. Reagan used the peroration many
times in the fall campaign, most notably in his closing statement during the
debate with Carter: "I would like to have a crusade today, and I would like
to lead that crusade with your help. And it would be one to take Government off the backs of the great people of this country, and turn you loose
again to do those things that I know you can do so well, because you did
them and made this country great" ("Text of Presidential Debate Between
Carter and Reagan," *Congressional Quarterly* (Nov. 1, 1980): 3289.

8. "Carter-Reagan Debate Text," p., 3289.

9. Robert Dallek, *Ronald Reagan: The Politics of Symbolism* (Cambridge, Mass.: Harvard University Press, 1984), pp. vii–viii.

10. Henry Plotkin, "Issues in the Presidential Campaign," in *The Election of 1980*, ed. Gerald Pomper (Chatham, N.J.: Chatham Publishing Co., 1981), p. 42.

11. Hill, p. 17.

12. William Tucker, "Environmentalism: The Newest Toryism," *Policy Review* (Fall, 1980): 140–52.

13. Edy, Peterson, and Evans quoted in Philip Shabecoff, "Major Environmental Leaders Back Carter Re-election Bid," *New York Times*, Sept. 28, 1980, Sec. A, p. 36.

14. Reagan quoted in Drew, p. 268.

15. "Convention Acceptance Speech," Republican National Convention, Detroit, Mich., transcript printed in *President Reagan* (Washington, D.C.: Congressional Quarterly, 1981), p. 100; "Carter-Reagan Debate Text," p. 3286.

16. "Carter-Reagan Debate Text," p. 3286.

17. For an example of the limited-growth philosophy applied to the management of natural resources, see Science Action Coalition with Albert J. Fritsch, *Environmental Ethics* (Garden City, N.Y.: Anchor Books, 1980), 171–98.

18. Shabecoff, p. 346.

19. Reagan quoted in John F. Stacks, *Watershed: The Campaign for the Presidency, 1980* (New York: Times Books, 1981), p. 184.

20. "Carter-Reagan Debate Text," p. 3286.

21. Reagan quoted in Drew, p. 114.

22. Reagan quoted in "Candidates All Endorse Energy Price Decontrol," *Congressional Quarterly* (Oct. 4, 1980): 2923. Reagan qualified the prediction, stating that "leading oil geologists will tell you that, with decontrol, we could be producing enough oil to be self-sufficient in five years." When experts discounted this prediction, the article concluded, "Reagan's advisers have also been quick to explain that he was only quoting others, not claiming they were correct."

23. "Convention Acceptance Speech," p. 100.

24. Ronald Reagan, "Announcement of Candidacy," Nov. 13, 1979, transcript printed in *President Reagan*, p. 94; "Convention Acceptance Speech," p. 100.

25. Kathy Fletcher, "Where Does Carter Stand with Environmentalists?" *High Country News*, May 30, 1980, p. 2.

26. Nash, *Wilderness*, p. 272.

27. Carter quoted in "Candidates All Endorse Energy Price Control," p. 2923.

28. "1980 Democratic Party Platform Text," *Congressional Quarterly* (Aug. 16, 1980): 2409.

29. Ibid., p. 2410.

30. Carter quoted in Drew, p. 183.

31. Jimmy Carter, "Convention Acceptance Speech," Democratic National Convention, Aug. 14, 1980, New York City, transcript printed in *Facts on File* (Aug. 14, 1980): 613.

32. "Carter-Reagan Debate Text," p. 3286.

33. "1980 Democratic Party Platform Text," p. 2410.

34. "Carter-Reagan Debate Text," p. 3286.

35. Ibid., p. 2864.

36. Watt quoted in Ron Wolf, "New Voice in the Wilderness," *Rocky Mountain Magazine* (Mar.–Apr., 1981): 30; Watt also quoted in Robert Jones, "New Interior Chief: None Like Him," *Los Angeles Times,* May 31, 1981, Sec. I, p. 1.

37. Wolf, p. 34.

38. The secretary of the interior is one of the most powerful members of the cabinet. The secretary runs all national parks, the Bureau of Reclamation, wilderness areas, wildlife refuges, and the Bureau of Indian Affairs. The secretary is responsible for leasing the outercontinental shelf for oil exploration as well as the mineral rights on thousands of acres of national forest land. In 1982, the Interior Department had an annual budget of $6.2 billion and 52,000 employees. See Ronald Brownstein and Nina Easton, *Reagan's Ruling Class* (Washington, D.C.: Presidential Accountability Group, 1982), p. 107.

39. James J. Kilpatrick, "Why They Don't Like Watt," *Washington Post,* Aug. 12, 1981, Sec. A, p. 19.

40. See Dale Russakoff, "Watt as a Fundraiser: 'Magnet' That Can Repel," *Washington Post,* Apr. 12, 1982, Sec. A, p. 1; see also Dale Russakoff, "Watt, Who Once Relished Publicity, Now Keeping a Low Profile," *Washington Post,* July 15, 1982, Sec. A, p. 2.

41. Jones, p. 1.

42. Watt quoted in Kurt Anderson, "Always Right and Ready to Fight," *Time* (Aug. 23, 1982): 27.

43. Watt quoted in Tony Brown, "Watt: Development Right, Time Wrong," *Argus Leader* [Sioux Falls], Apr. 7, 1982, located in *Newsbank,* ENV 34: F13.

44. Watt's biographical history is detailed in Wolf, p. 30.

45. Ibid.

46. Watt quoted in Joanne Omang, "Choice for Interior an Agency Adversary," *Washington Post,* Dec. 16, 1980, Sec. A, p. 1.

47. Ibid.

48. Wolf, p. 33.

49. Timothy Lange, "New Kind of 'Public Interest' Group Pushes Growth," *High Country News,* Jan. 11, 1980, p. 2. (Nader quoted on p. 4.)

50. James Watt, speech delivered in Dallas, May 8, 1978, transcript printed in *Briefing by the Secretary of the Interior,* House Committee on Interior and

Insular Affairs, Feb. 5, 1981, No. 97-1, (Washington, D.C.: Government Printing Office, 1981), pp. 61, 67.

51. Watt, Speech in Dallas, pp. 60–68.

52. Senate Hearings, *James G. Watt Nomination,* testimony of James G. Watt, p. 107.

53. Joanne Omang, "Watt–A Promise to Support Environmental Laws," *Washington Post,* Jan. 8, 1981, Sec. A, p. 2.

54. "Watt: Reagan's Interior Man From Pro-Enterprise Group," *High Country News,* Dec. 26, 1980, p. 4.

CHAPTER 5

1. James Conway, "James Watt, In the Right with the Lord," *Washington Post,* Apr. 27, 1983, Sec. B, p. 13.

2. Lou Cannon, *Reagan* (New York: G.P. Putnam's, 1983), p. 359.

3. Haynes Johnson, "Watt's Goals Are Reached Through the Process, Not the Press," *Washington Post,* Mar. 20, 1983, Sec. A, p. 3.

4. Johnson, p. 3.

5. Cannon, p. 361.

6. Anderson, p. 26.

7. Conway, p. 13.

8. Ibid., p. 2.

9. Phil McCombs, "Watt's Own 'Persecution' Brings Support for Memorial," *Washington Post,* Aug. 13, 1983, Sec. A, p. 15.

10. Conway, p. 13. According to Watt, Hickel was "subjected to such a *brutal,* harsh, ugly attack that it changed his whole personality and style of behavior. . . . He raced to the left to prove to the environmentalists that he was one of them. He ran so far to the left that Nixon had to fire him. . . . Because of the victory the hard-line left achieved in attacking Governor Hickel, through the tool of environmental activism, they took on Governor Hathaway. It was ugly, demeaning, brutal, inhumane treatment. I was with him, I was at his side. He had a nervous breakdown and quit after six weeks."

11. The numerous legislature acts that make up the conservation consensus, such as the Federal Land Protection and Management Act of 1976, the Surface Mining Control and Reclamation Act, and the Alaska Land Bill, give the interior secretary broad administrative powers over the use of federal lands. Reviewing the administration's handling of the public lands in its first year, the *Congressional Quarterly* reported that Watt had used budget recommendations, administrative actions, and personnel shifts to alter Interior policy. The secretary shifted the department from "taking stock of the environment, wilderness and scenic value of federal lands and put them into developing oil, gas, minerals, and timber." For a full analysis, see Kathy Koch, "Reagan Shifts

U.S. Land Policies on Public Land Management," *Congressional Quarterly* (Oct. 3, 1981): 1899.

12. A transcript of the *Los Angeles Times* interview is published in *Public Papers of the President,* Jan. 21, 1982 (Washington, D.C.: Government Printing Office, 1983), p. 61.

13. "Californians Protest Decision for Drilling Off Scenic Coast," *Washington Post,* Feb. 13, 1981, Sec. A, p. 8; Joanne Omang, "Watt Launches Interior Cutback with Old Office," *Washington Post,* Feb. 20, 1981, Sec. A, p. 16; Joanne Omang, "Man with a Mission: Watt Targets Strip-Mine Law," *Washington Post,* Mar. 13, 1981, Sec. A, p. 7.

14. Joanne Omang, "Watt Finds Time to Hear Audubon Society," *Washington Post,* May 30, 1981, Sec. A, p. 7.

15. Bill Prochnau, "The Watt Controversy," *Washington Post,* June 30, 1981, Sec. A, p. 1; David Broder, "Watt Says He's Reined In Udall on Hostile Hearings," *Washington Post,* Aug. 19, 1981, Sec. A, p. 1.

16. Bill Prochnau, "Watt's in a Name?" *Washington Post,* June 30, 1981, Sec. A, p. 13; James Dickinson and Paul Taylor, "Watt Tells Farmers House is Riddled with a Bunch of Liberals," *Washington Post,* Nov. 30, 1981, Sec. A, p. 5; Mary Battinta, "Executive Notes," *Washington Post,* Dec. 3, 1981, Sec. A, p. 25; Mary Battinta, "Watt Used Lee Mansion For Parties," *Washington Post,* Dec. 31, 1981, Sec. C, p. 1.

17. James G. Watt, Speech to the 46th Annual North American Wildlife and Natural Resources Conference, Washington, D.C., Mar. 23, 1981; James G. Watt, Speech to the Outdoor Writers of America Association, Louisville, Ky., June 15, 1981. Unless noted, all speech manuscripts were obtained from the Department of the Interior and are in the author's possession.

18. James G. Watt, Speech to the National Association of Realtors, Miami, Fla., Nov. 16, 1981.

19. Watt, Outdoor Writers of America speech.

20. James G. Watt, Speech to the National Coal Association, St. Louis, Mo., June 15, 1981; James G. Watt, Speech to the Associated Press Managing Editors Annual Meeting, Toronto, Canada, Oct. 23, 1981.

21. James G. Watt, Speech to the National Association of Counties, Louisville, Ky., July 12, 1981; James G. Watt, Speech to the National Petroleum Council, Washington, D.C., Dec. 3, 1981.

22. James G. Watt, Speech to the National Recreation and Park Association, Minneapolis, Minn., Oct. 27, 1981.

23. "Field and Stream Talks With Interior Secretary Watt," *Field and Stream* (Dec., 1981): 59; Watt, National Recreation and Park speech; Watt, Associated Press Editors speech. In the interview with *Field and Stream,* Watt (p. 59) noted that the Reagan administration would move land use decisions from the government to the private sector, a fundamental goal among leaders of the New Right: "We are changing the philosophy of the Department of the Interior.

We think that instead of the social planners in Washington saying what lands are most attractive for coal mining or oil and gas development on the Over-thrust Belt area or the Outer Continental Shelf, we should let the market-place determine what the most attractive lands are."

24. Jack Anderson, "This Land is Your Land, Or is It?" *Washington Post,* July 18, 1982, Sec. B, p. 7.

25. Philip Shabecoff, "Reagan to Open More Public Lands for the De-velopment of Minerals," *Louisville Courier-Journal,* Apr. 6, 1982, Sec. A, p. 3.

26. Ben A. Franklin, "5-Year Old Mining Act is Still Bothering Watt," *New York Times,* Aug. 4, 1982, Sec. A, p. 9.

27. "Off-shore Oil-leasing Plans Get Watt's Final Approval," *New York Times,* July 22, 1982, Sec. A, p. 13.

28. Peter Stoler, "Land Sale of the Century," *Time* (Aug. 23, 1982): 16.

29. William Kronholm, "House Panel Cites Watt for Contempt," *Louis-ville Courier-Journal,* Feb. 10, 1982, Sec. A, p. 3; "Suit Seeks to Halt Watt from Altering Mine Rules," *Louisville Courier-Journal,* Feb. 4, 1982, Sec. B, p. 3.

30. William Kronholm, "Watt is Directed to Reimburse U.S. for Cost of Two Christmas Parties," *Louisville Courier-Journal,* Feb. 25, 1982, Sec. A, p. 2.

31. Dale Russakoff, "Watt Letter to Israelis Causes Stir," *Washington Post,* July 24, 1982, Sec. A, p. 1; Charles Austin, "Watt Reportedly Apologized for His Note to Israeli Envoy," *New York Times,* July 29, 1982, Sec. A, p. 1.

32. George F. Will, "Protecting the Land," *Pantagraph* [Bloomington, Ill.], Aug. 19, 1982, Sec. A, p. 11; Seth King, "Low Wattage Votes Show Power Source," *Herald-Review* [Decatur, Ill.], Aug. 19, 1982, Sec. A, p. 10; Dale Russakoff, "Panel Votes to Curb Wilderness Area Leases," *Washington Post,* Sept. 24, 1982, Sec. A, p. 8. Watt also angered one of his most powerful sup-porters earlier in 1982. Attempting to reorganize the Bureau of Indian Affairs, Watt announced the closure of numerous reservation schools as well as six of the bureau's twelve regional offices. Sen. James McClure advised the secre-tary that such an action could not be taken without congressional approval. Significantly, McClure's action represented the beginning of congressional ef-forts to restrict Watt's administrative reforms. See "Congressmen Nip Watt's BIA Plan," *Missoulian,* March 28, 1982, Sec. A, p. 15.

33. Dale Russakoff, "Western Governors Rap Watt Over Coal Leasing Policies," *Washington Post,* Sept. 4, 1982, Sec. A, p. 1.

34. Dale Russakoff, "Inside: Interior," *Washington Post,* Dec. 2, 1982, Sec. A, p. 25.

35. Russakoff, "Watt, Who Once Relished Publicity," p. 2. Watt canceled the speeches "following White House warnings that his presence could hurt Republican candidates' prospects. The shift began, Interior officials said, after White House warnings showed Watt with the lowest approval rating of any cabinet officer other than Labor Secretary Ray Donovan."

36. James G. Watt, Speech to the Conservative Forum, Washington, D.C., Jan. 22, 1982.

37. Several economists affiliated with the New Right argued that Watt's confrontational manner was counterproductive to the movement's larger goals. For example, see John Baden, "Environmental Barometer Unsteady," *Los Angeles Times*, Sept. 28, 1983, Sec. II, p. 7; Steven M. Hanke, "Watt Never Did Believe in Privatizing U.S. Land," *Wall Street Journal*, Aug. 5, 1983, p. 20.

38. James G. Watt, Speech to the Independent Petroleum Association of America, Dallas, Oct. 15, 1982. Contrasting Carter's natural resource record with Reagan's, Watt concluded: One choice was a "gloomy pathway toward greater government spending, more government regulation, excessive locking away of natural resources needed for economic progress and national security —a course predicated on the theory that we are in an era of shortages." In contrast, Reaganism sought to "rebuild our economic base" and "restore stewardship of resources" in order to "revitalize the great engine of America's enterprise system."

39. James G. Watt, Speech to the National Public Lands Council, Reno, Nev., Sept. 21, 1982; Watt, Independent Petroleum Association speech.

40. Watt, National Public Lands Council speech.

41. Mary Battinta, "Watt Detractors Take Exception to Virginia Speech," *Washington Post*, Sept. 20, 1982, Sec. A, p. 2.

42. Field and Stream interview, p. 59.

43. Geoffrey O'Gara, "In Wyoming's One-Shot Antelope, Watt Finds it Takes Two," *Washington Post*, Sept. 20, 1982, Sec. A, p. 2.

44. James G. Watt, Speech to the American Association of Blacks in Energy, Atlanta, Feb. 5, 1982; Watt, Independent Petroleum Association speech.

45. Watt, National Public Lands Council speech.

46. Robert Sangeorge, "Watt Unleashes Barb at Indian Reservations," *Washington Post*, Jan. 19, 1983, Sec. A, p. 7; William Raspberry, "Watt's Indian Problem," *Washington Post*, Jan. 24, 1983, Sec. A, p. 13.

47. "Watt Says Foes Want Centralization of Power," *New York Times*, Jan. 21, 1983, Sec. A, p. 10; "Environmentalists: More of a Political Force," *Business Week*, Jan. 24, 1983, p. 85.

48. Bill Thomas, "Forget the Beach Boys: Watt Wants Wayne Newton," *Chicago Sun-Times*, Apr. 7, 1983, p. 108.

49. Richard Cohen, "Watt's Wrong," *Washington Post*, Apr. 7, 1983, Sec. B, p. 1; Richard Cohen, "Wattspeak," *Washington Post*, Apr. 28, 1983, Sec. B, p. 1; Art Buchwald, "Watt a July Fourth," *Washington Post*, Apr. 14, 1983, Sec. D, p. 1; Ellen Goodman, "Watt's Greatest Hits," *Washington Post*, Apr. 16, 1983, Sec. A, p. 23; Judy Mann, "Ignorance," *Washington Post*, Apr. 8, 1983, Sec. C, p. 1; Judy Mann, "Watt is a Household Name Once Again, and Votes May be Lost," *Washington Post*, Apr. 11, 1983, Sec. A, p. 7; Mary McGrory, "In the

Beach Boys Brouhaha, Other Outrages are Obscured," *Washington Post,* Apr. 12, 1983, Sec. A, p. 3.

50. Phil McCombs and Richard Harrington, "Watt Beached on July 4 Music Ban," *Washington Post,* Apr. 8, 1983, Sec. A, p. 1.

51. Dale Russakoff, "Advisers to Watt Blackballed by GOP Committee," *Washington Post,* Mar. 27, 1983, Sec. A, p. 1; Dale Russakoff, "Watt Acknowledges Consulting RNC," *Washington Post,* Mar. 28, 1983, Sec. A, p. 3; Dale Russakoff, "Interior Aide's Memo on Wilderness Policy Ordered Quashed," *Washington Post,* Apr. 2, 1983, Sec. A, p. 3.

52. Dale Russakoff, "Interior Department Officials Deny Leasing U.S. at 'Fire Sale' Prices," *Washington Post,* Apr. 28, 1983, Sec. A, p. 2; Matt Yancey, "Watt Barred From Selling Coal Leases," *Missoulian,* Aug. 4, 1983, Sec. A, p. 1. When asked to justify the controversial leases, Watt argued that any effort to curtail the department's leasing program could harm the nation's "economic development, environmental protection, and national security." Waiting for the highest bids on leases, he observed, would lead to disaster. See James G. Watt, Speech to the Rocky Mountain Coal Mining Institute, Vail, Colo., June 28, 1983.

53. Lou Cannon, "Reagan to Define Policy on Environment," *Washington Post,* Mar. 23, 1983, Sec. A, p. 5; Dale Russakoff, "Watt's 'Truth' Campaign Hits Snags," *Washington Post,* Apr. 11, 1983, Sec. A, p. 1. Reagan defended Watt in his weekly radio address to the nation. Arguing that the secretary had been subjected to unfair treatment by the media and environmentalists, Reagan observed that if "Jim discovered a cure for cancer, there are those who would attack him for being pro-life." Transcript published in *Public Papers of the President* (Washington, D.C.: Government Printing Office, 1983), p. 852.

54. James G. Watt, Speech to the American Society of Newspaper Editors, Denver, Colo., May 11, 1983. Audiotape supplied by Cecil Andrus.

55. James G. Watt, Speech to the National Congress of American Indians Executive Board, Washington, D.C., Jan. 25, 1983.

56. James G. Watt, Speech to the Game Conservation International Association, San Antonio, Tex., Mar. 7, 1983.

57. James G. Watt, Speech to the Grand Coulee Dam Golden Anniversary, Grand Coulee, Wash., July 16, 1983.

58. Charles S. Johnson, "Watt Hurts President in the West, Pollster Says," *Great Falls* [Mont.] *Tribune,* June 29, 1983, Sec. A, p. 1.

59. Rick Crone, "Watt Recites Administration's Resource 'Successes,'" *Daily Interlake* [Kalispell, Mont.], June 29, 1983, Sec. A, p. 1; Charles S. Johnson, "Democratic Governors Spar with Watt," *Great Falls Tribune,* June 30, 1983, Sec. A, p. 1; "Watt Evades Governor's Wrath," *Helena* [Mont.] *Independent,* June 29, 1983, Sec. A, p. 1; "Watt: No Huge Land Sale Planned," *Billings Gazette,* June 30, 1983, Sec. A, p. 1.

60. Charles S. Johnson, "Supporters, Critics Meet Watt," *Great Falls Tribune,*
June 29, 1983, Sec. A, p. 1.
61. Charles S. Johnson, "Democratic Governors Spar with Watt," *Great
Falls Tribune,* June 30, 1983, Sec. A, p. 1; "Schwinden: Watt Glosses Over
Problems," *Great Falls Tribune,* June 30, 1983, Sec. A, p. 2.
62. Don Schwennsen, "Watt Pledges to Help Protect Glacier," *Missoulian,*
July 15, 1983, Sec. A, p. 2.
63. "Watt Plans to See Funds for Park Land," *Great Falls Tribune,* July 15,
1983, Sec. A, p. 4.
64. Mark Brunson, "Watt's Antagonism Toward Press Part of Road Show,"
Daily Interlake, July 15, 1983, Sec. A, p. 1. As usual, Watt could not leave the
trip to Montana on a positive note. Rep. Pat Williams attacked the secretary's
plan to increase oil and gas exploration in wilderness areas. Williams charged
that Watt sought to drill test sites in the Bob Marshall Wilderness Area until
the Congress prohibited such measures. Watt told local reporters that the charge
was a "phony issue" created by Williams to "draw out and mislead the American people and the press on the issue." The goal of such phony issues, noted
Watt, was to "whip up hatred to raise dollars" for environmental organizations. "It's a closed issue," the secretary concluded, "but they keep stirring
it, because it's a big money-raiser." Don Schwennsen, "Watt: Bob Marshall
Exploration 'Phony' Issue," *Missoulian,* July 16, 1983, Sec. A, p. 1.
65. "Watt Pulls Agency Out of Reagan Land-Sale Plan," *Missoulian,* July 28,
1983, Sec. A, p. 2; "Land Removed From Sale Plan," *Great Falls Tribune,* July 28,
1983, Sec. A, p. 1.
66. Ron Corday, "Watt is Expected to Resign," *Washington Post,* Feb. 11,
1983, Sec. A, p. 1.
67. Dale Russakoff, "Watt's Off-the-Cuff Remark Sparks Storm of Criticism," *Washington Post,* Sept. 22, 1983, Sec. A, p. 1; Dale Russakoff, "Watt's
Support on the Hill Erodes," *Washington Post,* Sept. 24, 1983, Sec. A, p. 1.
Watt's loss of support in the West sealed his fate. According to the *Great Falls
Tribune:* "Of the 18 Republican senators in the region, 10 are still supporting
the embattled secretary but eight, who have leaped to his defense in the past,
have either attacked Watt or chosen to remain silent." Some of the leading
Republicans who refused to support Watt included Paul Laxalt, Mark Hat-
field, and William Armstrong. Martin Crutsinger, "Watt Losing Western Base?"
Great Falls Tribune, Oct. 1, 1983, Sec. A, p. 2.
68. Philip Shabecoff, "Watt Played Incandescent Role," *Herald-Review*
[Decatur, Ill.], Oct. 14, 1983, Sec. A, p. 10.
69. "Watt Claims Record Land Gains," *Herald-Review,* Oct. 21, 1983, Sec. B,
p. 10.
70. "The Legacy of James Watt," *Time,* (Oct. 24, 1983): 25.
71. Bil Gilbert, "Alone in the Wilderness," *Sports Illustrated* (Oct. 3, 1983):
111.

CHAPTER 6

1. See David Broder, *Changing of the Guard: Power and Leadership in America* (New York: Penguin Books, 1981), p. 180. Broder observes that the Heritage Foundation was created in 1972 to provide "public-policy research on a timely basis for congressional debate and propaganda purposes." See also Crawford, *Thunder on the Right,* p. 12. Crawford concludes, the Heritage Foundation "surprised many observers by becoming a rather respectable research institution. . . . But it is unusual for a research institution to have a 'staff ideology,' as the Heritage Foundation has. Its studies invariably confirm the notions to which its conservative colleagues and trustees . . . are clearly committed."

2. Political Economy Research Center, Inc., "An Introduction," Aug. 22, 1983. The center is described as a think tank devoted to "advancing a society of individuals who are free and responsible in their relations with one another and their environment." Working with scholars, business people, and government officials, the center transmits research "to the policy arena through books, articles, lectures, and conferences." A copy of this document was supplied by the center.

3. Baden quoted in Dan McIntyre, "Right Face: John Baden and MSU's Libertarian Think Tank," *Montana Magazine* (Sept. 1981): 58.

4. For an analysis of the function and goals of one such supporter of PERC, the Cato Institute, see David Remnick, "Nurturing Unorthodox Views At a 'Think Tank for Yuppies,'" *Washington Post National Weekly Edition,* Sept. 9, 1985, pp. 14–15.

5. McIntyre, pp. 56, 60; Nancy Shute, The Movement to Sell America," *Outside Magazine* (Sept., 1983): 38–39; Peter Caughey, "America Examines Public Land Sales Policies," *Bozeman Daily Chronicle,* Aug. 14, 1983.

6. Baden quoted in David F. Salisbury, "Two Differing Views of US Resources—From Ecologists, Economists," *Christian Science Monitor,* Aug. 17, 1982, p. 14. Salisbury concludes that the PERC's New Resource Economics is "an attempt to provide an underpinning in economic theory for the politically conservative belief that a market approach to the management of natural resources is generally preferable to the centralized 'scientific' planning that the federal government has been utilizing."

7. Manhattan Institute for Policy Research, "Privatizing Public Lands: The Ecological and Economic Case for Private Ownership of Federal Lands," May, 1982. A copy of this document was supplied by Steven H. Hanke.

8. For a description of the scope of the Reagan administration's asset management program and the numerous problems it encountered, see Gordon T. Lee, "What if the Government Held a Land Sale and Hardly Anybody Showed Up?" *National Journal* (Sept. 25, 1982): 1624–30.

9. Shute, p. 40; McIntyre, p. 52; Caughey, n.p.

10. John Baden, "Bulldozers and Bald Eagles," *Chicago Tribune* (May 6, 1983): Sec. I, p. 25.

11. Hanke quoted in Ann Crittenden, "Exodus of the Supply Siders," *New York Times,* July 25, 1982, Sec. F, p. 6.

12. Hanke quoted in Patrick Cox, "Land Sales Man," *Reason* (Nov., 1982): 40.

13. Steven H. Hanke, "Would the Real Mr. Reagan Please Stand Up?" *Christian Science Monitor,* Mar. 23, 1983, p. 23.

14. Steven H. Hanke, "Privatize Those Lands! A Message to Sagebrush Rebels," *Reason* (Mar., 1982): n.p.

15. John Baden, "Introduction" and "Property Rights, Cowboys and Bureaucrats," *Earth Day Reconsidered,* ed. John Baden (Washington, D.C.: Heritage Foundation, 1980): pp. 5, 81.

16. John Baden, Randy Simmons, and Rodney D. Fort, "Environmentalists and Self-Interest: How Pure are Those Who Desire the Pristine," in Baden, *Earth Day Revisited,* pp. 13–14.

17. Bruce Johnson, "Concluding Thoughts," in Baden, *Earth Day Revisited,* p. 107.

18. Ibid., p. 105.

19. William Tucker, *Progress and Privilege: America in the Age of Environmentalism* (Garden City, N.Y.: Anchor Press, 1982), pp. 156, 170. The public response to Tucker's book indicated the polarized atmosphere of the conservation debate. See Jerome Zukosky, "A Devastating Attack on Environmental 'Purity,'" *Business Week* (Sept. 11, 1982): 11–12; Wallace Stegner, "Regress and Pillage," *New Republic* (Aug. 30, 1982): 35–37. Concluding that the book is no mean diatribe, Zukosky wrote, "Tucker propounds an attractive, optimistic faith in our capacity to harness technology, and he extolls the virtues of applying pricing mechanisms to the solution of environmental problems." On the other hand, Stegner charged, "I have never read a book as biased, confused, and intermittently informed as this one, or one more likely to be dangerous if taken seriously, as this is certain to be by the ideologues of the Reagan Administration. It reads as if it had been written on a fellowship provided by James Watt."

20. Anderson and Baden quoted in McIntyre, pp. 58–59. Anderson attempted to put his remarks in the context of scholarly objectivity: "As a backpacker, I should be charged for the use of the wilderness areas. I'm happy that I'm not, but as an economist, I sincerely believe that the backpackers of the world do not have any inalienable rights to the wilderness."

21. For example, see Steven H. Hanke, "Grazing for Dollars," *Reason* (July, 1982): 44.

22. Marie Ruemenapp, "Privatization Offers Best Hope to Sheep Producers," *National Wool Grower* (Sept., 1983): 19.

23. Tucker, pp. 181, 190.

24. Steven H. Hanke, "The Privatization Debate: An Insider's View," *Cato Journal* 2 (1982): 660. Hanke observed that "there is strong evidence to suggest that government bureaucrats have been effectively protecting their asset-hoarding bias and undermining the President's privatization efforts. Some of the President's appointees have even expressed their reluctance to use the term 'privatization.'" Asking for the president's help in changing the attitude of many bureaucrats, Hanke concluded, "If the President's program is to be a success, the bureaucratic bias toward asset hoarding and the double talk about privatization must be recognized and effectively dealt with. The cancer from within must be arrested."

25. Tucker, p. 244.

26. Baden quoted in Caughey, n.p.

27. John Baden and Laura Rosen, "The Environmental Justification of Privatization," *Environment* 25 (Oct., 1983): 38.

28. Baden quoted in the *Manhattan Report on Economic Policy.*

29. Richard L. Stroup and John Baden, "Endowment Areas: A Clearing in the Policy Wilderness?" *Cato Journal* 2 (1982): 699.

30. Steven H. Hanke, "Environmental Myths Cloak Possible Sale of Forestland," *Los Angeles Times,* Apr. 13, 1983, Sec. II, p. 7.

31. Baden quoted in "Privatizing Public Lands," Manhattan Institute.

32. Steven H. Hanke, "Wise Use of Federal Land," *New York Times,* May 6, 1983, Sec. A, p. 31. Steven H. Hanke, letter to the editor, *Wall Street Journal,* Aug. 29, 1983, p. 13.

33. Baden and Stroup, "Endowment Areas," p. 702.

34. Baden quoted in Caughey, n.p.

35. Tucker, pp. 30, 139–40.

36. Tucker quoted in "Privatizing Public Lands," Manhattan Institute.

37. John Baden, "'America the Beautiful,' Private Ownership of Natural Resources is the Way to Go," *Barron's* (May 2, 1983): 11.

38. Hanke, "The Privatization Debate," p. 662; Hanke quoted in Cox, p. 40.

39. Steven H. Hanke, "Privatizing the Public Lands: There is Way," *Cattleman* (Mar., 1983): 124.

40. Baden and Rosen, p. 36; Baden, "'America the Beautiful,'" p. 11.

41. Ruemenapp, p. 20.

42. Tucker, p. 131.

43. John Baden and Richard Stroup, "Saving the Wilderness: A Radical Proposal," *Reason* (July, 1981): 35–36.

44. Ruemenapp, p. 21.

45. Christopher K. Leman, "How the Privatization Revolution Failed, and Why Public Land Management Needs Reform Anyway," in Francis and Ganzel, p. 113.

46. John Baden, "Environmental Barometer Unsteady," *Los Angeles Times,* Sept. 28, 1983, Sec. II, p. 7; Baden, "Bulldozers," Sec. I, p. 25.

47. Hanke quoted in Cox, p. 40; Steven H. Hanke, "A Case for Privatization," *Baltimore Sun,* May 10, 1983.

48. Steven H. Hanke, "Watt's Liberal Sins," letter to the editor, *New York Times,* July 3, 1983, Sec. E, p. 12. Claiming that it was time for the secretary "to stop talking and begin acting in an authentically conservative way," Hanke demanded that Watt "roll back the frontier of state ownership and privatize some of the 73 million acres of Federal park land." Such a proposal was anathema to Watt, who had claimed repeatedly that he had no designs on developing any parks or recreation areas.

49. Steven H. Hanke, "Watt Never Did Believe in Privatizing U.S. Lands," *Wall Street Journal,* Aug. 5, 1983, p. 20. Hanke found Watt's good neighbor program to satisfy the Sagebrush Rebellion contradictory to conservative ideals: "Why does the (self-proclaimed) most conservative and loyal member of the president's cabinet oppose Mr. Reagan's land sales program? This opposition arises because Mr. Watt, a celebrated 'sagebrush rebel,' believes in public land ownership—but at the state rather than the federal level. That is why the secretary calls his 'Good Neighbor Policy' a program that allows state and local governments to buy federal property at a 'discount' for 'community needs.' This position is quite similar to the one taken by socialists, who prefer decentralized, rather than centralized, state farms: e.g. *kolkhozy* rather than *sovkhozy,* in the U.S.S.R." In a strange twist of events, privatization's leading advocate implied that James Watt was a policy maker more akin with the Soviet Union than with the New Right.

50. C. Ford Runge, "An Economist's Critique of Privatization," in *Public Lands and the U.S. Economy: Balancing Conservation and Development,* ed. George M. Johnson and Peter M. Emerson (Boulder, Colo.: Westview Press, 1984), pp. 70–71.

51. M. Rupert Cutler, "The Wilderness System Isn't Broken and Doesn't Need Fixing," in *Public Lands and the U.S. Economy,* ed. Johnson and Emerson, pp. 77, 79.

52. See Salisbury, "Two Differing Views," p. 14.

53. Leman, p. 115.

54. Ibid., p. 111.

CHAPTER 7

1. For an analysis of Leopold's importance among environmentalists, see Stegner, "Living on Our Principal," pp. 15–21. According to Stegner, Leopold hoped for the "gradual spread of a 'land ethic,' built upon scientific understanding of the earth and earth processes, but infused with a personal, almost religious respect for life and for the earth that generates and supports it" (p. 15).

2. Aldo Leopold, *A Sand County Almanac* (New York: Oxford University Press, 1966), pp. 239–40.
3. Leopold, p. 211.
4. Ibid., p. 217.
5. Ibid., pp. 272, 279.
6. William Turnage, "James Watt and the New Barbarians: The Anti-Environmental Policies of the Reagan Administration," Yale School of Forestry and Environmental Affairs, Feb. 9, 1982. Transcript in the author's possession.
7. Leopold, pp. 246, 278.
8. Leopold, p. 251.
9. Edward Abbey, "Thus I Reply to Rene Dubois," in *Down the River* (New York: E. P. Dutton, 1982), pp. 118–19.
10. Abbey, pp. 120–21.
11. Wallace Stegner, "The Gift of Wilderness," in *One Way to Spell Man* (Garden City, N.Y.: Doubleday and Co., 1982), p. 167. In a letter to the author, Mar. 22, 1984, Stegner reported: "I gave the speech called the 'Gift of Wilderness' at a meeting at Muir College, U.C. San Diego, and also the Loma Prieta Chapter of the Sierra Club and the annual meeting of the Trust for Public Land in San Francisco, before I published it piecemeal in California Magazine and put it back together again as the final essay in the book of essays called *One Way to Spell Man.*"
12. Stegner, p. 167.
13. Ibid., pp. 170, 176.
14. See Fox, pp. 333–57, for a discussion of the role of the radical amateur in the historical and contemporary conservation debate. Fox believes that "amid the changing issues and personalities, the role of the radical amateur was the driving force in conservation history. The movement depended on professional conservationists and government agencies for expertise, staying power, organization, and money. The amateurs by contrast provided high standards, independence, integrity. Unhampered by bureaucratic inertia or a political need to balance constituencies and defend old policies, they served as the movement's conscience." Typical radical amateurs included Charles Lindbergh, Rachel Carson, Joseph Wood Krutch, and William O. Douglas.
15. "The World From the Grass Roots: Weed Watt Out!!!" *Outdoor America* (Sept.–Oct., 1981): 4.
16. "Watt's Wrongs," *Living Wilderness* (Fall, 1981): 40.
17. Brock Evans, "The Environmental Community Response to the Reagan Administration Program," *Vital Speeches* 48 (1982): 240. Evans's speech was delivered at the National Symposium on Public Lands and the Reagan Administration, Denver, Colo., Nov. 19, 1981.
18. Stuart Langton, "The Future of the Environmental Movement," in *Environmental Leadership,* ed. Stuart Langton (Lexington, Mass.: D.C. Heath and Co., 1984), p. 2. According to Langton: "the antienvironmental antics of

the Reagan administration had several salutary spin-offs for the environmental movement. First, many environmental groups that had experienced some erosion in paid memberships because of the decline in the economy in the late 1970s suddenly experienced a swell of new memberships. Second, environmental groups, in the face of a common enemy, began to cooperate with one another as never before. Third, environmentalists discovered quickly how important it was to monitor existing environmental regulations and practices to protect their hard-fought victories of earlier years."

19. Russell W. Peterson, "Keynote Address," Regional Conference of the Audubon Society, North Midwest Region, Lake Delton, Wisc., Oct. 9, 1982 (transcript in the author's possession). According to Peterson: "the original plume hunters plied their trade around the turn of the century, when feathers were much in demand to decorate women's hats. The commercial hunting of plumed birds . . . was taking a terrible toll. These beautiful creatures were being hunted to the brink of extinction." As a result, several thousand people, calling themselves the Audubon Society, "advertised and publicized and lobbied; they raised money and they raised hell; and they eventually won their battle. They were among the first environmental activists—and they were exceedingly effective. . . . But now, three generations later, the plume-hunter mentality has made an alarming comeback."

20. Turnage, "Watt and the New Barbarians."

21. William Turnage, "Benefit for Idaho," Idaho Conservation League, Boise, Nov. 17, 1981 (transcript in the author's possession).

22. Evans, "Environmental community Response," p. 238. Russell Peterson, Oral Statement to the Senate Subcommittee on Public Lands and Reserved Water, Sept. 23, 1982 (transcript provided by Peterson).

23. Turnage, "Benefit for Idaho."

24. Peterson, Oral Statement.

25. Gaylord Nelson, "A Gross Exaggeration," *Living Wilderness* (Winter, 1981): 7.

26. Evans, "Environmental Community Response," p. 237.

27. Editorial, "Move to Guard Bob Marshall Puts Real Values Before Rhetoric," *High Country News*, (May 29, 1981): 14.

28. Gaylord Nelson, "Rethinking the Federal Lands," speech to Rethinking the Public Lands Conference, Portland, Oreg., Sept. 10, 1982 (transcript in the author's possession).

29. Nelson, "Rethinking the Federal Lands."

30. Nelson, "A Gross Exaggeration," pp. 4, 6.

31. "Ansel Adams Denounces Watt," *Living Wilderness* (Winter, 1981): 43; Susan K. Reed, "Ansel Adams Takes on the President," *Saturday Review* (Nov., 1981): 33.

32. Stegner and Etulain, p. 183; Stegner, "The Gift of Wilderness," p. 177.

33. Wallace Stegner, "The Best Idea We Ever Had," *Wilderness* (Spring, 1983): 4, 13.

34. Abbey quoted in Stewart McBride, "The Real Monkey Wrench Gang," *Outside* (Dec.–Jan., 1983): 71.

35. Edward Abbey, *Beyond the Wall* (New York: Holt, Rinehart and Winston, 1984), p. xiv.

36. Abbey, *Beyond the Wall,* p. xvi.

37. For an analysis of *The Monkey Wrench Gang* and the novel's relationship with the real-world environmental debate, see Brant Short, "Saving the Wild and the Free: The 'Monkey Wrench' Rhetoric of Edward Abbey," in *In Search of Justice: The Indiana Tradition in Speech Communication,* ed. Richard J. Jensen and John Hammerback (Amsterdam: Rodopi, 1987), pp. 285–301.

38. Dan Whipple, "Blowing It: 'Ecotage' in Jackson Hole," *High Country News* (May 1, 1981): 10.

39. Dan Whipple, "Earth First! Says It's Time to be Tough," *High Country News* (April 17, 1981): 11.

40. "Cecil Andrus on Windmills and Balance," *High Country News* (Nov. 13, 1981): 16.

41. Cecil Andrus, Speech to the annual conference of the American Newspaper Editors, May 11, 1983, Denver, Colo. (audiotape supplied by Andrus).

42. Stewart Udall, Speech to the Institute of the American West, Sun Valley, Ida., Apr. 15, 1983 (audiotape supplied by the Institute of the American West).

43. Udall, Speech to the Institute of the American West.

44. Ibid. Udall was a frequent critic of the Reagan administration, speaking across the country and granting interviews. In one interview he concluded: "I'm against the whole attitude Watt exemplifies–that the oil industry subscribes to these days–that we just have to go out there and find all the oil there is and use it up. I just had my second grandchild born last week and I'd like my grandchildren to have a little bit of oil 30 years from now to do those things with." Ken Olson, "Stewart Udall: Watt's Interior Contrary to the Tide of History," *High Country News,* (Nov. 13, 1981): 10.

45. To demonstrate Utah's collective commitment to its tourist industry, in 1985 the state changed automobile license plates to include the image of a downhill skier and the slogans "Ski Utah" and "The Greatest Snow on Earth" across the top and bottom of each plate. State police officers, declining to advertise for the state, have their own special plates.

46. "Wilderness for Utah: How Much is Enough?" *Deseret News* [Salt Lake City], Nov. 18, 1981, Sec. A, p. 5; "Cuts Too Deep in Utah Wilderness Proposals," *Deseret News,* Jan. 9, 1982, Sec. A, p. 12.

47. Joseph Bauman, "Don't Be Stingy on Wilderness for Utah," *Deseret News,* Jan. 11, 1982, Sec. A, p. 5.

48. Joseph Bauman, "Utahns Favor Bigger Chunk for Wilderness," *Deseret*

News, Feb. 1, 1982, Sec. B, p. 1. Religion presented an interesting variable. For those residents with no religious preference, 72 percent favored 2.6 million acres of wilderness; 61 percent of Catholics favored the proposal; Protestants, 55 percent; and Mormons, 44 percent.

49. Roland Robison and Dick Carter, "How Much Wilderness Should Be Set Aside Against Development?" *Deseret News,* Mar. 12, 1983, Sec. A, p. 5.

50. Dick Carter, "Delegation's Wilderness Proposals Simply Don't Do Proper Justice," *Salt Lake City Tribune,* July 17, 1983, Sec. A, p. 18.

51. Joseph Bauman, "S.L. Speakers Want More Wilds Protected," *Deseret News,* July 13, 1983, Sec. B, p. 1.

52. Joseph Bauman, "Environmentalists Back Bill to Protect 706,736 Acres," *Deseret News,* Nov. 19, 1983, Sec. B, p. 1.

53. Jim Robbins, "Battle for the 'Bob,'" *Living Wilderness* (Winter, 1981): 19–25.

54. Don Schwennsen, "He's Worried About the Bob," *Missoulian,* May 11, 1982, Sec. A, p. 13; Robert Jones, "Conservationists Get New Backing," *Los Angeles Times,* Nov. 22, 1982, Sec. I, p. 3.

55. Udall quoted in Olsen, p. 10.

56. Marj Charlier, "'Battle of the Bob' Linked to the Undoing of Watt," *Billings Gazette,* Jan. 4, 1984. Environmentalists used the Bob Marshall controversy to substantiate the need for legislative reforms. The *High Country News* editorialized that the battle between the administration and the Congress to determine possible leasing in the nation's wilderness areas highlighted the inherent contradictions within the Wilderness Act of 1964. The report noted that one section of the law supported preservationist values and that another section seemed to endorse developmental policies. Declaring that it "is time to clean up our wilderness act," the newspaper concluded, "Let us see some corrective legislation and let us see how the big talkers vote." "Congress Puts On a Bad Act With Wilderness Backdrop," *High Country News* (Nov. 27, 1981): 15.

57. Bert Lindler, "Government to Study Sale of Forest Lands," *Great Falls Tribune,* Mar. 16, 1983, Sec. A, p. 1.

58. Bert Lindler, "Proposed Land Sales Draw State, National Heat," *Great Falls Tribune,* Mar. 17, 1983, Sec. A, p. 13.

59. "'Keep Out' Plague Threatens," *Great Falls Tribune,* Mar. 27, 1983, Sec. A, p. 10.

60. Jim Robbins, "'I Can't Believe They Want to Sell the Crazies,'" *Billings Gazette* Apr. 3, 1983, Sec. D, p. 1.

61. JoAn Mengal, "Public Land Sales are Sinking," *Bozeman Daily Chronicle,* Apr. 17, 1983, p. 33. The perceptions offered by the various Montanans reflected the rhetoric of many national environmental groups. For example, see "The Public Lands Sell Out," *Outdoor America* (July–Aug., 1982): 4. The editorial writer, representing the Izaak Walton League, argued that privatization

162 Notes to Pages 123–126

would mean "long-term economic and environmental loss. The accessibility and value of public lands contribute, directly and indirectly, to the quality of life of every American. From a purely economic standpoint, grazing, timber, mineral and other leases return billions of dollars to the U.S. Treasury each year. From a recreational and environmental viewpoint, the public lands provide unparalleled scenic beauty, wildlife habitat, cultural resources, and varied recreational opportunities."

62. "Advisability of Land-Sales Scheme Questioned," *Great Falls Tribune*, (May 7, 1983), Sec. A, p. 15.

63. "Land Sales Threaten Wildlife Habitat, Says Wildlife Official," *Bozeman Daily Chronicle*, May 20, 1983, p. 15.

64. JoAn Mengal, "Ex-Forest Service Employee Digs into BLM Resource Plans," *Bozeman Daily Chronicle*, May 29, 1983, p. 3.

65. "Public Prefers Trades to Land Sales," *Bozeman Daily Chronicle*, May 5, 1983, p. 6.

66. "Conservationist: Land Sales May Neglect Wildlife, Public," *Bozeman Daily Chronicle*, Oct. 13, 1983, p. 4.

67. "Federal Land Sales a Failure," *Bozeman Daily Chronicle*, Oct. 13, 1983, p. 4.

68. In late July, 1983, Watt decided to eliminate the Interior Department's participation in the federal land sales program. See "Land Removed from Sale Plan," *Great Falls Tribune*, July 28, 1983, Sec. A, p. 1. See also "Watt Pulls Agency Out of Reagan Land-Sale Program," *Missoulian*, July 28, 1983, Sec. A, p. 2.: "the program has fallen far short of those estimates and only a few thousand acres of land have been sold. Despite the lackluster record, the administration had come under a great deal of criticism from Western ranchers concerned they might lose valuable grazing rights on millions of acres of federal land and from environmentalists who believed the land would be sold for development."

69. Andy Pasztor, "Reagan Policies Spur Big Revival of the Environmental Movement," *Wall Street Journal*, Aug. 2, 1982, Sec. II, p. 15.

70. Robert L. Jones, "In Search of Leaders," *Missoulian*, Dec. 30, 1984, Sec. A, p. 1.

71. Philip Shabecoff, "Watt's Successor Offers Olive Branch to Critics," *New York Times*, Dec. 8, 1983, Sec. A, p. 14.

72. Tom Morganthau, "Environment: A Cleaner Act?" *Newsweek* (Jan. 30, 1984): 23. Clark also worked to keep many in the West happy with the Reagan administration. Speaking to 500 menbers of the Montana Stockgrowers Association in 1984, Clark promised to continue working with the commercial users of the nation's grazing lands. See T. J. Giles, "Interior Secretary Lauds 'Partnership,'" *Great Falls Tribune*, May 1, 1984, Sec. A, p. 1.

73. "Reagan Sells Environmental Record, But Some Aren't Buying," *Louisville Courier-Journal*, July 12, 1984, Sec. A, p. 4. Reagan attempted to re-

fute charges that he was insensitive toward environmental issues in a series of speeches during the summer of 1984. Speaking at a wildlife refuge in Maryland, Reagan complained that his concern for the environment was "one of the best kept secrets" of his presidency. See Michael Putzel, "Environmental Issues of 'Great Interest' to Him, Reagan Says," *Louisville Courier-Journal*, July 11, 1984, Sec. A, p. 5. Reagan also took his message on the road, speaking to 20,000 mobile home campers attending a convention in Kentucky. He told the campers that his "administration will never respond by trying to keep the American people from using the great outdoors." See Carol Marie Cropper, "President Takes Offensive on Environment, Criticizes Past Efforts," *Louisville Courier-Journal*, July 13, 1984, Sec. A, p. 4.

74. For example, see "Conservationists Rap Reagan Stance," *Louisville Courier-Journal*, June 26, 1984, Sec. A, p. 3. Six major conservation groups, including the Sierra Club, the National Audubon Society, and the Friends of the Earth signed a letter to Reagan, calling his environmental record "dismal" and demanding many changes in administration policy, including a reduction of offshore and coal leasing and more funds for the development of renewable energy sources.

75. Evans, "Environmental Community Response," p. 236.

CHAPTER 8

1. James G. Watt, Dallas speech, May 8, 1978, transcript printed in "Briefing by the Secretary of the Interior," *House Committee on Interior and Insular Affairs*, Feb. 5, 1981, No. 97-1, (Washington, D.C.: Government Printing Office, 1981), p. 107.

2. Sheldon S. Wolin, "From Progress to Modernization: The Conservative Turn," *democracy* (Fall, 1983): 9.

3. Arthur A. Ekirch, *The Idea of Progress in America, 1815–1860* (New York: Peter Smith, 1951), pp. 11, 37.

4. Wolin, p. 10.

5. See Nash, *Wilderness*, pp. 182–99.

6. See Arrandale, passim.

7. Linda Medcalf and Kenneth Dolbeare, *Neopolitics: American Political Ideas in the 1980s* (New York: Random House, 1985), p. 165. Paul Weyrich quoted in Viguerie, p. 56.

8. Clyde N. Wilson, "Citizens or Subjects?" in *The New Right Papers*, ed. Robert W. Whitaker (New York: St. Martin's Press, 1982), p. 123. He concluded that "New Rightists do not intend to establish a religion of the dollar bill. This clearly distinguishes them from certain elements of the Old Right and from libertarians."

9. Thomas Fleming, "Old Rights and the New Right," in Whitaker, p. 196.

10. Richard Slotkin, *The Fatal Environment* (New York: Atheneum, 1985), p. 33.

11. Ekirch, p. 11.

12. Udall, *Quiet Crisis,* p. 202.

13. Robert Rienow and Leona Train Rienow, *Moment in the Sun* (New York: Ballantine Books, 1967), pp. 236–39; Paul Sears, "Ecology—A Subversive Science," *Bioscience* (July, 1964), cited in Rienow and Rienow, p. 213; Barry Commoner, *The Closing Circle* (New York: Bantam Books, 1971), p. 273; Science Action Coalition, p. 183.

14. Broder, p. 162.

15. Samuel T. Francis, "Message from MARS: The Social Politics of the New Right," in Whitaker, pp. 76, 81.

16. "Carter-Reagan Debate Text," p. 3289.

17. The Science Action Coalition (p. 177), for example, observed: "Many cultural anthropologists locate the antecedents of the predominant growth philosophy of our culture in the Old Testament of the Bible. . . . But Israel and its culture were unique. It was a nation going somewhere. Yahweh's people were part of a covenant and destination. For them time was linear—directional. They *became* a special or chosen people who give direction to their world by free choices."

18. Russel B. Nye, *This Almost Chosen People* (Lansing: Michigan State University Press, 1966), p. 3.

19. According to Slotkin (p. 15): "The Myth of the Frontier is arguably the longest-lived of American myths, with origins in the colonial period and a powerful continuing presence in contemporary culture. Although the Myth of the Frontier is only one of the operative myth-ideological systems that form American culture, it is an extremely important and persistent one."

20. See for example Rushing, pp. 14–32; Barry Alan Morris, "The Ponderosa Presidency: Reagan's Western Melodramatic Form," *Speaker and Gavel* 19 (1981–1982): 31–37.

21. Smith, p. 6.

22. Slotkin, p. 33.

23. Sacvan Bercovitch, "The Rites of Assent: Rhetoric, Ritual, and the Ideology of American Consensus," in *The American Self,* ed. Sam B. Girgus (Albuquerque: University of New Mexico Press, 1981), p. 23.

24. Slotkin, p. 41.

25. Girgus, p. 10.

26. Ibid., 10–11.

Bibliography

NEWSPAPERS

Argus Leader, Sioux Falls, S. Dak.
Billings Gazette, Billings, Ida.
Blackfoot Morning News, Blackfoot, Ida.
Bozeman Daily Chronicle, Bozeman, Mont.
Christian Science Monitor.
Daily Interlake, Kalispell, Mont.
Deseret News, Salt Lake City.
Great Falls Tribune, Great Falls, Mont.
Helena Independent, Helena, Mont.
Herald-Review, Decatur, Ill.
High Country News.
Idaho State Journal, Pocatello.
Idaho Statesman, Boise.
Indianapolis Star.
Lewiston Morning Tribune, Lewiston, Ida.
Los Angeles Times.
Louisville Courier-Journal.
Minidoka County News, Rupert, Ida.
Missoulian, Missoula, Mont.
Moab Times Independent, Moab, Utah.
Montana Standard, Butte.
New York Times.
Pantagraph, Bloomington, Ill.
Salt Lake Tribune, Salt Lake City.
Times-News, Twin Falls, Ida.
Wall Street Journal.
Washington Post.
Wood River Journal, Hailey, Ida.

UNPUBLISHED SOURCES

Andrus, Cecil. Speech to the annual conference of the American Society of Newspaper Editors, Denver, Colo., May 11, 1983.

Babbitt, Bruce, Letter to Leo Corbet, President of the Arizona State Senate, Apr. 8, 1980.

———. "An Alternative to the Sagebrush Rebellion." Speech to the Man and His Resources Symposium, Dillon, Mont., Nov. 14, 1980.

Cawley, Malcom. "The Sagebrush Rebellion." Dissertation. Collorado State University, 1981.

Colorado Legislative Council. "Recommendations for 1981 Committee on Agriculture." Dec., 1980, pp. 1–47.

Grose, Richard. Letter to the author, Mar. 27, 1984.

Hatch, Orrin. "The Sagebrush Rebellion is Real! Utah for Utahns, Not the Washington Bureaucrats." Congressional newsletter to residents of Utah. Copy available at the University of Utah Library, Salt Lake City.

———. "A Second American Revolution." Speech to the Western Coalition on Public Lands, Reno, Nev., Spet. 6, 1979.

Lamm, Richard. "Public Resource Management Under the Reagan Administration." Speech to the USC Law Center, Los Angeles, Feb. 5, 1982.

Laxalt, Paul. "The Sagebrush Rebellion: A Backgrounder from Senator Paul Laxalt." Congressional newsletter to residents of Nevada, Feb., 1980.

Legislative Council Bureau, State of Nevada. "How to Organize a Grassroots Group." Position paper.

———. "Sagebrush Rebellion Presentation." Sample speech for pro-Rebellion speakers.

———. Sample Letters Supporting the Sagebrush Rebellion.

McClure, James. Speech to the Western Colonies in Revolt Symposium, Sun Valley, Ida., July, 1981.

Manhattan Institute for Policy Research. "Privatizing the Public Lands: The Ecological and Economic Case for Private Ownership of Federal Lands." Proceedings of a Conference on Public Lands Ownership, New York, May, 1982.

Montana Democratic Party Issue Brief No. 6. "The Sagebrush Rebellion." 1981. Copy available at Carroll College Library, Helena, Mont.

Nelson, Gaylord. "Rethinking the Federal Lands." Speech to the Rethinking the Federal Lands Conference, Portland, Oreg., Sept. 10, 1982.

———. Speech to the Montana Wilderness Association, Great Falls, Mont., Dec. 5, 1981.

Nelson, Robert. "Making Sense of the Sagebrush Rebellion." Paper distributed by the Legislative Council Bureau, State of Nevada. Apr. 1982.

Peterson, Russell. "Keynote Address." North Midwest National Audubon Society meeting, Lake Delton, Wisc., Oct. 9, 1982.

————. Oral statement to the Senate Subcommittee on Public Lands and Reserved Water Hearings, Sept. 23, 1982.

Political Economy Research Center, Inc. "An Introduction." Bozeman, Mont., Aug. 22, 1983.

Robison, Ken. Speech to the Western Colonies in Revolt Symposium, Sun Valley, Ida., July, 1981.

Sagebrush Rebellion, Inc. *Sagebrush Rebellion, Inc., Newsletter.* 1980–84.

Turnage, William. "Benefit for Idaho." Speech presented to the Idaho Conservation League, Boise, Ida., Nov. 17, 1981.

————. "James Watt and the New Barbarians: The Anti-Environmental Policies of the Reagan Administration." Speech to the Yale School of Forestry and Environmental Studies, New Haven, Conn., Feb. 9, 1982.

Udall, Stewart. Speech to the American Institute of the West, Sun Valley, Ida., Apr., 1983.

Utah Foundation. "Utah and the Sagebrush Rebellion." Research Report No. 399. Jan., 1980. Copy available at the University of Utah, Salt Lake City.

Watt, James G. Speech to American Association of Blacks in Energy, Atlanta, Feb. 5, 1982.

————. Speech to American Mining Congress, Denver, Sept. 28, 1981.

————. Speech to American Society of Newspaper Editors, Denver, May 11, 1983.

————. Speech to Anchorage Chamber of Commerce, Anchorage, Aug. 10, 1981.

————. Speech to Associated Press Managing Editors Annual Meeting, Toronto, Oct. 23, 1981.

————. Speech to Conservative Forum, Washington, D.C., Jan. 22, 1982.

————. Speech to 46th Annual North American Wildlife and Natural Resources Conference, Washington, D.C., Mar. 23, 1981.

————. Speech to Game Conservation International Association, San Antonio, Mar. 7, 1983.

————. Speech to Government Affairs Conference of the National Newspaper Association, Mar. 11, 1983.

————. Speech to Grand Coulee Dam Golden Anniversary, Grand Coulee, Wash., July 16, 1983.

————. Speech to Independent Petroleum Association of America, Dallas, Oct. 15, 1982.

————. Speech to National Association of Counties, Louisville, Ky., July 12, 1981.

————. Speech to National Association of Realtors, Miami, Nov. 16, 1981.

————. Speech to National Coal Association, St. Louis, Mo., June 15, 1981.

————. Speech to National Congress of American Indians, Bismarck, N.Dak., Sept. 27, 1982.

————. Speech to National Congress of American Indians Executive Board, Washington, D.C., Jan. 25, 1983.

————. Speech to National Petroleum Council, Washington, D.C., Dec. 3, 1981.

————. Speech to National Public Lands Council, Reno, Nev., Sept. 21, 1982.

————. Speech to National Recreation and Park Association, Minneapolis, Oct. 27, 1981.

————. Speech to National Water Resources Association, Albuquerque, Nov. 2, 1981.

————. Speech to National Water Resources Association, Salt Lake City, Oct. 26, 1982.

————. Speech to Outdoor Writers of America Association, Louisville, Ky., June 15, 1981.

————. Speech to Rocky Mountain Coal Mining Institute, Vail, Colo., June 28, 1983.

————. Statement by Secretary James G. Watt, North Atlantic Lease Offering, Sale 52, Feb. 23, 1983.

Wengert, Norman. "Land, People, and Policy: The Western Connection." Paper presented to Soil Conservation Society of America, Spokane, Wash., Aug. 2–5, 1981.

Western Conference, Council of State Governments. "Western Involvement in the Sagebrush Rebellion." Resolution No. 80-1, no date.

Western Democratic Governors. "Reagan and the West." Policy statement supplied by Gov. Richard Lamm, with letter dated Mar. 27, 1984.

GOVERNMENT DOCUMENTS

Bureau of the Census. *Statistical Abstract of the United States: 1981.* Washington, D.C.: Government Printing Office, 1981.

Public Papers of the President, 1982 (Washington, D.C.: Government Printing Office, 1983).

U.S. Congress, House. Subcommittee on Mines and Mining. *Sagebrush Rebellion: Impacts on Energy and Minerals.* 96th Cong. 2nd sess. H. Rept. 96-39. Washington, D.C.: Government Printing Office, 1980.

————. Committee on Interior and Insular Affairs. *Briefing by the Secretary of the Interior.* 97th Cong., 1st sess. H. Rept. 97-1. Washington, D.C.: Government Printing Office, 1981.

U.S. Congress, Senate. Committee on Energy and Natural Resources. *James G. Watt Nomination Hearings.* 97th Cong. 1st sess. S. Rept. 97-1. Washington, D.C.: Government Printing Office, 1981.

U.S. Department of the Interior. *1980 National Survey of Fishing, Hunting, and*

Wildlife Associated Recreation. Washington, D.C.: Government Printing Office, 1982.

ARTICLES

Adler, Jerry. "James Watt's Land Rush." *Newsweek* (Aug. 29, 1981): 23–27.
Anderson, Kurt. "Always Right and Ready to Fight." *Time* (Aug. 23, 1982): 27–28.
Andrus, Cecil. "The Attack on Federal Lands." *National Parks and Conservation* (Apr., 1980): 9–10.
"Ansel Adams Denounces Watt." *Living Wilderness* (Winter, 1981): 43.
Babbitt, Bruce. "Federalism and the Environment: An Intergovernmental Perspective of the Sagebrush Rebellion." *Environmental Law* 12 (1982): 847–61.
Baden, John. "Agricultural Land Preservation: Threshing the Wheat from the Chaff." *Proceedings of the Southwestern Legal Foundation* 21 (1983): 171–202.
———, and Laura Rosen. "The Environmental Justification of Privatization." *Environment* 25, No. 8 (October, 1983): 7+.
———, and Richard L. Stroup. "Entrepreneurship, Energy and the Political Economy of Hope." *Proceedings of the Southwestern Legal Foundation* 19 (1981): 337–60.
———, and ———. "Saving the Wilderness: A Radical Proposal." *Reason* (July, 1981): 35–36.
Beck, Tom. "The Angry West." *Newsweek* (Sept. 17, 1979): 35–39.
Blakemore, Richard E., and Robert E. Ericson. "The Sagebrush Rebellion." *Journal of Soil and Water Conservation* 36 (1981): 146–48.
Bureau of Land Management. "Federal Lands Being Transferred for Community Expansion." *Nevada Government Today* (Winter, 1981): 24.
Callison, Charles. "The Great Sagebrush Rally." *Audubon* (Jan., 1981): 113–15.
"Candidates All Endorse Energy Price Decontrol." *Congressional Quarterly* (Oct. 4, 1980): 2923.
Carter, Jimmy. "Convention Acceptance Speech." *Facts on File* (Aug. 14, 1980): 612–13.
Carter, Marsha, and Roseanne Carter. "West Tangles with East in Sagebrush Rebellion." *Phoenix Magazine* (June, 1980): 73–75.
Cox, Patrick. "Land Sales Man." *Reason* (Nov., 1982).
DeVoto, Bernard. "The West Against Itself." *Harper's* 194 (Jan., 1947): 1–13.
Dobra, John L., and George A. Uhimchuk. "Property Rights, Legal Efficiency, and the Political Economy of the Sagebrush Rebellion." *Nevada Review of Business and Economics* 5 (1982): 2–12.
Evans, Brock. "The Environmental Community Response to the Reagan Administration." *Vital Speeches* 48 (1982): 235–41.
Gilbert, Bil. "Alone in the Wilderness." *Sports Illustrated* (Oct. 3, 1983): 111.

————. "Inside Interior: An Abrupt Turn." *Sports Illustrated* (Sept. 26, 1983): 67–80.

Hanke, Steven H. "Grazing for Dollars." *Reason* (July, 1982): 43–44.

————. "On Privatization's Myths." *Environmental Forum* (May, 1983): 33–34.

————. "The Privatization Debate: An Insider's View." *Cato Journal* 2 (1982): 653–62.

————. "Privatize Those Lands! A Message to Sagebrush Rebels." *Reason* (Mar., 1982).

————. "Privatizing the Public Lands: There Is a Way." *Cattleman* (Mar., 1983): 124–26.

————. "Selling the Federal Lands." *Reason* (Sept., 1982): 22–23.

Ivie, Robert. "Speaking 'Common Sense' about the Soviet Threat: Reagan's Rhetorical Stance." *Western Journal of Speech Communication* 48 (Winter, 1984): 39–50.

Kinkead, Gwen. "James Watt's Self-Made Storm." *Fortune* (Nov. 30, 1981): 138–50.

Koch, Kathy. "Reagan Shifts U.S. Land Policies on Public Land Management." *Congressional Quarterly* (Oct. 3, 1981): 1899–1904.

"The Legacy of James Watt." *Time* (Oct. 24, 1983): 25.

McBride, Stewart. "The Real Monkey Wrench Gang." *Outside* (Dec.–Jan., 1983): 36+.

McCloskey, Michael. "Wilderness Movement at the Crossroads, 1945–1970." *Pacific Historical Review* 41 (1972): 346–61.

McConnell, Grant. "The Conservation Movement: Past and Present." *Western Political Science Quarterly* 7 (1954): 463–78.

McGee, Michael Calvin. "The 'Ideograph': A Link between Rhetoric and Reality." *Quarterly Journal of Speech* 66 (1980): 1–16.

McIntyre, Dan. "Right Face: John Baden and MSU's Libertarian Think Tank." *Montana Magazine* (Sept., 1981): 56–61.

Morganthau, Tom. "Environment: A Clean Act." *Newsweek* (Jan. 30, 1984): 30.

Morris, Barry Alan. "The Ponderosa Presidency: Reagan's Western Melodramatic Form." *Speaker and Gavel* 19 (1981–82): 31–37.

Nash, Roderick. "American Environmental History." *Pacific Historical Review* 41 (1972): 363–72.

————. "John Muir, William Kent, and the Conservation Schism." *Pacific Historical Review* 36 (1967): 423–33.

————. "Path to Preservation." *Wilderness* 48 (1984): 5–11.

Nelson, Gaylord. "A Gross Exaggeration." *Living Wilderness* (Winter, 1981): 4–9.

Nelson, Robert H. "Why the Sagebrush Revolt Burned Out." *Regulation* (May–June, 1984): 34.

Ognibene, Peter J. "Sagebrush Senators." *Rocky Mountain Magazine* (July–Aug., 1981): 43–48.

Oravec, Christine. "John Muir, Yosemite, and the Sublime Response: A Study in the Rhetoric of Preservationism." *Quarterly Journal of Speech* 67 (1981): 245–58.

O'Riordan, Timothy. "The Third American Conservation Movement." *Journal of American Studies* 5 (1971): 155–71.

Popper, Frank J. "The Timely End of the Sagebrush Rebellion." *Public Interest* 76 (1984): 61–73.

Rakestraw, Lawrence. "The West, States' Rights, and Conservation." *Pacific Northwest Quarterly* 48 (1957): 89–99.

Reed, Susan K. "Ansel Adams Takes on the President." *Saturday Review* (Nov., 1981): 32–39.

Reese, Michael. "Watt Defuses a Rebellion." *Newsweek* (Sept. 21, 1981): 48.

Richardson, Elma. "The Interior Secretary as Conservation Villain: The Notorious Case of Douglas 'Giveaway' McKay." *Pacific Historical Review* 41 (1972): 333–45.

Robbins, Jim. "Battle for the 'Bob.'" *Living Wilderness* (Winter, 1981): 19–25.

Ruemenapp, Marie. "Privatization Offers Best Hope to Sheep Producers." *National Wool Grower* (Sept., 1983): 19–23.

Rushing, Janice Hocker. "The Rhetoric of the American Western Myth." *Communication Monographs* 50 (1983): 14–32.

Sharpe, Maitland. "Liquidating the Land." *Outdoor America* (July–Aug., 1982): 10–26.

———. "The Sagebrush Rebellion." *Outdoor America* (Sept.–Oct., 1980): 5–7+.

Shute, Nancy. "The Movement to Sell America." *Outside Magazine* (Sept., 1983): 38–39.

Tucker, William. "Environmentalism: The Newest Toryism." *Policy Review* (Fall, 1980): 141–52.

———. "Is Nature Too Good for Us?" *Harper's* (Mar., 1982): 27–35.

Turbak, Gary. "America's Sagebrush Rebellion." *Kiwanis Magazine* (Feb., 1981): 28–31.

Unger, Sanford J. "The 'New Conservatives.'" *Atlantic Monthly* (Feb., 1979): 20–24.

"Unrest in the West: Who Owns This Land?" *Changing Times* (July, 1981): 31–32.

Wald, Johanna H., and Elizabeth H. Temkin. "The Sagebrush Rebellion: The West against Itself–Again." *UCLA Journal of Environmental Law and Policy* 2 (1982): 187–207.

Watkins, T. H. "James Gaius Watt: An Idea Whose Time Has Gone." *Living Wilderness* (Winter, 1981): 24–28.

Watt, James G., "Interview with Field and Stream." *Field and Stream* (Dec., 1981): 60+.

———. "Interview with U.S. News." *U.S. News and World Report* (June 14, 1982): 41–43.

————. "When James Watt Speaks Out." *U.S. News and World Report* (June 6, 1983): 55.
"Watt's Wrongs." *Living Wilderness* (Fall, 1981): 40.
"West Senses Victory in Sagebrush Rebellion." *U.S. News and World Report* (Dec. 1, 1980): 29.
Wolf, Ron. "New Voice in the Wilderness." *Rocky Mountain Magazine* (Mar.– Apr., 1981): 30+.
Wolin, Sheldon S. "From Progress to Modernization: The Conservative Turn." *democracy* (Fall, 1983): 9–21.
"The World from the Grass Roots: Weed Watt Out!" *Outdoor America* (Sept.– Oct., 1981): 4.
Young, Cliff. "What's Behind the Sagebrush Rebellion?" *National Wildlife* (Aug.–Sept., 1981): 31–34.
Zukosky, Jerome. "A Devastating Attack on Environmental 'Purity.'" *Business Week* (Sept. 11, 1982): 11–12.

BOOKS

Abbey, Edward. *Abbey's Road*. New York: E. P. Dutton, 1979.
————. *Beyond the Wall*. New York: Holt, Rinehart and Winston, 1984.
————. *Desert Solitaire*. New York: Ballantine Books, 1968.
————. *Down the River*. New York: E. P. Dutton, 1982.
Arrandale, Tom. *The Battle for Natural Resources*. Washington, D.C.: Congressional Quarterly, 1983.
Baden, John, ed. *Earth Day Reconsidered*. Washington, D.C.: Heritage Foundation, 1980.
————, and Richard L. Stroup, eds. *Bureaucracy vs. Environment*. Ann Arbor: University of Michigan Press, 1981.
Barrett, Laurence I. *Gambling with History*. New York: Penguin Books, 1983.
Berry, Wendell. *The Unsettling of America*. San Francisco: Sierra Club Books, 1977.
Broder, David. *Changing of the Guard: Power and Leadership in America*. New York: Penguin Books, 1981.
Brownstein, David, and Nina Easton. *Reagan's Ruling Class*. Washington, D.C.: Presidential Accountability Group, 1982.
Cannon, Lou. *Reagan*. New York: G. P. Putnam's, 1983.
Commoner, Barry. *The Closing Circle*. New York: Bantam Books, 1971.
Crawford, Alan. *Thunder on the Right*. New York: Pantheon, 1980.
Dallek, Robert. *Ronald Reagan: The Politics of Symbolism*. Cambridge: Harvard University Press, 1984.
Drew, Elizabeth. *Portrait of an Election*. New York: Simon and Schuster, 1981.

Ekirch, Arthur A. *The Idea of Progress in America, 1815–1860.* New York: Peter Smith, 1951.

Elder, Charles D., and Roger W. Cobb. *The Political Uses of Symbols.* New York: Longman Books, 1983.

Fox, Stephen. *John Muir and His Legacy.* Boston: Little, Brown and Co., 1981.

Francis, John G., and Richard Ganzel, eds. *Western Public Lands: The Management of Natural Resources in a Time of Declining Federalism.* Totowa, N.J.: Rowman and Allanheld, 1984.

Germond, Jack, and Jules Witcover. *Blue Smoke and Mirrors: Why Reagan Won and How Carter Lost the 1980 Election.* New York: Viking Books, 1981.

Girgus, Sam B., ed. *The American Self.* Albuquerque: University of New Mexico Press, 1981.

Hays, Samuel P. *Conservation and the Gospel of Efficiency.* Cambridge: Harvard University Press, 1959.

———. *American Political History as Social History.* Knoxville: University of Tennessee Press, 1980.

Holiwell, Richard N., ed. *Agenda '83: A Mandate for Leadership Report.* Washington, D.C.: Heritage Foundation, 1983.

Jensen, Richard J., and John C. Hammerback, eds. *In Search of Justice: The Indiana Tradition in Speech Communication.* Amsterdam: Rodopi, 1987.

Johnson, George M., and Peter M. Emerson, eds. *Public Lands and the U.S. Economy: Balancing Conservation and Development.* Boulder, Colo.: Westview Press, 1984.

Lamm, Richard D., and Michael McCarthy. *The Angry West.* Boston: Houghton Mifflin Co., 1982.

Langton, Stuart, ed. *Environmental Leadership.* Lexington, Mass.: D.C. Heath and Co., 1984.

Leopold, Aldo. *San County Almanac.* New York: Oxford University Press, 1966.

Medcalf, Linda, and Kenneth Dolbeare. *Neopolitics: American Political Ideas in the 1980s.* New York: Random House, 1985.

Nash, Roderick. *Wilderness and the American Mind.* New Haven: Yale University Press, 1982.

Nye, Russel B. *This Almost Chosen People.* Lansing: Michigan State University Press, 1966.

Petulla, Joseph. *American Environmental History.* San Francisco: Boyd and Fraser, 1977.

———. *American Environmentalism.* College Station: Texas A&M University Press, 1980.

Pomper, Gerald, ed. *The Election of 1980.* Chatham, N.J.: Chatham Publishing Co., 1981.

Reid, Ronald F., *The American Revolution and the Rhetoric of History.* Annandale, Va.: Speech Communication Association, 1978.

Rienow, Robert, and Leona Train Rienow. *Moment in the Sun.* New York: Ballantine Books, 1967.

Robison, Ken. *The Sagebrush Rebellion: A Bid for Control.* Blackfoot, Ida.: D and S Publishing, 1981.

Rowley, William. *U.S. Forest Service Grazing and Rangelands: A History.* College Station: Texas A&M University Press, 1985.

Science Action Coalition with Albert Fritsch. *Environmental Ethics.* Garden City, N.Y.: Anchor Books, 1980.

Slotkin, Richard. *The Fatal Environment.* New York: Atheneum, 1985.

Smith, Henry Nash. *Virgin Land.* Cambridge, Mass.: Harvard University Press, 1950.

Stacks, John F. *Watershed: The Campaign for the Presidency, 1980.* New York: Times Books, 1981.

Stegner, Wallace. *One Way to Spell Man.* Garden City, N.Y.: Doubleday, 1982.

————. *The Sound of Mountain Water.* Garden City, N.Y.: Doubleday, 1969.

————, and Richard Etulain. *Conversations with Wallace Stegner.* Salt Lake City: University of Utah Press, 1983.

Tucker, William. *Progress and Privilege: America in the Age of Environmentalism.* Garden City, N.Y.: Anchor Press, 1982.

Udall, Stewart D. *The Quiet Crisis.* New York: Avon Books, 1963.

Viguerie, Richard. *The New Right: We're Ready to Lead.* Falls Church, Va.: Viguerie Co., 1981.

Voight, William, Jr. *Public Grazing Lands.* New Brunswick, N.Y.: Rutgers University Press, 1976.

Whitaker, Robert W., ed. *The New Right Papers.* New York: St. Martin's Press, 1982.

Index

Ronald Reagan and the Public Lands was composed into type on a Compugraphic digital phototypesetter in ten point Galliard with two points of spacing between the lines. Galliard was also selected for display. The book was designed by Jim Billingsley, typeset by Metricomp, Inc., printed offset by Thomson-Shore, Inc., and bound by John H. Dekker & Sons. The paper on which the book is printed is designed for an effective life of at least three hundred years.

Texas A&M University Press : College Station